Studies in Scripture

VOLUME SIX Acts to Revelation

Edited by Robert L. Millet

DESERET
BOOK

Salt Lake City, Utah

The following articles © The Church of Jesus Christ of Latter-day Saints are used by permission:

"The Forty-Day Ministry of Christ," S. Kent Brown and C. Wilfred Griggs, Ensign, August 1975, pp. 6–11.

"Unto All Nations: Teaching the Book of Acts," Robert J. Matthews, Church Educational System Symposium on the New Testament, 1984, pp. 32–39.

"Walking in Newness of Life: The Epistle of Paul to the Romans," Robert L. Millet, CES Symposium on the New Testament, 1984, pp. 40–43.

"The Book of Revelation—Three Keys for Making It a Book of Revelation," Gerald N. Lund, CES Symposium, 1980, pp 114–22.

Cover painting: "Behold My Hands and Feet" by Harry Anderson © The Church of Jesus Christ of Latter-day Saints. Used by permission.

First printing in hardbound 1987
First printing in paperbound 2003

Visit us at deseretbook.com

Library of Congress Catalog Card Number 87-070686

ISBN 0-87579-084-4 (hardbound)
ISBN 1-59038-261-7 (paperbound)

Printed in the United States of America   72076-022P
Publishers Printing, Salt Lake City, UT

10   9   8   7   6   5   4   3   2   1

Studies in Scripture

VOLUME SIX Acts to Revelation

Studies in Scripture series

Vol. 1: The Doctrine and Covenants
Vol. 2: The Pearl of Great Price
Vol. 3: Genesis to 2 Samuel
Vol. 4: 1 Kings to Malachi
Vol. 5: The Gospels
Vol. 6: Acts to Revelation
Vol. 7: 1 Nephi to Alma 29
Vol. 8: Alma 30 to Moroni

CONTENTS

Preface vii

1 The Saga of the Early Christian Church, *Robert L. Millet* . 1

2 The Postresurrection Ministry, *S. Kent Brown and
   C. Wilfred Griggs* 12

3 "Unto All Nations," *Robert J. Matthews* 24

4 The Just Shall Live by Faith, *Robert L. Millet* 45

5 "Is Christ Divided?" Unity of the Saints through Charity,
   David R. Seely 57

6 Concern, Correction, and Counsel for Converts,
   George A. Horton, Jr. 83

7 Grace, Mysteries, and Exaltation, *Rodney Turner* 107

8 "Work Out Your Own Salvation," *H. Dean Garrett* . . . 125

9 The Preeminence of Christ, *Clyde J. Williams* 136

10 Hope for the "Children of Light" as the Darkness Descends,
   Jo Ann H. Seely 146

11 From Unprofitable Servant to Beloved Brother in Christ,
   David R. Seely 165

12 The Pastoral Epistles, *Bruce A. Van Orden* 178

13 Jesus Christ, Symbolism, and Salvation, *Joseph F. McConkie* . 192

Contents

14 A String of Gospel Pearls, *Larry E. Dabl* 207

15 The Sublime Epistles of Peter, *Monte S. Nyman* 225

16 The Epistles of John, *Thomas W. Mackay* 236

17 Refuge in God's Love, *Catherine Thomas* 244

18 "Things Which Must Shortly Come to Pass,"
    Gerald N. Lund 256

19 Whither the Early Church, *S. Kent Brown* 276

    Scripture Index 285

    Subject Index 297

PREFACE

"We are witnesses of all things which [Christ] did both in the land of the Jews, and in Jerusalem; whom they slew and hanged on a tree," Peter boldly declared to the household of Cornelius the Gentile. "Him God raised up the third day, and shewed him openly; not to all the people, but unto witnesses chosen before of God, even to us." (Acts 10:39-41.)

The story of the early Christian church—the drama associated with the initial growth and struggles of Christianity after the ascension of Jesus Christ into heaven—is an inspiring collection of testimonies, a scriptural convocation of chosen witnesses. Jesus had risen from the dead. The Holy Ghost had been given in pentecostal power. Now these chosen messengers set out to deliver the proclamation of peace "in Jerusalem, and in all Judaea, and in Samaria, and unto the uttermost part of the earth." (Acts 1:8.)

Studies in Scripture, Volume 6: Acts to Revelation is another book in a series intended to enhance and supplement one's personal study of the revelations and truths found in the standard works of The Church of Jesus Christ of Latter-day Saints. Recognizing that there is no substitute for a sincere and serious study of the scriptures themselves, this series is presented as a resource, an aid in pointing Latter-day Saints toward the profound realities to be discovered in the books that comprise our scriptural canon.

Sincere appreciation is expressed to many persons, without whose active involvement and enthusiastic support this project would not have been possible. The contributors have willingly shared their talents and the results of many years of research and teaching. Gratitude is also extended to Ronald A. Millett, Eleanor Knowles, and the staff at Deseret Book for their interest and editorial and production expertise in this work. And, as always, I owe a special debt of gratitude to my wife and children, who have been more than supportive through the entire series.

This volume consists of essays written to give deeper insight into the historical backgrounds and doctrinal significance of the messages contained in the second half of the New Testament, Acts to Revelation. These essays have been written by Latter-day Saints who have commitment to the Lord Jesus Christ and loyalty to his anointed servants in the Restored Church. We make no apology for the fact that this book has been compiled with a bias of belief; it is an expression of testimony, a statement of faith.

All of the contributors are responsible for their own conclusions, and this collection is a private endeavor and not a production of either Brigham Young University or The Church of Jesus Christ of Latter-day Saints. Although the writers and editor have sought to be in harmony with the teachings of the scriptures and the leaders of the Church, the reader should not regard this work as a primary source for gospel understanding but should turn instead to the scriptures and the words of modern prophets for authoritative doctrinal statements.

It is hoped that this book will make a meaningful contribution in bringing Latter-day Saints to a greater understanding of and appreciation for the Savior and his early followers in the first century Christian church. It is also hoped that those who read it will be inspired and motivated to pattern their lives and teachings after those chosen messengers who gave their all to build up and establish the kingdom of God in the meridian of time, for the clarion call of our Lord in our day is to "Go . . . and do likewise."

ROBERT L. MILLET

1

THE SAGA OF THE
EARLY CHRISTIAN CHURCH

Robert L. Millet

The church established by our Savior in the meridian of time continued for a time after his death and ascension into heaven. The keys of the kingdom of God had been delivered to Peter, James, and John on the mount of transfiguration (Matt. 16:19; 17:1-8);[1] a missionary plan was set in motion (Matt. 10); and the chosen witnesses of the Christ began to spread the proclamation of peace in an orderly but systematic fashion: in Jerusalem, in all Judea, in Samaria, and unto the uttermost parts of the known world (Acts 1:8).

Notable Achievements of the Early Church

1. *Growth in Organization.* If we were to reason and extrapolate from the experience of the Restored Church, we might suppose that the Meridian Church developed organizationally in a gradual, line-upon-line fashion. In this dispensation the Lord appointed Joseph Smith and Oliver Cowdery as the first and second elders and also as apostles of Jesus Christ in April 1830, at the time of the organization. (D&C 20:2-3.) The first high priests were ordained in June 1831. (Preface to D&C 52.) The First Presidency was established in March 1832. (Preface to D&C 81.) And the Quorum of the Twelve Apostles

---

Robert L. Millet is assistant professor of ancient scripture and New Testament area coordinator at Brigham Young University.

and Quorum of the Seventy were not selected for five years, until February 1835.

In the four Gospels, the only church officers mentioned are apostles and seventies. It is worthy of note that as late as Matthew 16:16-18, the time of Peter's confession at Caesarea Philippi—only six months before the crucifixion—Jesus had spoken of the establishment of his church as a future eventuality: "Upon this rock I will build my church." It is Paul who indicates that the Lord provided an organization, such as evangelists, pastors, bishops, teachers, and deacons, for the perfecting of the saints and the work of the ministry. (See Eph. 4:11-14; 1 Tim. 3:1-7; 2 Tim. 4:5; Titus 1:7-9.) Perhaps a key to understanding the Lord's process for church organization is to be found in the early verses of Luke's Acts of the Apostles: The Lord Jesus, through the Holy Ghost, gave commandments to those early apostles, "to whom also he shewed himself alive after his passion [suffering] by many infallible proofs, being seen of them forty days, and *speaking of the things pertaining to the kingdom of God.*" (Acts 1:2-3; emphasis added.) It may be, therefore, that the Savior provided the more complex church organization (similar to what we know in the latter-day church) during his forty-day ministry.[2]

With the death of Judas Iscariot, there was a vacancy in the Twelve. In the presence of a number of disciples, Peter—the senior member of the quorum and president of the church—called for nominations, recommendations of a man who would be of apostolic stature, one to stand with the other eleven as a witness of the resurrection of their Master. Joseph Barsabas and Matthias were nominated. After sincere prayer, the voice of the Spirit indicated the mind of the Lord: Matthias was chosen and the apostles gave forth their lots—their sustaining votes—in support of the one the Lord had selected.[3] (Acts 1:15-26.) For a season at least, the principle of apostolic succession was in operation in that day, and the Church of Jesus Christ continued in an uninterrupted manner. The divinely given laws were set and the principles of a theocratic religious system among the saints were in place.

With the growth of the Church and the consequent discovery of further needs, organizational developments continued. In the sixth chapter of Acts, "seven men of honest report, full of the Holy Ghost

2

and wisdom," were chosen as *diakona,* special assistants to the leaders of the church in ministering to the welfare needs of a group of widowed Greek-speaking Jews. (Acts 6:1-5.) Of this number were two noble and capable preachers of righteousness: Stephen, who would soon bear witness of Jesus Christ to the Jewish council and become one of the early martyrs of Christendom, and Philip, one who ministered in the spirit of Elias and who discoursed and performed miracles with mighty power. (Acts 7–8.)[4]

2. *Growth Beyond Traditional Bounds.* There was nothing more firmly established in the minds of Jews (even Christian Jews) in the meridian of time than the concept that God had chosen the House of Israel—according to his own infinite foreknowledge and in harmony with the doctrine of election in the flesh—to be his own peculiar people. Even Jesus, with his universal vision and sense of mission to all mankind, had provided during his mortal ministry specific instructions that his own proselyting effort, as well as that of the Twelve, was to be directed toward the "lost sheep of the house of Israel." (Matt. 10:5-6; 15:24.)

There were, of course, those prophetic utterances which hinted at the possibility that one of the major assignments delivered to Israel by Jehovah was to reach beyond the limits of the covenant people to the *goyim,* the nations or the Gentiles; to bring the knowledge of the one true God to the understanding of all men on earth; and to dispense to the world those moral and ethical edicts laid down by the God of Sinai. Through Isaiah the Lord had declared: "It is a light thing [too little, not enough] that thou [Israel] shouldest be my servant to raise up the tribes of Jacob, and to restore the preserved of Israel: *I will also give thee for a light to the Gentiles,* that thou mayest be my salvation *unto the end of the earth.*" (Isa. 49:6; emphasis added.) And even Jesus had said before his ascension into heaven that the Twelve were to go unto *all nations* and make converts to Christianity. (Matt. 28:19-20.) Few members of the church seemed ready, however, for the revelation that came to Peter and Cornelius (Acts 10) and for the zealous manner in which Paul carried the message of Christianity to the Gentiles.

Tradition in the first century, like that of any age, was stiff and extremely resistant to change. But the Lord had spoken, the light of a new day was bursting upon the early church, and changes were to be forthcoming: the gospel message was now to go forth to the Gentiles, and the crumbs of bread from the royal table were being gathered and feasted upon by the "dogs" of the nations outside Israel. Those who gave heed to the words of the living oracles and received their declarations as if from the mouth of the Lord himself became grounded and rooted in the faith; those who were more governed by their traditions and those of their forebears either lived and died weak in the faith or left the faith entirely.

3. *Growth in Spiritual Power.* Two significant events following the death of Jesus Christ proved to be of inestimable worth in building and shaping the faith of the struggling band of Christians: the resurrection of the Master and the gift of the Holy Ghost.

"Why seek ye the living among the dead? He is not here, but is risen." (Luke 24:5-6.) This divine announcement from the mouths of angels affirmed the hopes and stilled the fears of a troubled lot of early Christian disciples. One of the greatest messages in all eternity was the message of the empty tomb, the announcement that a God had died, ministered in the world of spirits, and come back to life; that the effects of the rising of the Sinless One would pass upon all; that death and hell and endless torment had no hold on mankind; and that every soul could glory in the reality of immortality, with those who believe and obey gaining the added assurance of eternal life. Christ had risen from the dead! He had broken the bands of death! Now it all seemed so much more comprehensible for the Twelve and the disciples; now things began to make sense; suddenly the significance of the central moment in the divine drama—a drama acted out in time's meridian—loomed larger and brighter and clearer.

Following the day of Pentecost and the remarkable spiritual outpouring associated with that singular occasion, vision replaced partial blindness; insight and perception and quiet resolve overcame the ignorance and fear that had so characterized the disciples during the Master's mortal ministry. As President Joseph F. Smith taught, "Not one of the disciples possessed sufficient light, knowledge nor wisdom, at the time of the crucifixion, for either exaltation or condemnation; for it was afterward that their minds were opened to understand the scriptures, and that they were endowed with power from on high;

without which they were only children in knowledge, in comparison to what they afterwards become under the influence of the Spirit."[5]

Simon Peter serves as the classic illustration of this principle. Whereas in the Gospels we see Peter as noble and loyal and dedicated, we are also made privy to his weaknesses: he doubts and denies. After the resurrection and the day of Pentecost, Peter is a different man entirely: his zeal is fortified with wisdom, his loyalty buttressed with an indefatigable and undeniable witness of his Lord and Master. When his testimony of the Christ is challenged, he responds: "We ought to obey God rather than men. The God of our fathers raised up Jesus, whom ye slew and hanged on a tree." With boldness he attests: "We are his witnesses of these things; and so is also the Holy Ghost, whom God hath given to them that obey him." (Acts 5:29-30, 32.)

One of the primary messages of the New Testament is how the gospel of Christ can renovate the human personality. One who is born of the Spirit becomes a new creature in Christ, has crucified the old man of sin, and has, like his Redeemer, risen to a newness of life and assumed a higher standard of existence. Having learned that the Lord is better able to create righteousness in a human soul than any man or woman could do, the true believer surrenders his will to Him who knows all things. The disciple discovers—as Paul and Moroni taught—that as he comes to Christ, He who is omnipotent is not only able to reveal weakness but also able to transform weaknesses into strengths.

Saul, the same who became Paul the Apostle, serves as the classic illustration of this principle. Zealous but misguided in his defense of the law and his battle of Christianity, this former Pharisee was turned about midstream: he was given new direction on the road to Damascus and received a call to serve in an opposite cause, a call issued by Him who had been the focus of Saul's persecution. Conversion took place and weakness became strength. Luke, the author of the Acts of the Apostles, set out to demonstrate that Paul's actions and works constituted him as every bit the apostle that Peter was. One need only compare the following scriptural sources to realize the power of Christ to change men's souls:

Peter	Paul
Acts 3:1-8	Acts 14:8-12

Acts 5:14-15 . . Acts 19:11-12
Acts 8:18-23 . . Acts 13:6-11
Acts 9:36-42 . . Acts 20:7-12
Acts 12:6-7 . . . Acts 16:25-26

Challenges Faced by the Early Church

In the midst of noticeable growth in the first-century church, there were also formidable obstacles that tested the mettle of the saints. These challenges were both internal and external; they represented an attack upon both the structure and the heart of the Christian faith.

1. *Internal Struggles: The Jews.* The Jewish establishment considered Jesus of Nazareth to be revolutionary and unorthodox; they viewed the organization he set in motion as a heretical and apostate form of Judaism. When Jesus told the woman at the well that "salvation is of the Jews" (John 4:22), he seemed to be laying stress upon the fact that Judaism was the closest approximation to the truth: at least the Jews worshiped the true God and accepted the whole of the Old Testament (as contrasted with the Samaritans).[6] But in a myriad of ways the Jewish nation had fallen into apostasy and was in dire need of reform and restoration.[7] Jesus came not only to work out the infinite and eternal atonement, but also to restore Christianity to its pristine purity, to bring back that which had been divinely delivered in the earliest ages of time.

An even greater deterrent to the progress that might have been enjoyed by the Christian church was provided by those Jews who had become Christians, but who could not release their grasp upon Judaism. "The Judaizers," as they were called, were a constant stumbling block to Paul and the apostles of the first century. Their incessant insistence upon continued loyalty and adherence to the law of Moses—and particularly the practice of circumcision—led to the Jerusalem Conference (Acts 15) and occupied a significant amount of the time and energy of Paul (see Gal. 2), who contended that the law had been fulfilled in Christ and that neither circumcision nor uncircumcision were relevant matters when it came to discussing the substantive issues associated with salvation.

2. *External Struggles: Persecution of the Christians.* The earliest

form of persecution faced by the Christians came from the Jews. The leaders of the faith were frequently hailed before the Jewish Sanhedrin for their Messianic proclamation. "Did not we straitly command you that ye should not teach in this name [the name of Christ]?" the council demanded of Peter and John. "Behold," they continued, "ye have filled Jerusalem with your doctrine, and intend to bring this man's blood upon us." After it was decided that the apostles should not be put to death, they were beaten and once again warned concerning their preachments. "And they departed from the presence of the council, rejoicing that they were counted worthy to suffer shame for his name." (Acts 5:28-41.)

Stephen was tried and illegally executed for his witness of Christ—his powerful and persuasive testimony that Jesus of Nazareth was the fulfillment of the Prophets and that the murder of the Master sealed the doom of apostate Jewry. (See Acts 7.)

Paul, who was viewed as a heretic by the Jews, was often the object of Jewish wrath. In speaking of his own trials and persecutions, he wrote to the Corinthians: "Of the Jews five times received I forty stripes save one. Thrice was I beaten with rods, once was I stoned." (2 Cor. 11:24-25.) And yet this minister of peace could also write: "We are troubled on every side, yet not distressed; we are perplexed, but not in despair; persecuted, but not forsaken; cast down, but not destroyed." And then, acknowledging the source of his inner strength, Paul observed: "Always bearing about in the body the dying of the Lord Jesus, that the life also of Jesus might be made manifest in our body." (2 Cor. 4:8-10.)

The most serious form of persecution eventually came, of course, at the hands of the Romans. Formal persecution by the Romans may be said to have begun in the reign of Nero in A.D. 64 and to have continued until the close of the reign of Diocletian (A.D. 305). In writing of this external challenge to the church, Elder James E. Talmage observed:

> One of the principal reasons of the severity with which the Romans persecuted the Christians ... seems to have been the abhorrence and contempt with which the latter [the Christians] regarded the religion of the empire, which was so intimately connected with the form, and indeed, with the very es-

sence of its political constitution. For, though the Romans gave an unlimited toleration to all religions which had nothing in their tenets dangerous to the commonwealth, yet they would not permit that of their ancestors, which was established by the laws of the state, to be turned into derision, nor the people to be drawn away from their detachment to it. These, however, were the two things which the Christians were charged with, and that justly, though to their honor. They dared to ridicule the absurdities of the pagan superstition, and they were ardent and assiduous in gaining proselytes to the truth.[8]

One of the central messages of the Revelation (Apocalypse) of John is a plea for the children of light—the Christians, the members of the covenant community—to "hold on," to remain steadfast and secure in the faith in the midst of persecution. John stressed that the saints lived in the great day of Satan's power, but that the throes and onslaughts of wickedness would be brought to an abrupt halt by the intervention of God and the consequent introduction of a day of righteousness. The Beloved Disciple, looking through the stream of time, anticipated the day when the people of God would be freed from the effects of evil and persecution, a glorious era when "the kingdoms of this world are become the kingdoms of our Lord, and of his Christ; and he shall reign for ever and ever." (Rev. 11:15.)

3. *Internal Struggles: The Impact of Greek Philosophy.* Alexander the Great's empire, as a political entity, did not survive his death in 323 B.C. But the cultural empire he founded lasted for nearly one thousand years, until the rise of Islam and the Arab conquests in the seventh century A.D. Greek or Hellenistic influence was profound—upon the Roman Empire, upon the world of Judaism, and, unfortunately, upon the early Christian church. As Zenos had declared in prophetic vision, for a time the grafting of branches from the "wild olive tree" (Gentile influence) resulted in a season of strength for the Church. (See Jacob 5:17.) But it was only a matter of time before the doctrines of the prophets and the ideas of the philosophers came in conflict; those with eyes to see were aware that attempts to merge the revelations of the temple of God with the oracles of Delphi would be abortive to the true Christian faith. Ecumenism would lead to shared impotence. And so it did.

The Hebrew-Christian world view was dramatically different from that of the Greeks. Some areas of stress of the two groups were head or intellect (Athens) versus heart (Jerusalem); knowledge (Greeks) versus faith (Christians); and rhetoric or manner of speaking (Greeks) versus prophecy and revelation, a substantive message (Christians).[9] In a related but more serious vein, the Greek notion of God was in stark contrast to that revealed through Jesus Christ and the prophets. There were two conceptions of God entertained by the Greeks that, when eventually mixed with the truth, resulted in a heretical hybrid, a conceptual concoction foreign to the spiritually sensitive and certainly offensive to that God who delights in revealing himself to his children. First of all, the Greeks believed in a god who was totally *transcendent,* one too lofty, too holy to have communion with this world. In their minds, God was unknowable and unreachable. Secondly, God was *impassible,* the embodiment of pure activity. He was the First Great Cause, the Prime Mover, one over which nothing could exercise influence. God is thus void of feelings, passions, and compassion in behalf of humankind. In regard to the nature of the resultant composite—the Greek-Christian God—Elder Bruce R. McConkie taught:

> Let me . . . identify the original heresy that did more than anything else to destroy primitive Christianity.
>
> This first and chief heresy of a now fallen and decadent Christianity—and truly it is the father of all heresies—swept through all of the congregations of true believers in the early centuries of the Christian Era; it pertained then and pertains now to the nature and kind of being that God is.
>
> It was the doctrine, adapted from Gnosticism, that changed Christianity from the religion in which men worshiped a personal God, in whose image man is made, into the religion in which men worshiped a spirit essence called the Trinity. This new God, no longer a personal Father, no longer a personage of tabernacle, became an incomprehensible three-in-one spirit essence that filled the immensity of space.

"The adoption of this false doctrine about God," Elder McConkie further observed, "effectively destroyed true worship among men and ushered in the age of universal apostasy."[10]

Summary

A study of the first-century church and its leaders is of inestimable worth. For one thing, we are made privy to a crucial phase of earth's history; we learn from intimate sources (such as commissioned histories and letters) of what the world has come to know as the beginnings of Christianity. As Latter-day Saints, we appreciate the second half of the New Testament for what is preserved concerning the inspired workings of the apostles and prophets in what we now know from modern revelation to be one of the many dispensations of the gospel. More important, however, are the profound lessons—key doctrines, principles, and examples of courage in the face of danger and death—that may be learned from the lives and words of a people who counted all the allurements of the world to be but filth and dross when compared with the excellence of the knowledge of the Lord Jesus Christ. In short, they cherished the approbation of God more than the praises of the world and have left a legacy of faith and hope that will last forever.

Notes

1. See also *Teachings of the Prophet Joseph Smith,* comp. Joseph Fielding Smith (Salt Lake City: Deseret Book, 1976), p. 158.

2. Robert J. Matthews, *Unto All Nations: A Guide to the Book of Acts and the Writings of Paul* (Salt Lake City: Deseret Book, 1975), p. 1. See also S. Kent Brown and C. Wilfred Griggs, "The Postresurrection Ministry of Christ," chapter 2 in this volume, for a more detailed discussion of Christ's postresurrection teachings and ministry.

3. Bruce R. McConkie, *Doctrinal New Testament Commentary,* 3 vols. (Salt Lake City: Bookcraft, 1965-73), 2:32.

4. *Teachings of the Prophet Joseph Smith,* p. 336; McConkie, *Doctrinal New Testament Commentary* 2:81.

5. Joseph F. Smith, *Gospel Doctrine* (Salt Lake City: Deseret Book, 1986), p. 433.

6. Stephen E. Robinson, "The Setting of the Gospels," in *Studies in Scripture, Volume 5: The Gospels,* ed. Kent P. Jackson and Robert L. Millet (Salt Lake City: Deseret Book, 1986), pp. 10-37.

7. Bruce R. McConkie, *The Mortal Messiah: From Bethlehem to Calvary,* 4 vols. (Salt Lake City: Deseret Book, 1979-81), 1:228-40.

8. James E. Talmage, *The Great Apostasy* (Salt Lake City: Deseret Book, 1975), p. 66.

9. Edwin Hatch, *The Influence of Greek Ideas on Christianity* (Gloucester, Massachusetts: Peter Smith, 1970); Talmage, *The Great Apostasy,* chapters 6, 7.

10. Bruce R. McConkie, "What Think Ye of Salvation by Grace?," *Brigham Young University Fireside and Devotional Speeches, 1983-84* (Provo, Utah: Brigham Young University Publications, 1984), p. 44.

2

THE POSTRESURRECTION MINISTRY

S. KENT BROWN AND C. WILFRED GRIGGS

Everyone knows that the Gospels of the New Testament do not present full biographies of Jesus. In their individual testimonies concerning the ministry, crucifixion, and resurrection of the Savior, the authors selectively drew upon those teachings and deeds of Jesus that supported their purpose in writing. That the purpose of all the Gospels is to present the redemptive story of Jesus rather than a biography can be easily seen by noting that only two Gospels present an account of Jesus' birth, only one has any information about his youth (and that most sparing), and none gives more than a hint here and there relating to his adult family life. We do emphasize, however, that the Gospels are comprised of details that properly belong to biographies, just as histories are full of geographical details; but in both instances such material is included as secondary to a primary and differing purpose.

Each Gospel gives a special perspective concerning Jesus and his redemptive ministry. Matthew's testimony is directed primarily toward Jews and displays many characteristics that would be relevant especially to such an audience, including repeated and formulaic references to Old Testament prophecies and their fulfillment in Jesus. Similar observations could be made about each of the Gospels, such as the energetic Messiah of Mark, the universalism and Gentile-oriented

S. Kent Brown is professor of ancient scripture and director of publications for the Religious Studies Center at Brigham Young University. C. Wilfred Griggs is professor of ancient scripture at BYU.

teachings and parables in Luke, and the language and symbolism of John.

In view of such differences in purpose and approach, the historicity of Jesus' life and ministry is strengthened by the harmonious picture of his teachings and deeds in the Gospels. The similarities in the Gospels are all the more remarkable in light of John's statement that "there are also many other things which Jesus did, the which, if they should be written every one, I suppose that even the world itself could not contain the books that should be written." (John 21:25.) Such a passage was also an open invitation for ancient writers to try to provide more details about Jesus' life either from a personal knowledge of events and teachings, from a misdirected sense of piety, or simply from charlatan motives.

The Problems of the Apocryphal Writings

Men throughout history have sought to create new and sensational information about Jesus. Perhaps the best-known modern example of such fraudulent attempts to embellish the Gospel accounts is the notorious *Archko Volume,* which purports to originate from ancient records.[1] Similar ancient attempts have become part of the apocryphal literature of the New Testament. Because the New Testament Gospels are rather precise and detailed in their descriptions of Jesus' miracles and teachings, most apocryphal writings do not attempt to add details to the period already covered by the Gospel narratives. Instead, many apocryphal works have concentrated on the youth of Jesus, the background of Mary and Joseph, and other related periods within the time frame of the New Testament. Such fanciful narratives are occasionally grotesque, since they dwell at length upon the sensational. The so-called Infancy Gospels exploit the youth of Jesus to such an extent that he often appears to be a miracle-working delinquent, quite in contrast to the self-controlled and compassionate healer portrayed in the Gospels.

Another period of Jesus' life that provided an obvious invitation for apocryphal writing is referred to in Acts 1:3, where Luke mentions the forty-day ministry of the resurrected Jesus among his disciples. One of the major differences between the earlier periods of Jesus' life, which have drawn such speculative interest, and the time after the resurrection is that in the latter instance the resurrected Jesus was by then well-known and surrounded by disciples who would certainly be witnesses of his forty-day ministry. By contrast, the lives of Jesus' parents and the period of his youth would certainly not have drawn widespread interest and attention until many years later, when Jesus had become well-known. Therefore, works that deal with these early periods are likely to be much less credible simply because they were far removed from contemporary eyewitnesses.

Luke states that during the forty-day ministry the Savior spoke "of the things pertaining to the kingdom of God." But there are only vague hints in other New Testament writings as to the nature and content of these teachings. The preaching of Jesus to the spirits in prison (see 1 Pet. 3:19 and 4:6) and the doctrine of baptism for the dead (see 1 Cor. 15:29) are two examples of teachings that best fit the context of Acts 1:3. Although few, if any, works pertaining to the forty-day ministry of Acts 1:3 were known a century ago, modern discoveries have produced a virtual library of such writings. Many claim to be authored by such apostles as Peter, John, Philip, Thomas, and James, while others, for example, are simply entitled "The Accounts of the Great Ministry," "Concerning the Resurrection," and "Dialogue of the Redeemer." Many of these documents provide a time reference to the forty-day ministry when they claim to contain teachings of the *Living Jesus.* In this literature the word *living* is often a technical term that refers to the resurrected and glorified Christ.

There are many difficulties in establishing or refuting the authenticity of such writings. One predicament concerns the varied kinds of doctrinal ideas found in them. In some instances, these ideas either expand or differ from those found in the New Testament writings. But there is no point in arguing that the teachings and activities of the risen Jesus must have been the same as those of the mortal Jesus, since Luke states that it was after the resurrection that the Savior "opened ... their [the disciples'] understanding, that they might understand the scriptures [Old Testament]." (Luke 24:45.) John adds that the resurrected Lord did many marvels that were not recorded in his writings. (John 20:30.)

Another complication centers on the claimed authorship of many of the forty-day documents. The apostles mentioned above would be the very ones by whom such records would predictably be composed, and one must decide whether these texts indeed came from the apostles or were falsely attributed to them. The observation that many recently found texts date from the third or fourth centuries is itself not conclusive proof against early origins, for almost all extant documents from antiquity come from copies made centuries after the original composition was published. In addition, the majority of these writings contain no allusions or references to any contemporary historical circumstances that would tell us whether they were composed near the time of Jesus or many decades afterward. Since the dating problem persists in the case of almost every apocryphal text, judgment concerning authenticity must be made on other grounds.

A third difficulty arises because these documents were not widely read and circulated. But this circumstance cannot form a decisive argument against their authenticity, for most of them claim to contain secret teachings reserved for a righteous minority within Christianity.

In view of these problems, most scholars have tacitly adopted the following standard for determining the value of such documents: if they correspond to something already known to "orthodox" Christianity, they are assumed to have been derived from Christianity; if they do not correspond to "orthodox" Christianity, they were probably not Christian in origin. The difficulty with this standard is agreeing on a definition of "orthodox" Christianity. Although scholars differ on such a definition, they are generally agreed that most of what is contained in the forty-day literature is *not* fully Christian.

The Doctrine and Covenants provides Latter-day Saints with an opportunity to look for elements of truth in this literature with a better standard of comparison than is available to others. When the Prophet Joseph Smith inquired of the Lord whether he should translate the Old Testament Apocrypha as a part of his work on the Bible, he was given the revelation contained in section 91. Although the forty-day literature is not part of the apocrypha known to Joseph Smith, it presents to modern-day readers the same problems as the Old Testament Apocrypha in its relationship to the scriptures. The revelation states that "there are many things contained therein that are true" and "there are many things contained therein that are not true." (D&C 91:1-2.)

To be sure, although we cannot tell any more about the history or society of the people who wrote these texts than can the scholars, we can examine some of the traditions and beliefs in their writings and note how they correspond to the restored gospel. This examination leads to greater insights into the nature of early Christianity than before possible and gives further evidences of the apostasy or rebellion within the church.

We are certain that one item of which Jesus spoke during his forty-day visit concerned the disciples' approaching missions. In the New Testament, Luke records that at the end of the forty days the resurrected Jesus forbade the disciples to leave Jerusalem for their missions until they had received the Spirit. (See Acts 1:4-5; Luke 24:46-49.) Luke then recounts Jesus' final words to the disciples to the effect that they would be witnesses of the Savior's resurrection "unto the uttermost part of the earth." (Acts 1:8. See also Acts 1:22; 2:32.)

The accounts of the Gospel writers agree with this picture. For example, Matthew writes that the risen Jesus met with his disciples for the last time on earth in order to send them to "teach all nations, baptizing them." (Matt. 28:19.) Mark concurs that Jesus' final instructions to his disciples included the charge to go "into all the world, and preach." (Mark 16:15.) According to Luke's Gospel, when the resurrected Lord opened the scriptures to the understanding of his disciples, he told them that "repentance and remission of sins should be preached ... among all nations, beginning at Jerusalem." (Luke 24:47.)

It is unfortunate that we possess so little information about the missionary activities of the apostles when we know that Jesus spent time preparing them for this significant effort. Apart from a few scattered accounts in the early chapters of Acts, virtually all of the stories that concern missionary work in the New Testament are told about Paul. Even Eusebius, who published the first extant history of the Church in about A.D. 325, knew but little information about a few disciples, and much of this he obtained from apocryphal traditions. He noted that "when the holy apostles and disciples of our Savior were dispersed over the whole world, Parthia was allotted to Thomas, according to tradition, while Scythia was allotted to Andrew, and Asia to John. . . . But Peter, it seems, preached in Pontus and Galatia and Bithynia, in Cappadocia and Asia. . . . He also at last came to Rome."[2] Of Paul, Eusebius merely notes in the same source that he preached the gospel "from Jerusalem to Illyricum" in western Greece. Because Eusebius knew no other traditions about the apostles' proselyting labors between Jesus' death and about A.D. 65, he assumed that "during all these years the greater number of the apostles and disciples . . . made their abode in the city of Jerusalem."[3] Against this "orthodox" view of Eusebius rests the weight of so-called apocryphal traditions that generally affirm that the disciples did indeed fulfill the Lord's charge to take the gospel to the world.

The *Pseudoclementina*, a collection of early Christian documents whose picture of the earliest church has been argued to be almost as reliable as that in Acts, focuses primarily on the apostle Peter's missionary activities that ultimately led him to Rome. One section recounts that the apostles used to gather annually to Jerusalem at Passover to report on their missionary activities.[4] This clearly implies that all of the apostles were engaged in missionary work in some measure. In the *Apocryphon of James*, a secret apocryphal letter that the Lord's brother James allegedly wrote to an unknown person, the idea of the apostles all going on missions is so strong that this text claims that they all departed *before* the day of Pentecost except for James himself, who returned to Jerusalem alone. In the recently discovered apocryphal *Letter of Peter to Philip*, Peter wrote urgently to Philip to inform him that the Savior had directed the apostles to gather together before they left on their missions. When the apostles met on the Mount of Olives, Jesus appeared and repeated the command that they preach to the world. In this alleged letter of Peter, we find the idea repeated that the disciples again met after having preached for a period.

To be sure, the apocryphal works offer us little more reliable information regarding where the disciples preached than we have from such "orthodox" sources as Eusebius. Although the sources do not strictly agree on the exact destination of Thomas, for example, they all concur that he went to the east.

The *Acts of Thomas*, a work originally composed in Syriac at an unknown date, claims to chronicle Thomas's activities as the apostle to India. Many students of Christian history have dismissed the *Acts of Thomas* as legendary fiction both because its Christian character seems perverted owing to the mention of ceremonial washings and anointings (the very things that other texts claim that Jesus gave to the disciples during the forty days) and because many legendary elements appear to embellish the stories of Thomas's miracles. It is remarkable that the historical and geographical details in the *Acts of Thomas* agree with those known from the middle of the first century A.D., the period when Thomas would have been actively proselytizing.

According to the apocryphal *Acts of Andrew,* an account of this apostle's missionary work written about A.D. 150, Andrew spent the bulk of his mission in northern Asia Minor and in Greece, finally suffering martyrdom in the Greek city of Patrae.

The *Acts of John,* in correlation with many other so-called apocryphal and orthodox accounts, places the ministry of John the apostle in Asia Minor, especially in and near Ephesus.

In the *Acts of Peter,* we find assertions that Paul traveled to Spain after spending time in Rome, and that Peter spent considerable time in Rome before his own martyrdom.

In the view of the *Acts of Philip,* Peter and John are also said to have visited Parthia, where Philip supposedly proselytized for a time in addition to his missionary labors in Palestine, Asia Minor, and Greece. Philip purportedly was martyred in Hierapolis, a city in western Asia Minor.

The traditions about where Matthew preached in such works as the *Acts of Andrew and Matthias* and the *Martyrdom of Matthew* merely specify that this apostle proselytized among cannibals and spent time among them in a city called Myrna, otherwise unknown.

For the rest of the apostles, one can generally say that not even legend has enshrined their missionary efforts.

Like the *Acts of Thomas,* all of the works just mentioned are considered fiction by most students of early Christianity. Once again, this judgment is made partially on such bases as (1) that some doctrines (such as the premortal existence of all people) are not present in the New Testament and, therefore, are non-Christian, and (2) that the religious ceremonies (such as washings, anointings, and receiving special clothing) were not part of the worship services in the earliest church and, hence, their presence in these texts must be due to pagan influences. Latter-day Saints, who understand these doctrines and ordinances, should probe deeper. When available historical and geographical details in these texts agree with what is known about the first century A.D., it is clear that we have to give them more serious consideration than simply calling them pious legend.

Common Themes in the Apocryphal Accounts

Although the apocryphal writings found during the past century derive from many different geographical settings and theologically diverse sects, there are a number of themes common to virtually all of these writings, regardless of origin. The similarity of themes in these texts, despite the wide-ranging theological differences of the sects that used them, both argues for their development out of an authentic historical and theological setting and invites our careful examination. It is all the more remarkable that these similarities occur, considering the lack of many of these themes in the New Testament and other early Christian literature.[5] A very brief examination of a few of the more prominent themes in this literature would include the following:

The most popular Old Testament subject for apocryphal speculation is the creation story found in Genesis. In addition to entire works dealing specifically with the creation of the world, lengthy segments on the creation are included in such works as the *Hypostasis of the Archons* and the *Apocryphon of John.*

The *Hypostasis* begins with a quotation from Paul's epistle to the Ephesians (6:12) that establishes the purpose of the text—to explain that man's struggles in this life are really against the powers of darkness. There follows a description of the heavenly council, the rebellion in heaven, and the casting out of Satan and his rebellious followers. Next, the account of the creation of the earth and subsequent events includes a dramatic dialogue between God, Satan, Adam, and Eve. The detailed accounts of the temptation, the partaking of the forbidden fruit, and the expulsion of Adam and Eve from the garden are followed by the esoteric and embellished account of earth's history to the time of Noah. Some of the details included in this interesting manuscript most certainly are due to speculation and imagination. But not all. Enough remains to indicate that there were once ordinances associated with the basic story of the text. In this light, it is quite likely that when the ordinances associated with the text were lost, the resulting deficiency was compensated in part by such imaginative additions.

In the *Apocryphon of John* a similarly involved account of a heavenly council, a war, and an expulsion of rebellious offspring of God is recounted. This time the telling of the story is placed in the context of the glorified Jesus explaining to John "things which are, which have been, and which will be." Accordingly, this text concerns itself with history from the time of Adam until Noah, and also includes detailed descriptions of the eternal destinies of man. These descriptions occur near the end of the text and are in the form of a dialogue: John asks Jesus about those who will be saved, those who have not known in mortality "to whom they belong," and those "who have come into the knowledge but have turned away." In answer to the preceding questions the Savior explains that some will become perfect, purifying themselves from all evil, and will inherit eternal life. Those who do not know in mortality to whom they belong will go to a prison after this life, where they will be able to obtain knowledge and be saved.

At this point, John asks how the spirit can return to the mortal body (implying that more than knowledge is necessary for salvation), but the Savior responds that a spirit in prison can be saved by "being connected with another in whom the spirit of Life is," and will not have to return to a mortal body. Further along in the text, Jesus explains to John that after his death he went to the spirit prison and taught salvation to those who were there. Variations on this popular theme can be found in numerous other apocryphal texts.

Another common element in apocryphal literature is the secrecy enjoined upon those who receive these teachings. The *Gospel of Thomas* begins: "These are the secret words which the Living Jesus spoke," and *Thomas the Contender* begins with the "secret words that Jesus spoke to Judas-Thomas." The *Apocryphon of John* opens with "the secret teachings," and *Second Jeu* has an entire page devoted to a charge by Jesus to his disciples that they "not give these things for anything of the world." It is obvious that the people who wrote or copied these documents did not intend for them to become widely read.

References to rituals abound in this large body of material. In addition to baptisms and sacred meals, there are also numerous references to washings, anointings, and special garments. In the *Acts of Thomas,* those who are baptized also request the "seal" from the apostle Thomas, which consists of an anointing with oil. In the famous *Hymn of the Pearl* from the same work, the plan of redemption is portrayed in amazing detail and clarity. The son of God is sent to the world (symbolized by Egypt) with the charge to bring back the pearl (his soul). Although he falls into a spiritual coma by partaking of the food and raiment of the world, his heavenly parents, after holding a great council to plan his redemption, send the message of salvation and its attendant power to their son. The son awakens, exercises his new power over the serpent who rules the world, rescues his pearl, and accomplishes the long, hard journey back to his parents' home. There, according to the promises given before he made the journey, the son receives a heavenly garment and a beautiful robe, which admit him into the company of the great ones of heaven.

Marriage as a requirement for those who would achieve the highest of the three heavens is a teaching found in the *Gospel of Philip,* and the sanctity of marriage is alluded to in other documents. On some occasions the resurrected Jesus is portrayed as giving sacred teachings to the apostles and their wives, as in *Second Jeu.* From the variations of the rituals perceived in apocryphal literature, it appears evident that the different sects probably changed the ordinances, perhaps because they no longer understood their significance.

Finally, one of the recurring messages in this body of literature is the gloomy future that is in store for the true believers. In the *Epistle of Peter to Philip,* when the disciples are walking back to Jerusalem after being instructed by the risen Lord on the Mount of Olives, Peter explains to the others that they will suffer greatly. The voice of the Lord is then heard from heaven and confirms what Peter has said, adding that persecution is necessary for one to become like the Savior. In the *Apocryphon of James,* Jesus explains to James that, by suffering persecution and doing the will of the Father, one can be made equal to

Christ. James later asks how the apostles are to respond to those asking for prophecy, and Jesus replies that prophecy has already been taken from the earth. Later in the same work Peter expresses concern that the Savior was not very encouraging, to which the Lord responds that the disciples should not be concerned with anything but the promise of eternal life.

In the *Apocalypse of Peter,* Jesus explains that even Peter would be blasphemed in the future by deceivers who would depart from the truth, leading multitudes after them. These false teachers, continues the Savior, make merchandise of his (the Savior's) word, oppress their brothers with the defilement of apostate religion, and even use Peter's name to lead the souls of men astray. All is not lost, however, for the Savior states that there is a time appointed for the false teachers (who are characterized as "waterless canals") and the fulfillment of their deception, after which the "agelessness of immortal thought will be renewed." The deception will be pulled out by its roots and righteousness will prevail at his coming.

In these works the disciples are assured that through the death and resurrection of Jesus, they need not fear suffering, persecution, or death in this life. What they learned and received in the forty-day ministry would be the means for obtaining salvation and eternal life.

Even though often spurious in origin and detail, these apocryphal writings bear a united testimony of missionary activity by the risen Jesus' most trusted companions. In addition, much of what they taught according to these accounts not only continues several prominent themes already found in the scriptures but also augments and adds other doctrines. Many such teachings have been shown to be true by the restoration of the gospel and have been buttressed by the recent discovery of ancient texts long lost. Moreover, ordinances and ceremonies thought to have been pagan in inspiration are shown to have been an integral part of the original tapestry of earliest Christianity in the light of the gospel ordinances restored through Joseph Smith. Thus, the documents that claim to chronicle the expanding ministry after Jesus' resurrection should not be dismissed out of hand. Further, the invitation is open to all to examine them in accordance with the observations made by the Lord to the Prophet: "Therefore, whoso readeth it, let him understand, for the Spirit manifesteth truth;

and whoso is enlightened by the Spirit shall obtain benefit therefrom; and whoso receiveth not by the Spirit, cannot be benefited." (D&C 91:4-6.)

Notes

1. See Richard L. Anderson's expose of this fraud in "Imitation Gospels and Christ's Book of Mormon Ministry," in C. Wilfred Griggs, ed., *Apocryphal Writings and the Latter-day Saints* (Provo, Utah: Religious Studies Center, Brigham Young University, 1986), pp. 53-107.

2. Eusebius, *History of the Church* III.I.1-2.

3. Ibid., III.7.8.

4. *Recognitions* I.43-44.

5. For a thorough summary, see Hugh Nibley, "The Forty-day Mission of Christ—the Forgotten Heritage," *When the Lights Went Out* (Salt Lake City: Deseret Book, 1970), pp. 33-54.

3

"UNTO ALL NATIONS"
(Acts)

ROBERT J. MATTHEWS

The book of Acts covers a period of about thirty years and is a continuation of the Gospel of Luke. It is a sequel to the Gospels and was written by Luke to tell what the leaders of the Church did after Jesus' ascension into heaven, especially in missionary work among the Gentiles. (Acts 1:1-2.) Luke was a Gentile and was the natural one to write about missionary work among the Gentiles because he was there when it all began.

Acts is a dramatic and moving story about how the early church taught the gospel of Jesus Christ first to the Jews, next to the Samaritans, and then to the Gentiles. Considerable preparation, conditioning, and struggling were required of many Jewish members of the church before they were willing to accept Gentiles by virtue of the gospel without the law of Moses. Many Jewish Christians vigorously insisted that a Gentile had to become a Jew before he could become a Christian. The whole matter of gentile converts had to be dealt with not only in terms of doctrine but also in terms of culture and emotion.

Acts and the writings of Paul are firsthand accounts of how this was done gradually, a half step at a time, within the framework of the established authority of the priesthood and the administration of the church. We also get an insight into the cultural and emotional resistance that had to be overcome within the church in order for the gospel of Jesus Christ to be extended to the Gentiles, specifically to the

Robert J. Matthews is professor of ancient scripture and dean of Religious Education at Brigham Young University.

Greeks and the Romans. The word *gentiles* means "the nations, and eventually came to be used to mean all those not of the house of Israel," the covenant people. (Bible dictionary, s.v. "gentile.") Genealogically, *gentile* refers to the descendants of Japheth, son of Noah. (Gen. 10:1-5.)

Since Luke had a specific purpose in writing about missionary work, he did not give an account of all of the Twelve, but he selected those things basic and necessary to the development of his particular theme. Thus, Acts 1 through 8 tells about calling a new member to the Quorum of the Twelve, extensive conversion among the Jews, appointing seven men to administer welfare activities, taking the gospel to the Samaritans and others, and the preaching of Peter and John. These early chapters are interesting by themselves, but they are especially important as a foundation for understanding properly the middle chapters (Acts 9–15), which deal primarily with the conversion of Paul and the entry of Gentiles into the Church, and the later chapters (Acts 16–28), which give an account of Paul's work as the Apostle of the Gentiles. The major portion of Acts deals with Paul and his travels and does not equally represent the labors of the original Twelve. Luke was writing, not a general church history, but a recitation of how the gospel was made available to the Gentiles. The Acts of the Apostles is not the title given to the work by Luke himself and is not an accurate description of the contents. The earliest manuscripts do not bear this title; the book was originally called simply Acts.

Some casually think of the book of Acts as history and of the Epistles as doctrine, but this classification is too simplistic. All of the books are rich in both history and doctrine: there is much doctrine in Acts and much history in the Epistles. These writings demonstrate the diligent efforts of the church leaders in proclaiming the gospel of Jesus Christ to both Jew and Gentile. The brethren were determined and enthusiastic, alive with the spirit of missionary work and the testimony of Jesus. They knew they had the most important message in the world for their day, and they proceeded to give it.

Jesus' Forty-day Ministry

During the forty-day period following his resurrection, the Savior visited frequently with the Twelve, "speaking of the things pertaining to the kingdom of God" (Acts 1:3) and giving instructions concerning their ministry to "the uttermost part of the earth" (Acts 1:8), which they were to accomplish after receiving the Holy Ghost.

It is probable that during this forty-day period the church was organized into quorums and various offices. The four Gospels contain no reference to a complex church organization during Jesus' mortal ministry and tell only of a Quorum of the Twelve (Luke 6:12-16) and the seventy (Luke 10:1-17). A similar situation is seen with the church in this dispensation, in which the offices of bishop, seventy, patriarch, Quorum of the Twelve, and First Presidency were added years after the original organization.

Increased Missionary Effort

When the Twelve were sent on missions during the ministry of Jesus, they were instructed to go only to the people of Israel and were specifically told not to go among the Gentiles or to the Samaritans. (Matt. 10:5-6; 15:24. See also 3 Ne. 15:21-24.) Jesus ministered briefly among the Samaritans, but he primarily taught the Jews. (John 4:3-43.) As a result of this restricted missionary activity, the church at the time of Jesus' death was almost exclusively Jewish. After his resurrection, however, Jesus commanded the Twelve to go and "teach all nations" (Matt. 28:19), but they were to wait in Jerusalem until they were "baptized with the Holy Ghost," which would occur "not many days hence" (Acts 1:5). After receiving the Holy Ghost, they were to become "witnesses unto [Jesus] both in Jerusalem, and in all Judaea, and in Samaria, and unto the uttermost part of the earth." (Acts 1:8.) This injunction is the key to the book of Acts and clearly forecasts an extension of the missionary effort and a change in policy regarding the Samaritans and the Gentiles. This change in program is not contradictory, but it indicates that the Lord has a timetable in offering the gospel to various people and races. Acts 1:8 sets the pattern for the entire book: the Jews were taught first, then the Samaritans, and finally the Gentiles.

When Matthias was appointed to fill the vacancy in the Quorum of the Twelve created by the death of Judas Iscariot, Peter explained that the office of apostle is to be a special witness for the resurrection of Jesus Christ. This responsibility is conspicuous in the subsequent preaching of the Brethren. (See Acts 1:21-22; 2:32; 3:15; 4:33; 5:29-32.) Within a few months, thousands were brought into the church, notably on the day of Pentecost (Acts 2:41, 47) and in similar conversions through the preaching of the gospel by the Twelve (Acts 4:4; 6:7). Peter, who had been given the keys of the presidency, took the lead in all of these events. He indicated that most, if not all, of the Twelve had earlier been followers of John the Baptist. (Acts 1:21-22.) This discipleship is consistent with John's mission to prepare a people for Christ. It would be good economy for John to begin the preparation of those who would later become the Twelve by teaching them their first lessons in the gospel.

Although the membership of the Church was almost completely of Jewish lineage at the time of these early events, it is evident that a number of people of Gentile lineage soon came into the church. For example, the people who had gathered at Jerusalem on the day of Pentecost were from sixteen surrounding provinces and countries and had come to Jerusalem to attend the feast. (Acts 2:6-12.) They are spoken of as being "Jews and proselytes." (Acts 2:10.) To understand this statement, we must know that a proselyte was a person of Gentile lineage who had joined the Jewish religion by obedience to the requirements of the law of Moses, including circumcision, baptism, sacrifice, and attending to the dietary laws. It is certain there were Gentile proselytes among the three thousand persons converted and baptized into the church on the day of Pentecost. They were among the first people of Gentile ancestry in the Christian church; but of course, they had earlier become Jews by religion. Later, when the seven were chosen to assist with the distribution of food, one of them is identified as "Nicolas a proselyte of Antioch." (Acts 6:5.) He was a Gentile who had accepted Judaism before he became a Christan. (See Bible dictionary, s.v. "proselyte".) There was another class of Gentile believers called "Godfearers." (Bible dictionary, s.v. "proselyte.") These, although they believed in the God of Israel, did not actually become Jews by ceremony, such as by circumcision. (See Acts 13:16, in which Paul addresses those who are "of Israel" and those "that fear God.")

When the Holy Ghost came upon the Twelve on the day of Pentecost, they spoke with new tongues. But even more significant, the

27

Holy Ghost caused a great change in their hearts. This change is especially noticeable in Peter because we have more information about his activities than about the activities of the other members of the original Twelve. On the night prior to Jesus' crucifixion, Peter is characterized as fearful and hesitant. (John 18:15-27.) But after the day of Pentecost he is bold and forthright, not fearing the Jewish council, imprisonment, or death. (Acts 2—4.) This change can be attributed to the effect of the Holy Ghost, which purifies, emboldens, strengthens, comforts, and in every way prepares a servant of the Lord for the work that is required of him. He is born again.

Although many scriptures illustrate Peter's forthright witness of Jesus, perhaps the best known is his testimony before the Jewish Sanhedrin, when he was arrested for healing a lame man and for preaching the resurrection of the dead through Jesus. (Acts 4:8-12.) This witness was an official testimony of Peter and John to the highest Jewish court. Other aspects of Peter's testimony of Jesus include a strong emphasis that (1) Jesus is the Son of God, (2) he has been raised from the grave (Acts 2:24, 31-36; 3:13-15), (3) he was heir to the throne of David (Acts 2:29-32), (4) he was the prophet spoken of by Moses (Acts 3:20-24), and (5) God had made him both Lord and Christ (Acts 2:36; 5:29-32; 10:38-42).

The Administrative Organization Is Enlarged

As church membership increased, it became necessary to increase the number of administrative offices. One of these offices was established because of a problem in the distribution of food and clothing to the Grecian widows. (A Grecian was not a Greek but a Jew who spoke Greek. These Grecians were generally Jews of the Diaspora and were not indigenous to Jerusalem or Palestine.) Seven men were appointed to attend to the temporal needs of the church so that the Twelve might be free to attend to spiritual affairs. (Acts 6:1-6.) This action was not the same type of administrative action that occasioned the appointment of Matthias to the Twelve, for he filled a vacancy in a quorum already extant. The appointment of these seven was the creation of a new body with specific and limited jurisdiction under the Twelve. (Acts 6:2-3.)

Because seven men were appointed, some have wondered if their office is analogous to that of the seven Presidents of the First Quorum of the Seventy in the church today. This analogy appears unlikely since the seven were especially appointed to serve tables, whereas the calling of a seventy is to preach the gospel. It is probably only coincidental that this group consisted of seven men. At this point many editions of the Bible contain a heading identifying these seven men as deacons. This heading is an interpretation by the editors and translators and is not part of the biblical text itself. The English word *deacon,* however, comes from the Greek *diakonos,* meaning a servant or an assistant. Although these seven men were assistants, their calling should not be equated with the ordained office of deacon in the Aaronic Priesthood.

Luke does not give us an account of the work of these seven men in their assignment to serve tables. He does, however, follow the activities of two of the seven, Stephen and Philip, in preaching the gospel to nonmembers. It might be that Stephen and Philip were called to do missionary work in addition to the welfare assignment, or they may simply have been reassigned. In the church today, most calls to service are temporary, and a person is likely to serve in several different callings in the period of a few years. Thus, a man who was once Presiding Bishop might later become a member of the Twelve; one serving as a bishop might be called as a stake president. Nothing suggests that the seven men who were called and set apart to assist in the daily ministration of food were to remain in that capacity for the remainder of their lives. Had Stephen and Philip remained in their original callings, we might have heard nothing further of them since it was their preaching activities that caused Luke to provide a detailed account about them.

The Preaching of Stephen

Stephen is described as "a man full of faith and of the Holy Ghost" (Acts 6:5) and "full of faith and power" (Acts 6:8). He performed miracles, and his hearers "were not able to resist the wisdom and the spirit by which he spake." (Acts 6:10.) He was taken before the Sanhedrin and was accused of having said that "Jesus of Nazareth shall destroy this place [Jerusalem and the temple], and shall change the customs which Moses delivered us." (Acts 6:14.) There was probably some substance in the charge, for Jesus had prophesied earlier of the destruction of Jerusalem and of the temple (Matt. 24) and had explained that the law of Moses would be fulfilled (Matt. 5:17). Stephen's enemies, however, made it appear that he was speaking "blasphemous words against Moses, and against God. . . . against this holy place, and the law." (Acts 6:11, 13.) His defense before the council was well-conceived. After making a short summary of the history of Israel from Abraham to David, Stephen pointed out that the true prophets had always been rejected by the people and that now the Son of God himself had been rejected by the children of those who had persecuted and killed the prophets. (Acts 7:51-52.) Stephen's words were so cutting that the people "gnashed on him with their teeth." (Acts 7:54.) When he declared that he could see a vision of Jesus on the right hand of God, they stoned him to death. (Acts 7:55-58.)

Under the law of Moses, stoning was the prescribed punishment for blasphemy. (Leviticus 24:11-16; Acts 6:11-13.) Stephen was stoned, not for his preaching, nor even for his scolding of the people, but for saying he had had a vision of the Father and the Son. He was stoned for proclaiming that he had received revelation. Stephen foreshadowed the work of Paul and is the earliest person mentioned in the New Testament to imply that the law of Moses was fulfilled and that its rites and customs should come to an end.

The Preaching of Philip

Luke states that at the same time as the death of Stephen there was a great persecution of Christians throughout Judea and Samaria. This scattering actually stimulated missionary activity, for "they that were scattered abroad went every where preaching the word." (Acts 8:4.)

Philip went to Samaria, where he preached the gospel of Jesus Christ, baptized, performed miracles, and brought many to a knowledge of Jesus. "When the apostles which were at Jerusalem [Peter and John] heard that Samaria had received the word of God" (Acts 8:14), they came from Jerusalem and laid hands on those whom Philip had baptized, giving them the Holy Ghost, and then they returned to Jerusalem (Acts 8:15-17, 25). Philip continued his missionary labors—not in Samaria (north of Jerusalem), but in the region of Gaza (south and west of Jerusalem). There he met, taught, and baptized an Ethiopian who "had come to Jerusalem for to worship." (Acts 8:27.) He was returning to his home, which was evidently in Ethiopia. This man was not of Israelite lineage but was a convert to Judaism, a proselyte.

Philip's activities represented a new dimension in the missionary work because the gospel was now being deliberately taken to other people—people who already had the law of Moses. Up to now, non-Jews were taught incidentally as part of the mission to the Jews; but now missionary work was being done overtly among non-Jewish people, fulfilling the second step of missionary work outlined in Acts 1:8.

The mission to the Samaritans, the offspring of Israelites intermarried with other people, was also a new dimension in the missionary outreach, for the Samaritans were a people who were partly of Israel but who were not Jewish. The Samaritans already had the law of Moses and practiced circumcision; thus, their entry into the church did not raise any new questions about the law. It was a half step toward taking the gospel to non-Israelite people.

The distinction between the powers of the Aaronic and the Melchizedek priesthoods is illustrated in Philip's preaching and baptizing at Samaria. But it was Peter and John, not Philip, who conferred the gift of the Holy Ghost. "In the case of Philip when he went down to Samaria, when he was under the spirit of Elias, he baptized both men and women. When Peter and John heard of it, they went down and laid hands upon them, and they received the Holy Ghost. This shows the distinction between the two powers."[1] This same difference was explained by John the Baptist when he restored the Aaronic Priesthood to Joseph Smith. (JS–H 1:70-72.)

The Conversion of Saul of Tarsus

Saul was born in Tarsus in Cilicia to Jewish parents of the tribe of Benjamin. Early in life he was sent to Jerusalem for schooling, where he studied under the famous Gamaliel, "a doctor of the law." (Acts 5:34.) Both Saul and Gamaliel were Pharisees. (Acts 22:3; Philip. 3:4-6.)

As a young man Saul persecuted the Christians from city to city and observed the stoning of Stephen at Jerusalem. Soon thereafter, when he was on his way from Jerusalem to Damascus with authority from the chief priest to bind and imprison all in that city who believed in Jesus, the Lord appeared to Saul in a vision. Saul both heard and saw the Savior and received instructions from him. (Acts 9.) The experience left Saul physically blind and very much humbled in spirit. The physical blindness was probably given to him as a symbol of his spiritual blindness.

Saul was later healed of his blindness and baptized by Ananias, a disciple at Damascus. While in Damascus Saul persuaded many at the synagogue to believe that Jesus was the Christ. His success angered the Jews, who by this time looked upon him as a traitor, and they sought to kill him. He then went into the deserts of Arabia for a time. (Gal. 1:17-18.)

Three years after his conversion, Saul went to Jerusalem (Gal. 1:17-18), but he found that the members of the church there were "afraid of him, and believed not that he was a disciple" (Acts 9:26). Fortunately, a notable disciple named Barnabas introduced him to the apostles and told them of his conversion and his preaching at Damascus. While in Jerusalem Saul conferred for fifteen days with Peter and James, the Lord's brother. The scriptures do not give an account of what they talked about. We assume that in addition to discussing the scriptures and points of doctrine, Saul must have asked many things about Jesus and his ministry. How thrilling to ask the chief apostle about when Jesus raised Lazarus from the dead, walked on water, opened the eyes of the blind, healed the sick, fed the five thousand, challenged the teachings of the Pharisees, suffered in the Garden of Gethsemane, and visited with the eleven for forty days following his resurrection. What an opportunity to ask James about Jesus as a boy, about Mary and Joseph and Jesus' other half-brothers and half-sisters, and about other things that James would know firsthand. Surely the diligent and intelligent Saul would, with propriety, ask these and other questions of two men who would be able to answer so well from personal experience.

Because some in Jerusalem were so opposed to Saul that "they went about to slay him" (Acts 9:29), the Brethren counseled him to return to his home city, Tarsus, which he did (Acts 9:30).

There is a discrepancy in the reports of Saul's vision on the road to Damascus. In Acts 9:7 we read that "the men which journeyed with him stood speechless, hearing a voice, but seeing no man." In Acts 22:9, however, we read: "They that were with me saw indeed the light, and were afraid; but they heard not the voice of him that spake to me." The Joseph Smith Translation corrects the account in Acts 9 to agree with that in Acts 22. The men who were with Saul saw the light but they did not hear the voice, nor did they see the Lord. This version is surely the correct one, because both the message and the vision of the Lord were intended only for Saul. His companions saw the light, however, and knew for themselves that something unusual was taking place. They could testify to this event and thus help support Saul's declaration of it.

Ananias was probably the presiding officer of the church in Damascus. Since the Lord came to Ananias and instructed him to seek out Saul, teach him the gospel, and heal his blindness, Ananias must have been the person in charge of the church in that area. It is likely that he was the man Saul would have desired most to imprison. It is an ironic turn of events that the very disciple Saul wished to silence should become the one who taught, healed, and baptized him.

Though Saul had seen and talked with the glorified, resurrected Jesus and had been healed of his physical blindness by a servant of the Lord, he still had to be baptized of water for the remission of sins to remedy his spiritual blindness. This ordinance is required of all, no matter how many other spiritual experiences and manifestations they may have had. (See Acts 9:17-19; 22:12-16.)

Ananias was reluctant to go to Saul, even though the Lord had asked him to. But the Lord could see what Ananias could not: Saul's potential for future service. (Acts 9:13-16; cf. 1 Sam. 16:7.) The Lord could see what Saul was capable of becoming. Men and women are called to the service of the Lord, not as a reward for what they have already done, but for what they are able to do in the future if given the proper opportunity. The Lord said that Saul was a chosen vessel and would yet suffer much for the sake of Jesus. (Acts 9:10-16.) Saul was suited by temperament, training, lineage, and experience to serve the Lord at a time when the church was about to reach out to the Gentile world. He was a Jew by lineage, trained as a Pharisee, learned and strict in the law of Moses and the traditions of his fathers, a Roman citizen politically, acquainted with the ways of the Greeks, reared in the Gentile city of Tarsus, and skilled in both the Hebrew and Greek languages. Above all, he had a determined, dedicated soul. His greatest asset was a capacity to love both man and God. For the thirty years remaining to him, he gave the Lord his complete devotion.

The Prophet Joseph Smith described Saul as being "about five feet high; very dark hair; dark complexion; dark skin; large Roman nose; sharp face; small black eyes, penetrating as eternity; round shoulders; a whining voice, except when elevated, and then it almost resembled the roaring of a lion. He was a good orator, active and diligent, always employing himself in doing good to his fellow man."[2]

Cornelius—Another New Dimension

Cornelius, a centurion of the Italian band, was a devout, God-fearing man with a good reputation among the Jews; but he was not a proselyte to Judaism. That is, he had not been circumcised. While fasting and praying, Cornelius was visited by an angel who told him to send for Peter, who would tell him what he should do. Cornelius was living in the seacoast town of Caesarea; Peter was visiting the city of Joppa about forty miles to the south. At this time Peter was given a vision in which he was commanded to kill and eat some beasts that were considered unclean under the Mosaic code. (Acts 10:10-16.) He did not at first know the meaning of the vision, but by subsequent events he came to recognize that the Lord was about to open the gospel to the Gentile nations.

Cornelius sent messengers to contact Peter, who, hearing of the situation and being instructed by the Spirit, started for Caesarea accompanied by six Jewish Christian brethren. When Peter arrived at Cornelius's home, he found a large gathering, for Cornelius "had called together his kinsmen and near friends." (Acts 10:24.) During the meeting the Holy Ghost came upon the Gentiles present, and they spoke in tongues. This astonished the Jewish Christian brethren, for they were amazed that the Holy Ghost would come upon uncircumcised Gentiles. Peter told the gathering that Gentiles were as eligible for baptism as were the Jews. (Acts 10:44-47.)

When Peter returned to Jerusalem, he was criticized by Jewish Christian brethren who had heard about his eating with Gentiles and keeping company with them. But Peter rehearsed the matter and was able to show them that by a number of revelations (the angel's visit to Cornelius, his own vision of the beasts, the voice of the Spirit to him, and the manifestation of the Holy Ghost at the meeting), the Lord had made it plain that the Gentiles should receive the gospel. We do not know the exact date of the events involving Cornelius, but Luke would probably have been acquainted with the proper chronology. He places the date of these events after the conversion of Saul but before a famine that came at about A.D. 44. Hence, the conversion of Cornelius would have been sometime between A.D. 35 and 43.

It was noted earlier that there were persons of Gentile lineage in the church as early as the day of Pentecost, several years before the conversion of Cornelius. What makes Cornelius and his household unique is that the earlier Gentiles were *all* proselytes to Judaism; Cornelius and his group were apparently the first nonproselytes and uncircumcised Gentiles to be baptized into the church.

Opening the door of the gospel to the Gentiles was another new dimension of missionary activity and the third step outlined in Acts 1:8. All previous conversions were of persons who held to the law of Moses and practiced circumcision. Even Paul's dramatic entrance into the church did not entail a new type of procedure, but Cornelius's entry signified a new day. It is important that it was Peter, the presiding officer of the church holding the keys of the kingdom, who began the proselytizing effort among the Gentiles. Only through the President of the Church does the Lord make such changes as the one involving Cornelius.

There is another significant feature of priesthood procedure in the account of Cornelius's conversion. The angel did not preach the gospel to Cornelius but directed him to Peter. The angel had sufficient knowledge, but it was not his calling to preach among mortals at that time. Peter was the living mortal administrator with the commission to take the gospel to men on the earth.

A similar circumstance is seen with the Lord's visit to Saul on the road to Damascus. He did not preach the gospel to Saul but told him it would be given to him in the city. Then the Lord sent Ananias to tend to it. Why did not Jesus do it? Because it is not the order of the priesthood for a heavenly being to preach to mortals when there is a qualified mortal with a priesthood commission able to do it. (This principle is alluded to in the parable of the rich man and Lazarus in Luke 16:19-31.) The Prophet Joseph Smith also taught this subject.[3]

Many have supposed that Cornelius was an exception to the order of heaven—that he received the gift of the Holy Ghost before baptism, whereas all others had to wait until after baptism. The wording of Acts 10:45 leads to this misconception. The Prophet Joseph Smith said Cornelius was not an exception and did not receive the gift of the Holy Ghost until after his baptism.[4]

Activity at Antioch:
Conversion of the Gentiles

Although Peter had opened the door for the Gentiles to come into the Church, missionary work proceeded slowly among them at first. Many Christians went forth throughout the cities of Phenice, Cyprus, and Antioch "preaching the word to none but unto the Jews only." (Acts 11:19.) About three hundred miles north of Jerusalem, however, at Antioch in Syria, there was lively activity resulting in the conversion of a great number of Greeks. Hearing of this, the Brethren sent Barnabas from Jerusalem to Antioch to look into the matter. After assessing the situation, he soon brought Saul from nearby Tarsus to assist him.

There is a faulty translation in the King James Version of Acts 11:20. The text states that the missionaries at Antioch preached to the Grecians. A Grecian, however, is a Jew who speaks Greek, whereas the sense of verse 20 and the verses following call for the word *Greek* instead of *Grecian*. Most modern translations of the Bible use the word *Greek*. *Grecian* adds nothing to the story, for Grecians had been in the

Church for years; but bringing Greeks into the Church was something new to write about.

Barnabas was probably selected for the assignment at Antioch because he was from Cyprus and, being from a Gentile environment, he would have common ground with Gentile converts. Likewise, his reason for wanting Saul to assist him would be that Saul's experience with Gentiles would make him an asset to the work.

Paul's First Missionary Journey

Saul and Barnabas stayed at Antioch "a whole year" and "taught much people." (Acts 11:26.) At about that time there came a great famine, and the saints in Judea were especially impoverished. The disciples at Antioch sent relief to the Judeans by the hands of Barnabas and Saul. The famine occurred in the days of Claudius Caesar, emperor from A.D. 41 to 54, and is generally thought to have occurred around A.D. 44. (Acts 11:25-30.) It had been ten years since the resurrection of Jesus, and the church had grown rapidly.

When Barnabas and Saul returned to Antioch from Jerusalem, they took John Mark (a nephew or cousin to Barnabas) with them. Shortly thereafter, having been called by revelation and set apart by the laying on of hands, they departed from Antioch and sailed to Cyprus and the cities of Galatia, part of the land known today as Turkey. Chief among the cities were Pisidian Antioch, Iconium, Lystra, and Derbe, which they visited in that order. The missionaries preached to Jews, proselytes, and Gentiles and encountered both strong opposition and outstanding success. At Cyprus, Saul (who at this point became known as Paul) found it necessary to smite an enemy with blindness in the name of the Lord. Paul knew well the stunning effect of blindness. At Antioch of Pisidia, the missionaries preached in the synagogue for at least two Sabbaths, and there "came almost the whole city together to hear the word of God." (Acts 13:44.) The Gentiles were pleased, but many of the Jews were not, and Paul and Barnabas were expelled from the city. A similar event occurred at Iconium. At Lystra, Paul and Barnabas were almost worshiped by the Gentiles, but the Jews from Antioch and Iconium stoned Paul and left him for dead. The strongest opposition in every city came from the unbelieving Jews because Paul taught that salvation came through Jesus Christ and not through the law of Moses. (Acts 13:23-42.)

The missionaries then visited the cities in reverse order and returned to Antioch of Syria. The mission had lasted perhaps a year, and the brethren had traveled over fourteen hundred miles—a small thing in our day, but a considerable accomplishment by sailboat and by foot through rough terrain. The probable date of the journey is A.D. 47-48.

There were two notable personal developments for Saul on this journey. The first is that while in Cyprus, Saul became known as Paul and is consistently called Paul thereafter. (Acts 13.) This renaming was probably because the Greek name *Paulos* would be more acceptable to Gentile audiences. The second development is that until the missionaries reached Cyprus, Barnabas seemed to be in charge. (Acts 11:30; 12:25; 13:2.) Beginning at Cyprus, Paul seemed to be the leader. (Acts 13:13, 50.) Most of the information about this first missionary journey centers around what Paul said and did; little is said about Barnabas.

On their first visit to each place, the missionaries preached and baptized. On the return journey, they "ordained elders in every church." (Acts 14:23.) These actions give a clue to missionary procedure and show that the church was organized with local priesthood leaders.

The Council at Jerusalem

The rapid influx of Gentile converts to Christianity in Antioch and in Galatia caused great concern among some of the Jewish members in the Jerusalem area. Paul and Barnabas had brought many Gentiles into the church by baptism, but they had not required circumcision. Certain men came to Antioch from Judea and taught (without authorization from the apostles) that "except ye be circumcised after the manner of Moses, ye cannot be saved." (Acts 15:1.) Paul and Barnabas had a great disputation with them, and the matter was finally taken to the apostles and elders at Jerusalem for settlement. Paul, Barnabas, and Titus, an uncircumcised Greek convert, went to Jerusalem for the scheduled council. There the strongest opposition to the Gentiles came from those members who had been Pharisees before becoming

Christians. (Acts 15:5.) In the council Peter rehearsed his experience with Cornelius. The decision was that Gentile converts need not be circumcised but that they should "abstain from meats offered to idols, and from blood, and from things strangled, and from fornication." (Acts 15:29.) This decision was clearly a vindication of the doctrine taught by Paul and Barnabas and was in harmony with the teaching that the law of Moses had been fulfilled by Christ. The Brethren at Jerusalem wrote an epistle to the saints in the vicinity of Antioch and Cilicia informing them of the decision of the council, and they sent Judas and Silas to confirm by word of mouth what the council had decided.

The action of the Jerusalem council involved a significant policy decision. Ever since Cornelius's conversion (possibly ten years), Gentile converts had been joining the church without circumcision; now it was an officially announced and written declaration. The decision that circumcision was not required of Gentiles categorically meant that circumcision was not a requirement for salvation. This affirmation had been years in coming. The council was held about A.D. 49-50. Cornelius had been baptized (without circumcision) as many as ten years earlier, and a number of Gentiles had been similarly admitted into the church at Antioch and throughout Galatia. Yet the matter was agitated by some. The evidence of Stephen's enlightened preaching and Peter's unmistakable experience with Cornelius makes it clear that the Brethren understood that the law of Moses was fulfilled in Christ, but evidently many members of the church did not understand. It was a matter of doctrine, tradition, culture, and emotion. Even though the Brethren had settled the matter doctrinally a decade before, considerable time passed before the matter was settled culturally and emotionally in the minds of some Jewish Christians. Furthermore, at least ten years after the council, many Jewish Christians in Jerusalem were still following the law of Moses. (Acts 21:17-25.)

The decision of the Jerusalem council was not definitive and did not forthrightly say that the law of Moses should be discontinued. Although it declared that Gentiles did not need circumcision for salvation, it did not say that Jewish members of the church need not circumcise their sons. This ambiguity was duly noted by the Jewish segment of the church in Jerusalem, for when Paul returned to

Jerusalem at the end of his third journey (about A.D. 60), he found many members still "zealous of the law." (Acts 21:20.) They pointed out that the Jerusalem council directed its decree only to the Gentiles and not to the Jews. (Acts 21:17-25.) The reason for this ambiguity seems to be that the Brethren did not wish to overly offend Jewish members. They wanted the Gentiles to be properly received, but they did not want to lose the Jewish Christians in doing so.

The Nephites in America had a much better understanding of the temporary and preparatory nature of the law of Moses than did the Jewish Christians, particularly the Jews of Jerusalem. Both Nephi and Abinadi had explained that the law of Moses should cease to be practiced after Jesus had made the atonement. (See 2 Ne. 25:24-27; Mosiah 12:24-32; 16:14-15.) Furthermore, Jesus told the Nephites after his resurrection that the law of Moses was fulfilled. (See 3 Ne. 9:17; 12:46; 15:2-8.) But the church members in Jerusalem did not understand. They were too bound by tradition or, as Paul said it, driven by a zeal without knowledge (Rom. 10:2), which rendered them impervious to the concept.

This imperviousness happened in other matters also. When the Lord tried to tell the Jews of his other sheep, they were not receptive and therefore were denied the understanding they might have had. The receptive Nephites gained the understanding. (See 3 Ne. 15:16-24; 16:4.) Since circumcision was originally the token of the covenant that God made with Abraham, the Jews of New Testament times looked upon it as the badge of their faith. Failing to understand that the token, but not the covenant, was done away in Christ, they doggedly pursued the old custom and missed the spiritual advancement they could have had by listening to Jesus, Peter, Paul, and the others.

From Paul's epistle to the Galatians, we learn interesting historical facts about the Jerusalem council that are not recorded in Acts. The most significant of these are that the council took place about fourteen years after Paul's conversion; that Paul traveled with Barnabas to the council; that Titus, an uncircumcised Greek convert, accompanied them as something of a test case. By revelation they went to Jerusalem and conferred privately with the Brethren before the council began, just to make certain they were in agreement. Titus was not compelled to be circumcised. The brethren at Jerusalem gave Paul and Barnabas the "right hands of fellowship" and commissioned them to "go unto the heathen" in their ministry. (Gal. 2:9.) This commission possibly gave rise to Paul's later definition of himself as "the apostle of the Gentiles." (Rom. 11:13. See also 2 Tim. 1:11.) Paul and Barnabas were given a special injunction to remember the poor in their ministry, to which Paul replied that he had a natural tendency to do that anyway.

Although Paul was opposed to circumcision as essential for salvation and he emphatically declared that it was not needful for Titus to be circumcised (Gal. 2:1-3), soon after the Jerusalem council Paul circumcised the young Timothy before taking him as a companion on the second mission (Acts 16:1-3). This action provides an insight into Paul's thinking. He saw a difference between necessity and convenience. With Titus, the question was whether or not circumcision was essential for salvation; thus, Paul opposed it. With Timothy it was a matter of rendering him acceptable to the non-Christian Jews where he would do missionary work. Paul was willing to allow circumcision as a concession, but not as a requirement, so that the Jews would be willing to listen to Timothy teach the gospel. This distinction reveals something of Paul's mind and method.

Paul's Travels among the Cities of the Empire

The Jerusalem council was held in about A.D. 49–50. At that time Paul received a special commission to "go unto the heathen" to preach the gospel. (Gal. 2:9.) He refers to this commission in Romans 11:13: "For I speak to you Gentiles, inasmuch as I am the apostle of the Gentiles." He spent most of his time and effort traveling throughout the Roman Empire preaching the gospel to the Gentiles. He made three major journeys as a missionary and another journey from Jerusalem to Rome as a prisoner of the state. He also contemplated a journey to Spain, but we do not know if he was able to bring it about. (Rom. 15:24-28.)

The chief areas of Paul's missionary activity throughout the Empire include visits to large centers of population, such as Ephesus, Corinth, Athens, Troas, Philippi, Thessalonica, the cities of Galatia (Antioch, Iconium, and Lystra), Antioch of Syria, and Rome. In each area he was intent on teaching especially the Gentiles, but he did not neglect his Jewish brethren, and in every city where possible he entered the synagogues and taught. (Acts 17:1-2.) Furthermore, a synagogue would be the best place to find Gentile proselytes who were ready for the gospel. They would have Gentile relatives and friends; the referral system for Gentiles would begin at the Jewish synagogue.

Paul's three major missionary journeys and his trip to Rome are chronicled in the book of Acts as follows (the dates and distances are estimated):

1. *First Missionary Journey.* (Acts 13–14.) He began and ended at Antioch of Syria, traveling approximately fourteen hundred miles, probably in A.D. 47–48.

2. *Second Missionary Journey.* (Acts 15:36–18:22.) He began and ended at Antioch of Syria, traveling a distance of approximately three thousand miles, probably in A.D. 51–53.

3. *Third Missionary Journey.* (Acts 18:23–21:15.) He began at Antioch of Syria and ended at Jerusalem, traveling approximately thirty-five hundred miles, probably in A.D. 54–58.

4. *Journey to Rome from Jerusalem.* (Acts 27–28.) This trip was approximately fourteen hundred miles; Paul traveled about A.D. 61.

5. *The Contemplated Journey from Rome to Spain.* This journey would have entailed an additional two thousand miles.

At Athens, having seen the pagan altar inscribed "TO THE UNKNOWN GOD," Paul showed characteristic originality and ingenuity by using the occasion as a missionary opportunity: "Whom therefore ye ignorantly worship, him declare I unto you." (Acts 17:23.) His audience listened patiently until he declared the resurrection of the dead, and then they left, shaking their heads.

After his third missionary journey, Paul was brought before the Sanhedrin in Jerusalem, where he gave an official testimony of his divine call and the reality of the resurrection of Jesus Christ. (Acts 22–

23.) The council was in an uproar because of his mention of the Resurrection. Perhaps the most important factor of his defense was that Paul the Apostle, the special witness for Jesus Christ, was standing where Jesus, Peter, John, and Stephen had stood—bearing witness of the resurrection of Jesus to the highest court in all Jewry.

When the Roman governor Festus was unable to ascertain what charges the Jews brought against Paul, he imprisoned him at Caesarea for two years and finally brought him before King Agrippa for examination. There Paul gave a most eloquent recitation of his early life, conversion, missionary labors, and testimony of Jesus and the Resurrection. Agrippa was moved by the power of the message and was almost persuaded to be a Christian. (Acts 26:28.) In chains, Paul replied that he wished not only the king but all mankind could be even as he (Paul) was, "except these bonds." (Acts 26:29.) Thirty years earlier the Lord had told Ananias that Paul was a chosen vessel to carry his gospel before Jews and Gentiles and before kings and rulers. The book of Acts clearly demonstrates the fulfillment of that call. Not only did Paul speak to multitudes but he personally testified of Christ to the highest leaders of both Jews and Gentiles.

The book of Acts closes with Paul in custody in Rome. The book is unfinished and incomplete, but we subsequently learn from Paul's epistles to Timothy that Paul also stood before Caesar in Rome and taught the gospel of Jesus Christ. He did as he was bidden by the Lord: he testified of Jesus Christ and suffered much for the name of Jesus.

Summary

Acts is a stirring recitation of major missionary accomplishments first among the Jews, then among the Samaritans, and finally among the Gentiles. It shows the role of the president of the church in handling major changes in policy and church developments. Acts chronicles the outreach of the church in half steps as the leaders testified of the resurrection of Jesus, implemented the gospel, and struggled with the cultures, prejudices, and weaknesses of the people. It shows that in spite of opposition, the Lord had men he could depend on, men who dared to bring about his purposes in an uncooperative and unfriendly world.

Notes

1. Joseph Smith, *Teachings of the Prophet Joseph Smith,* comp. Joseph Fielding Smith (Salt Lake City: Deseret Book, 1976), p. 336.
2. Ibid., p. 180.
3. Ibid., p. 265.
4. Ibid., p. 199.

4

THE JUST SHALL LIVE BY FAITH
(Romans)

ROBERT L. MILLET

Few men in the history of Christianity will have as much lasting effect on humanity and the course of world events as Paul the Apostle. Given a new direction and a proper channel for his misplaced zeal, Saul of Tarsus underwent a remarkable conversion in the prime of life—from persecutor and enemy of Christians to protector and defender, the friend of God. Having been born of God, Paul forsook position, recognition, and rabbinical preparation for the excellency of the knowledge of Jesus Christ "and him crucified." (1 Cor. 2:2.) His message for over thirty years was plain but poignant: salvation was to be had only in and through the atoning blood of Christ, the Messiah, who had "abolished death, and hath brought life and immortality to light through the gospel." (2 Tim. 1:10.)

With fire in his bones, Paul was given an apostolic commission to make and confirm converts to the Christian way of life. An energetic and indefatigable apostle to the Gentiles, he baptized, ordained, and established individuals in churches throughout the Roman Empire. And it was by means of his epistles—his letters—to the saints scattered abroad that he was able to regulate and set in order the affairs of the churches under his supervision.

Robert L. Millet is assistant professor of ancient scripture and New Testament area coordinator at Brigham Young University.

These epistles were regulatory letters and, for the most part, were written to handle specific problems or to clear up certain doctrinal misunderstandings. They were written to members of the church who had received and believed the fundamental doctrines of the faith. Because this was their purpose, Paul's epistles do not introduce or even expound upon theological backgrounds or foundations; such foundations were already firmly in place in the lives of those familiar with Paul's earlier teachings. Thus we could appropriately conclude that the Pauline Epistles are not, and were never intended to be, systematic theologies of the gospel of Jesus Christ; rather, they are what they were sent forth to be—regulatory correspondence to ensure a godly walk and conversation as well as orthodoxy in doctrine and practice among the members of the church. When read in conjunction with the book of Acts, the epistles help to supply valuable historical and doctrinal details in the work and ministry of Paul. There are truths and teachings in the Pauline Epistles that have universal value and are thus timeless in their import (for example, the Atonement and Christian conduct); these verities are as binding upon the Latter-day Saints as they were upon the former saints. There are other matters, however, that have specific, first-century reference, and whose focus—though timely and relevant to Paul's churches in a given day and culture—is not understood to be binding upon the restored church.

The epistles of Paul are organized in our present New Testament collection almost exclusively by length. The glaring exception is the Epistle to the Hebrews, whose authorship religious scholars of the world have debated for centuries; this epistle is thus placed at the end of the Pauline corpus. The Epistle to the Romans was written from Corinth during Paul's third missionary journey, in about A.D. 58–59. It is a masterpiece in Christian literature and contains a treasurehouse of understanding as to how the natural man may, through Christ, put off the old man of sin and rise unto a newness of life.

There are obviously many details that might be discussed in a more thorough treatment of the Epistle to the Romans. This chapter will concentrate briefly upon seven doctrinal matters put forward in this epistle and will attempt to penetrate to the core of the subjects to distill the essence of the principles.

Justification by Faith in Christ
(Romans 3–4)

In his letter to the Romans, Paul spoke to his readers at length regarding the meaning and cost of Christian discipleship. Having come out of the world and forsaken the sins of Babylon, Christians— through the "gospel of God" (Rom. 1:1)—are expected to press forward in righteousness, put on Christ, and overcome that nature of things which so easily beset them before baptism. Paul, quoting the ancient prophet Habakkuk, assured the Roman saints that "the just shall live by faith." (Rom. 1:17.) In describing the Apostle's challenge to turn the hearts of Jewish and pagan investigators to the Lord, Elder Bruce R. McConkie explained:

> On the one hand we are preaching to Jews who in their lost and fallen state have rejected their Messiah and who believe they are saved by the works and performances of the Mosaic law.
>
> On the other hand we are preaching to pagans—Romans, Greeks, those in every nation—who know nothing whatever about the messianic word, or of the need for a Redeemer, or of the working out of the infinite and eternal atonement. They worship idols, the forces of nature, the heavenly bodies, or whatever suits their fancy. As with the Jews they assume that this or that sacrifice or appeasing act will please the deity of their choice and some vague and unspecified blessings will result.
>
> Can either the Jews or the pagans be left to assume that the works they do will save them? Or must they forget their little groveling acts of petty worship, gain faith in Christ, and rely on the cleansing power of his blood for salvation?
>
> They must be taught faith in the Lord Jesus Christ and to forsake their traditions and performances. Surely we must tell them they cannot be saved by the works they are doing, for man cannot save himself. Instead they must turn to Christ and rely on his merits and mercy and grace.[1]

Paul stressed that salvation is through Christ and that the works of the Mosaic law and the works of the world are insufficient to justify man. For one thing, he stressed that the law of Moses was a system established to point out one's need for a redeemer. "By the deeds of the law," he wrote, "there shall no flesh be justified in his sight." Why should this be the case? The Apostle answered, "For by the law is the knowledge of sin." (Rom. 3:20.) One of the main functions of the law, with its myriad parts, was to demonstrate man's inability to live perfectly by every moral requirement. One translation of Romans 3:20 is as follows: "Indeed it is the straight edge of the Law which shows us how crooked we are." (Phillips Translation.) The law of Moses was given "to specify crimes" (Jerusalem Bible), that is, to establish right and wrong but also to delineate human limitations and to point up the need for divine assistance. "For all have sinned," Paul taught, "and come short of the glory of God; therefore being justified only by his grace through the redemption that is in Christ Jesus." (JST, Rom. 3:23-24.)

All persons, both Jews and Gentiles, must also come to the knowledge of the necessity but insufficiency of their own righteous actions. Their works, even the works of those within the Christian community, were to be viewed in perspective. "Therefore ye are justified of faith and works, through grace." (JST, Rom. 4:16.)

Christ as the Second Adam
(Romans 5)

Chapter 5 of Romans is a descriptive comparison of, and contrast between, Adam and Jesus Christ. It is a treatise on the grand gift of God through his Son; the saints are encouraged to "joy in God through our Lord Jesus Christ, by whom we have now received the atonement." (Rom. 5:11.) It was because of one man, Adam, that sin entered into the world: the Fall opened the door to mortality and made sin a reality. In addition, death, that universal commonality, entered upon the scene through the Fall, so that immortality might be offered by the Infinite One.

Even though Adam was a figure, or type, of the coming Messiah (Adam was the father of mortality; Christ, the father of immortality), yet their actions brought very different results. By the offense of Adam, all die; by the gift of Christ—the Atonement—all are made alive through the Resurrection, with those who believe and obey becoming the recipients of eternal life. Adam's act led to universal condemnation; Christ's gift opened the door to justification. Thus, even though one man's offense (Adam's fall) eventuated in universal death, Christ's abundant grace reigns over and conquers death in the end.

Walking in Newness of Life
(Romans 6)

Paul explained to the Romans that through the ordinance of baptism we evidence our acceptance of the atoning sacrifice; through going into the "watery grave," we participate symbolically in the Lord's burial and his subsequent rise from the tomb.

The concept of spiritual rebirth finds its greatest meaning when we consider further implications of the typology of baptism in regard to birth. The godly anguish and suffering of the repentant soul is typical of the excruciating pain experienced by the laboring mother as birth of the infant is imminent. The water used in the baptismal proceedings is symbolic of a body of water in which dirtiness and uncleanness are washed away. (See Acts 22:16.) Paul taught that the process of being taken down into the water is representative of Christ's burial in the tomb for three days. The rise from the watery grave is in the likeness of the Master's rise to a newness of life in the resurrected state. Further, the innocent and pure state of the new candidate for the kingdom is like unto the wholly innocent newborn at birth. Baptism thus becomes the channel by which one is both legally initiated into the church and also spiritually initiated into the blessings of the atonement of Christ. "Now if we be dead with Christ," Paul taught, "we believe that we shall also live with him." (Rom. 6:8.)

Members of the church are counseled to yield not only their hearts but also their whole bodies to the cause of truth. By so centering our souls upon the Lord and his divine purposes, we truly become servants of righteousness and are entitled to the wages of our Master. In the end we will receive a reward from him whom we have chosen to follow. "For the wages of sin is death; but the gift of God is eternal life through Jesus Christ our Lord." (Rom. 6:23.)

The Power of Christ to Change Lives
(Romans 7)

Chapter 7 of Romans might well be labeled "Paul: Before and After." It might also be classified as an explanation of how the power of Christ may change people's lives. First of all, Paul encourages the saints to recognize and accept the fact that the Mosaic law has found its perfect fulfillment in Christ and, having realized its purposes, has been done away in the atoning sacrifice. Just as a woman is not being unfaithful to a deceased husband by remarrying, neither is modern Israel unfaithful to the law of Moses by transferring allegiance to the Savior. The saints are now "married to another, even to him who is raised from the dead." (Rom. 7:4.)

Gross misunderstanding is frequently the result of reading Romans 7 without the invaluable assistance of the Joseph Smith Translation of the Bible. In the King James Version, this chapter depicts Paul as a helpless and largely depraved individual who has little power to choose good and live according to the things of God. Paul is "carnal, sold under sin." (Rom. 7:14.) Further, those things that he knows he should do, he does not do; that which he should not do, he does. "Now then it is no more I that do it," he adds, "but sin that dwelleth in me." (Rom. 7:17.) It is not difficult to understand how unenlightened Christians from Augustine to Luther could concoct from Romans 7 the notion of man's total depravity, particularly if they disregarded other scriptural statements indicating otherwise.

It is to the modern seer, Joseph Smith, that we turn for profound insights—the restoration of plain and precious truths, either of content or of intent. The Joseph Smith Translation stresses man's inabilities to effect righteousness without Christ:

> For we know that the commandment is spiritual; but when I was under the law, I was yet carnal, sold under sin.
>
> But now I am spiritual; for that which I am commanded to do, I do; and that which I am commanded not to allow, I allow not.
>
> For what I know is not right I would not do; for that which is sin, I hate. . . .
>
> Now then, it is no more I that do sin; but I seek to subdue that sin which dwelleth in me.

> For I know that in me, that is, in my flesh, dwelleth no good thing; for to will is present with me, but to perform that which is good I find not, only in Christ. (JST, Rom. 7:14-16, 18-19.)

Truly, through the Prophet Joseph's inspired revision of the Bible, we come to discern more clearly the character and accomplishments of Paul the Apostle.

Heirs of God, Joint Heirs with Christ (Romans 8)

Joseph Smith taught: "It is one thing to see the kingdom of God, and another thing to enter into it. We must have a change of heart to see the kingdom of God, and subscribe the articles of adoption to enter therein."[2] Individuals are born again to see the kingdom of God (cf. John 3:3) when the influence of the Holy Ghost leads to a spiritual recognition of the true church on earth. Such persons are born again to enter the kingdom of God (cf. John 3:5) when they obey the Spirit's instructions and submit to the "articles of adoption," the first principles and ordinances of the gospel. Faith, repentance, baptism, and the gift of the Holy Ghost are the articles of adoption in the sense that they provide the means whereby a person is initiated into the church and kingdom and also adopted into the family of the Lord Jesus Christ.

For many in the Christian world, being born again consists solely of a spiritual experience; for other groups, it is accomplished primarily through the sacraments of the church. Joseph Smith taught that truth lies in a road between these two extremes; he explained, simply, that "being born again, comes by the Spirit of God through ordinances."[3]

New members labor to enjoy the companionship of the Holy Ghost and in doing so begin the processes of spiritual rebirth. As a child of Christ, each one is a member of a new family. They take upon themselves a new family surname and are expected to abide by the rules and regulations of the family. In addition, they are in line to inherit, receive, and possess all the benefits of family membership.

It was never intended, however, that we remain children (even children of Christ) forever. Rather, the Lord desires that the members of his family mature, that they advance and progress in spiritual stature to the point where they qualify as equal inheritors, or "joint-heirs"

51

(Rom. 8:17), with Christ to all that the Father has. In speaking of those members of the Church who have been born again, Elder Bruce R. McConkie explained: "Then, if they press forward with a steadfastness in Christ, keeping the commandments and living by every word that proceedeth forth from the mouth of God, they qualify for celestial marriage, and this gives them power to become the sons of God, meaning the Father. They thus become joint-heirs with Christ who is his natural heir. Those who are sons of God in this sense are the ones who become gods in the world to come. (D&C 76:54-60)."[4]

These doctrinal verities are touched upon beautifully by Paul in Romans 8. Those who give themselves over to the direction of the Spirit and thus gain the mind of God eventually become the sons and daughters of God. They qualify to call upon the Father in an endearing and intimate manner: "Abba, Father." (Rom. 8:15.) As indicated, they are heirs, "heirs of God, and joint-heirs with Christ." (Rom. 8:17; see also vv. 13-16.)

Further, those saints who are divinely led have the additional blessing of having the Holy Ghost prompt and direct their very prayers to the Father. "Likewise the Spirit also helpeth our infirmities: for we know not what we should pray for as we ought: but the Spirit itself maketh intercession for us with groanings which cannot be uttered." (Rom. 8:26.)[5] In short, the Holy Ghost, who has the power to search the hearts of individuals, directs the adopted saint to pray for needs rather than desires; to pray for that which the Father would be pleased to grant. Through such a process, a person may come to a point not unlike the situation of Nephi, the son of Helaman, in the Book of Mormon. To such a person, the Lord can confidently decree: "All things shall be done unto thee according to thy word, for thou shalt not ask that which is contrary to my will." (Hel. 10:5.)

All of these rights and privileges are available because of the mediation of the Master, he who was called and prepared and foreordained to his messianic labors. Even though it is true that "unconditional election of individuals to eternal life was not taught by the Apostles," even so, "God did elect or predestinate, that all those who would be saved, should be saved in Christ Jesus."[6]

In speaking of Christ's divine preparation, Paul taught: "For him [Christ] whom he [the Father] did foreknow, he also did predestinate to be conformed to his own image, that he might be the firstborn among many brethren. Moreover, him whom he did predestinate, him he also called; and him whom he called, him he also sanctified; and him whom he sanctified, him he also glorified." (JST, Rom. 8:29-30.)

Christ and True Israel (Romans 9–11)

Chapters 9 through 11 of Romans provide a penetrating treatment of the subject, Who is Israel? Paul emphatically declared that despite the Jews' claims to preferred status because of lineal descent from Abraham, the true Israelite is the one who receives, by faith, Israel's promised Messiah. Circumcision or uncircumcision is an irrelevant matter; Jew or Gentile status is immaterial. What matters is whether the people of the first century A.D. (and all persons thereafter) turned their attention and affections toward Jesus of Nazareth, the God of ancient Israel and the Mediator of God's new covenant with mankind. In a very real sense, the Gentiles in Paul's day showed themselves more approved than did their Jewish counterparts. In Paul's words, the latter group, "which followed after the law of righteousness, hath not attained to the law of righteousness." Why? "Because they sought it not by faith, but as it were by the works of the law." (Rom. 9:31-32.) "For Christ is the end of the law for righteousness to every one that believeth" (Rom. 10:4); that is to say, Christ is the grand end to all of the law's myriad means, the fulfillment of the law's messianic ordinances and prophecies, and the real religion behind and beyond centuries of ritual.

Paul assured his readers that according to the "election of grace," a remnant of Israel will be spared and will come to the knowledge of their God. Elder Bruce R. McConkie wrote:

> This election of grace is a very fundamental, logical, and important part of God's dealings with men through the ages. To bring to pass the salvation of the greatest possible number of his spirit children the Lord, in general, sends the most righteous and worthy spirits to earth through the lineage of Abraham and Jacob. This course is a manifestation of his grace or in other words his love, mercy, and condescension toward his children.

53

This election to a chosen lineage is based on pre-existent worthiness and is thus made "according to the foreknowledge of God." (1 Pet. 1:2.) Those so grouped together during their mortal probation have more abundant opportunities to make and keep the covenants of salvation, a right which they earned by pre-existent devotion to the cause of righteousness.[7]

Gentiles are warned against haughtiness in their newfound status as adopted children of the covenant; theirs should be a profound sense of gratitude to Israel for opening the door of salvation. It was, needless to say, through the Jews that "the oracles of God" had been given to the world. (Rom. 3:1-2.)

Paul could have been referring to the allegory of Zenos (see Jacob 5–6) when he alluded briefly to the status of Israel as the natural branches of the olive tree and to the status of the Gentiles as the wild branches. (See Rom. 11:16-24.) Through baptism and adoption, the Gentiles are grafted into the mother tree, the house of Israel; they "come to the knowledge of the true Messiah, their Lord and their Redeemer." (1 Ne. 10:14.) Through subsequent righteousness, they begin to produce precious fruit that is acceptable to the Lord of the vineyard. This phenomenon is a great mystery: "that blindness in part is happened to Israel [through her callousness and insensitivity to the principles and presence of the Messiah], until the fulness of the Gentiles be come in." (Rom. 11:25; cf. 16:25; Eph. 3:3-6; Jacob 4:18.) Such an understanding must be received by the Gentiles with gratitude and humility. "Be not highminded, but fear" is Paul's counsel to the Gentiles; "for if God spared not the natural branches, take heed lest he also spare not thee." (Rom. 11:20-21.)

Newness of Life: A Process

Spiritual progress is a gradual thing, a process. We do well to understand that spiritual matters may be neither programmed nor rushed. Many of the dramatic events in the Book of Mormon and the New Testament that involve conversion or spiritual rebirth have a great effect upon the reader but represent an exception rather than a rule. Elder Bruce R. McConkie said:

We are born again when we die as pertaining to unrighteousness and when we live as pertaining to the things of the Spirit. But that doesn't happen in an instant, suddenly. That . . . is a process. Being born again is a gradual thing, except in a few isolated instances that are so miraculous they get written up in the scriptures. As far as the generality of the members of the Church are concerned, we are born again by degrees, and we are born again to added light and added knowledge and added desires for righteousness as we keep the commandments.[8]

There are few instant Christians or sudden disciples. The Holy Ghost generally brings about meaningful change in process of time, and unusual spiritual moments are granted according to the divine discernment of Him who knows us best: they generally come to us "in his own time, and in his own way, and according to his own will." (D&C 88:68.) Following baptism, our rise unto "newness of life" is frequently so gradual that we may not even notice the changes in our nature. But we must be appropriately patient with ourselves, knowing that the full measure of perfection will not be attained until we are well beyond the grave. Elder McConkie explained:

As members of the Church, if we chart a course leading to eternal life; if we begin the processes of spiritual rebirth, and are going in the right direction . . . then it is absolutely guaranteed—there is no question whatever about it—we shall gain eternal life. Even though we have spiritual rebirth ahead of us, perfection ahead of us, the full degree of sanctification ahead of us, if we chart a course and follow it to the best of our ability in this life, then when we go out of this life we'll continue in exactly that same course. We'll no longer be subject to the passions and the appetites of the flesh. We will have passed successfully the tests of this mortal probation and in due course we'll get the fulness of our Father's kingdom—and that means eternal life in his everlasting presence.[9]

Each of us needs to strike the appropriate balance between divine discontent (a constant urge to advance and improve) and what Nephi called "a perfect brightness of hope." (2 Ne. 31:20.) The gospel of Jesus Christ is "the power of God unto salvation" (Rom. 1:16), a power that in time may transform a character and renew a nature. Through patiently applying the principles of that gospel, we may thus participate in the noblest of all endeavors—the renovation of each man and woman.

Notes

1. Bruce R. McConkie, "What Think Ye of Salvation by Grace?" in *Speeches of the Year,* 1983-84 (Provo, Utah: Brigham Young University Press, 1984), pp. 47-48.

2. *Teachings of the Prophet Joseph Smith,* comp. Joseph Fielding Smith (Salt Lake City: Deseret Book, 1976), p. 328.

3. Ibid., p. 162.

4. Bruce R. McConkie, *Doctrinal New Testament Commentary,* 3 vols. (Salt Lake City: Bookcraft, 1965-73), 2:474. See also Bruce R. McConkie, "Households of Faith," *Speeches of the Year,* 1970 (Provo, Utah: Brigham Young University), December 1, 1970, pp. 5-6.

5. See also *Teachings of the Prophet Joseph Smith,* p. 278.

6. Ibid., p. 189.

7. Bruce R. McConkie, *Mormon Doctrine,* 2nd ed. (Salt Lake City: Bookcraft, 1966), p. 216.

8. Bruce R. McConkie, "Jesus Christ and Him Crucified," *Speeches of the Year,* 1976 (Provo, Utah: Brigham Young University, 1977), p. 399.

9. Ibid., pp. 400-401.

5

"IS CHRIST DIVIDED?"
UNITY OF THE SAINTS THROUGH CHARITY
(1, 2 Corinthians)

DAVID R. SEELY

Paul wrote his epistles to the Corinthians (1 and 2 Corinthians) from Ephesus and Macedonia in the spring and fall of the year A.D. 57, during his third mission to the Gentiles.[1] He addressed them to the members of the church at Corinth, which Paul had helped to found during his first mission in A.D. 50, and they represent two of the earliest (preceded only perhaps by the epistles to the Thessalonians), longest, and most doctrinally replete of the Pauline epistles. Paul wrote the letter found in 1 Corinthians to address the serious dissensions and immorality that had arisen in his absence among the saints there, and to answer some of their questions about church doctrine and practice. Shortly thereafter he wrote the letter found in 2 Corinthians, expressing his joy in hearing that many of the saints had repented and continuing his plea for repentance directed to those who had not.

Historical Background

The ancient Greek city-state of Corinth was strategically located in the center of the isthmus joining northern Greece to the Peloponnesus on the south, and controlled the port to the west on the Corin-

David R. Seely is assistant professor of ancient scripture at Brigham Young University.

thian Gulf and the port to the east on the Saronic Gulf. Because of its location, it was inseparably connected with the sea and derived its wealth primarily from shipping and trade. The isthmus was so narrow that small ships or cargoes headed west were often unloaded and dragged across the isthmus to continue their journey, thus avoiding the long journey around the Peloponnesus. Corinth heroically stood alongside her sister states of Athens and Sparta against the invasion from the east in the Persian Wars (490-478 B.C.); opposed the ensuing Athenian imperialism that resulted in the Peloponnesian War (431-404 B.C.); and, once again allied with her Greek sister city-states against the Spartan hegemony in the Corinthian War (395-387 B.C.). It is not surprising that eventually Corinth became the leader of the Achaian Confederacy, which came into conflict in the second century B.C. with the expanding military might of Rome. As a result of Roman supremacy and of Corinth's leading role in opposition, the Greek city was captured and burned by Rome in 146 B.C. and its citizens either killed or sold into slavery.

Therefore the Corinth of Paul's time was not the ancient Greek city but rather a Roman colony founded by decree of Julius Caesar in 44 B.C. on the ancient site, which had lain virtually desolate for more than a century. Its new population initially consisted of freedmen from Italy who were soon joined by Greeks and other foreigners, including many Jews, from the East. As in the past, Corinth quickly became an important center of industry and commerce, a center that in A.D. 27 became the capital of the Roman province of Achaia. Like any port city in ancient or modern times, Corinth at the time of Paul had the reputation of being cosmopolitan, worldly, and promiscuous— full of both philosophies and practices from every corner of the world. In fact, in Koine Greek "the verb *korinthiázein,* 'to live like a Corinthian' came to mean 'to live a dissolute life.'"[2]

Chapter 18 of the book of Acts narrates Paul's founding of the first Christian community in Corinth. In the year A.D. 50, Paul left Athens, near the end of his missionary journey, and traveled to Corinth, where he stayed for a year and a half. (Acts 18:11.)[3] At Corinth he met two Jewish converts, Aquila and his wife, Priscilla, who had recently been forced to leave Rome.[4] Because they were tentmakers like himself,

Paul moved in with them and presumably worked with them in their business while he pursued his missionary efforts there. While Acts 18:4 records that as he taught in the synagogue he "persuaded the Jews and the Greeks," it also implies that his message was more readily accepted by the Gentiles. (Acts 18:5-8.)[5] Nevertheless, the mixture of Jews and Gentiles may have been a factor in the contentions that soon arose within the church at Corinth. After Silas and Timothy came from Macedonia, Paul moved in with a Gentile named Justus, and many Corinthians believed in his words and were baptized, including Crispus, the "chief ruler of the synagogue." (18:8.)

The social conditions at Corinth were volatile even during Paul's ministry there, and we can only imagine some of the circumstances faced by the early saints in the fledgling church after he left. When Gallio was made "deputy of Achaia" (A.D. 51-52), many of the Corinthian Jews, enraged at Paul for "persuad[ing] men to worship God contrary to the law" (18:13), took him before Gallio for judgment. Gallio refused to get involved and sent the people away, implying that it was not his duty to get involved in a religious squabble. (18:14-16.) Shortly thereafter Paul left with Priscilla and Aquila and went to Ephesus, then continued alone to Antioch and eventually Jerusalem. (18:21.) While he was in Jerusalem, "a certain Jew named Apollos, born at Alexandria, an eloquent man, and mighty in the scriptures, came to Ephesus." (18:24.) After Aquila and Priscilla had "expounded unto him the way of God more perfectly" (18:26), Apollos was sent to Corinth with recommendations from "the brethren . . . exhorting the disciples there to receive him, . . . for he mightily convinced the Jews, and that publickly, shewing by the scriptures that Jesus was Christ" (18:27-28).

Within a relatively short time, news came to Paul of moral laxity among the Corinthian saints. He refers in 1 Corinthians 5:9 to a letter, no longer extant, that he had written previously advising them "not to company with fornicators." Further disturbing news of dissension among the saints came by way of messengers from the house of Chloe (1 Cor. 1:11) and a later delegation (1 Cor. 16:17), as well as by way of a letter from the church at Corinth asking his counsel on several of the divisive issues involved (1 Cor. 7:1). These reports provided the impetus for the writing of 1 Corinthians in which Paul addressed the issue of dissension as well as answered the doctrinal questions. He wrote 1 Corinthians in the early summer of A.D. 57, shortly before Pentecost (1 Cor. 16:8); and as a follow-up to this letter, he sent Timothy to see that his counsel was heeded and that the situation in Corinth improved (1 Cor. 16:10-11). The evidence in 2 Corinthians suggests, however, that things got worse before they got better. There are allusions in 2 Corinthians (2:1; 12:14; and 13:1-2) to a "second visit" by Paul, calling the members of the church to repentance, and to a harsh letter (possibly a reference to 1 Corinthians) that finally brought some results. Probably in the fall of A.D. 57, Paul got word that many at Corinth, humbled by his concern through his letters, had repented. He responded by writing the letter preserved in 2 Corinthians to further express his love for the Corinthian saints, his joy that many had responded to his rebuke, and his continued concern for those who still remained rebellious.

We have only a portion of one side of the correspondence between Paul and the saints at Corinth. But from these two letters we can learn much about the challenges faced by the small community of early saints as they sought to learn their identity as Christians in the most worldly of worlds at Corinth. It is not surprising that these letters contain much of value for saints in the latter days as well: faced with many of the same challenges, learning to accept and to love one another and seeking to come out from Babylon to build up Zion.

1 Corinthians: Structure and Contents

An outline of the contents of 1 Corinthians demonstrates that what at first glance may appear to be a random collection of Paul's teachings is really a carefully constructed letter of four parts:

    I. 1:1-9: Introduction
      A. Salutation (1:1-3)
      B. Thanksgiving/blessing (1:4-9)
    II. Chapters 1 to 6: Paul's response to reports from the house of Chloe
      A. Divisions in the church and a plea for unity
        (1:10—4:21)
        1. Dissensions at Corinth (1:10-17)

  2. The wisdom of the world and of the spirit
     (1:18–2:16)
  3. Teachers (3:1–4:21)
B. Immorality (chs. 5–6)
  1. Fellowship of sinners (ch. 5)
  2. Lawsuits and courts (6:1-8)
  3. Sexual laxity (6:9-20)
III. Chapters 7 to 15: Paul's response to questions posed by
   the church at Corinth
A. Marriage (ch. 7)
B. Idol sacrifices (8:1–11:1)
C. Divine worship and the new covenant (11:2–15:58)
  1. Women and worship (11:2-16)
  2. The Lord's Supper (11:17-34)
  3. Spiritual gifts (ch. 12–14)
     a. Charity (ch. 13)
     b. Speaking in tongues (ch. 14)
  4. Resurrection (ch. 15)
IV. Chapter 16: Conclusion
A. Exhortations (16:1-18)
B. Salutation (16:19-24)

The first part of the letter is a short formal introduction (1:1-9), followed by the body of the letter. The body of the letter is evenly divided between Paul's addressing the reports he had received from people in the house of Chloe of dissension and immorality that had crept into the church at Corinth (1:10–6:20), and his careful response to a series of questions written to him by the church (7:1) on subjects that had contributed to the contention in the church, such as marriage, idol sacrifices, the proper place of spiritual gifts, and the resurrection (chs. 7–15). The letter then ends with a formal conclusion. This study will systematically discuss each major section of the epistle, focusing on one of the major themes found throughout—unity among the saints.

I. Introduction: Salutation and Thanksgiving

Paul begins the first epistle to the Corinthians, just as he begins his other letters, with an introduction consisting of a salutation and a blessing (1:1-3) and a formal statement of thanksgiving (1:4-9). The salutation identifies Paul as the sender of the letter, writing in the official capacity of "an apostle of Jesus Christ through the will of God," along with Sosthenes, a fellow saint whom he identifies as "our brother." The letter is addressed to the members of the church at Corinth "that are sanctified in Christ Jesus." (1:2.) The salutation also contains the blessing or benediction "Grace [*cháris*] be unto you, and peace, from God our Father, and from the Lord Jesus Christ." (1:3.) This formulaic blessing is a unique Christian innovation in which Paul appears to have combined a modified form of the common Greek greeting *chaírein* with the common Hebrew greeting *shālôm*. Combining a Greek and a Hebrew greeting may have been a deliberate attempt to reflect the new order of Christian society, which was also a combination of Gentiles and Jews, and the words *grace* and *peace* that come from "God our Father and the Lord Jesus Christ" adequately summarize the gospel—the "good news"—of the atonement of the Lord Jesus Christ.[6]

Paul begins his thanksgiving by expressing gratitude for the grace of God that is given to the saints in Corinth by Jesus Christ. While gratefully acknowledging grace, a silent reference to the lack of harmony in Corinth and a foreshadowing of the rebuke that is to follow directly, is the conspicuous absence of any mention of its counterpart—peace. Paul then concentrates on the positive fruits of this grace that have been realized among the saints in Corinth—that they have been enriched in "all utterance, and in all knowledge" as well as spiritual gifts. (1:5, 7.) But once again the deafening silence regarding the fruits of faith, love, and righteousness lays the foundation for the body of the letter, which will deal with all of these expected fruits of the gospel. Ending on an optimistic note, he expresses his wish that in the end the saints may be able to stand "blameless in the day of our Lord Jesus Christ" (1:8), silently implying that repentance will be necessary. The final verse of thanksgiving (1:9) forms a transition from the introduction to Paul's first concern—the lack of unity among the saints in Corinth. He carefully sets the stage for his appeal for love and unity, noting that it is God who has called them "into fellowship of his Son Jesus Christ our Lord."

II. Paul's Response to Reports from the House of Chloe

Divisions in the Church and a Plea for Unity

Paul immediately addresses one of the disturbing developments at Corinth he has been advised of and makes his plea: "Now I beseech you, brethren, by the name of our Lord Jesus Christ . . . that there be no divisions among you." (1:10.) He has carefully prepared the rhetoric of his message. In verse 1 he indicates the official nature of this letter by referring to his apostolic calling and stewardship over the church in Corinth. At the same time he tempers the harsh nature of his rebuke throughout the letter with the constant use of the term *brethren*, emphasizing the intimate relationship enjoyed as members of the church and the common fellowship and commitment they enjoy through Jesus Christ.

Apparently the contentions and divisions among the members of the church had been manifested by the division into groups, each proclaiming their allegiance to Paul, Apollos, or Cephas. Paul's response to this situation is a series of rhetorical questions: "Is Christ divided? was Paul crucified for you? or were ye baptized in the name of Paul?" (1:13.) Once again Paul has prepared the rhetoric for his argument to follow, mentioning the name of Jesus Christ—who should be the sole focal point of allegiance—nine times in verses 1 through 9 before he explicitly reveals the subject of the letter in verse 10. At the same time he has carefully pointed out, as a model of oneness, the united efforts of God the Father and his Son Jesus Christ in administrating the gospel. (1:1, 3, 4, 9.)

It has been suggested that the factionalism in the church at Corinth may have been due in part to a division between the Greek (Gentile) and the Jewish members—the Greeks aligning themselves with Apollos, the charismatic and eloquent orator from Alexandria, and the Jews, originally from Syro-Palestine, identifying themselves with Cephas, the Apostle Peter. (John 1:42.)[7] At the same time, those who had been greatly influenced by Paul during his ministry at Corinth cited him as their champion. Ironically, members of one group seem to have distinguished themselves by identifying their faction as "of Christ." Paul responds to the division between the Jews and the Greeks, making the point that "the preaching of the cross" which is the "wisdom of God" is foolishness to all of the wise men of the world—both Jew and Greek. (1:18-21.)

Paul describes the doctrine of "Christ crucified" as a "stumblingblock" to the Jews, who "require a sign" (1:22-23), perhaps a reference to the widespread Jewish expectation of a powerful Messiah who, rather than dying the death of a criminal, was to have brought them mighty acts of political deliverance. To the Greeks who seek wisdom, the crucified Christ is "foolishness." (1:22-23.) But to those who are "called" (become members of the church), "both Jews and Greeks," Christ is the "power of God, and the wisdom of God." (1:24.) Just as there are not many "wise men after the flesh, not many mighty, not many noble" found in the congregation at Corinth (1:26), so God has chosen everywhere "the foolish things of the world to confound the wise; and . . . the weak things of the world to confound the things which are mighty" (1:27).

Paul's discussion about the wisdom of the world and the wisdom of the Spirit (1:18–2:16) is directed at the problem of dissension in the church. For members of the church to claim their allegiance to the wisdom of the Jews or Greeks, or to Apollos, Cephas, or even Paul, is to demonstrate a basic misunderstanding of the gospel message of Christ crucified, which transcends all worldly wisdom. Perhaps directing his remarks to those who claimed to be "of Paul," he points out that when he came, he purposely avoided preaching with "enticing words of man's wisdom, but in demonstration of the Spirit and of power: that [one's] faith should not stand in the wisdom of men, but in the power of God." (2:4-5.) True conversion, he explains, comes when the natural man—who "receiveth not the things of the Spirit of God: for they are foolishness unto him" (2:14)—is changed by the power of the Holy Ghost into a spiritual man, who is able to receive "the spirit which is of God," that he "might know the things that are freely given" to him by God (2:12).

The contention manifested at Corinth is a sure sign that the conversion process is not complete or is in a state of disintegration. In chapter 3 Paul describes the members of the church at Corinth as being in the infant stages of conversion—as "babes in Christ" who are "yet carnal: for . . . there is among [them] envying, and strife, and divisions." (3:1-3.) For this reason they must be fed with milk and not meat. (3:2.) Referring to the factionalism in the church, Paul proceeds to teach the proper place of teachers and other of the Lord's representatives on earth. Using a metaphor of agriculture, he explains: "I have planted, Apollos watered; but God gave the increase. So then neither is he that planteth any thing, neither he that watereth; but God that giveth the increase. Now he that planteth and he that watereth are one: and every man shall receive his own reward according to his own labour. For we are labourers together with God: ye are God's husbandry." (3:6-9.) He further compares the church to a building, the laborers as the builders, and the foundation as Jesus Christ. (3:9-15.) While each person's contribution to the building will be judged whether it be good or bad, the foundation—Christ—always remains secure, once again reminding the saints that true unity is achieved not by loyalty to each other but through the common bond of allegiance to God.

Paul concludes his teaching about the role of teachers with a summary of the whole principle: "Therefore let no man glory in men. For all things are yours; whether Paul, or Apollos, or Cephas, or the world, or life, or death, or things present, or things to come; all are yours; and ye are Christ's; and Christ is God's." (3:21-23.)

Immorality among the Saints

In chapters 5 and 6, Paul deals with the report of immorality among the saints in Corinth. He first turns to the specific charge of one who married his father's wife (stepmother). While in and of itself this constituted, according to the Mosaic law (Lev. 18:8; 20:11) and Roman law, the serious transgression of incest, Paul is first concerned with the fact that the members of the church have accepted such a transgressor. He notes that they are "puffed up" with pride in their sympathetic acceptance of this relationship when they should have "rather mourned" and cast such a transgressor out of their midst. (5:1-5.) Brotherhood and fellowship, so important to the unity of the saints, does not, however, extend to the casual acceptance of serious sin. He tells the Corinthian saints, "your glorying is not good." (5:6.)

Reversing the imagery of the well-known saying of Jesus (Matt.

13:33) comparing the kingdom of God, although small, to leaven that could influence the whole world for good, Paul compares the leaven to the one guilty of serious transgression who can also have a great influence on the whole: "Know ye not that a little leaven leaveneth the whole lump? Purge out therefore the old leaven, that ye may be a new lump, as ye are unleavened." (5:6-7.) In cases of serious sin, judgment is necessary and some may need to be cast out in order not to compromise the whole church.

At the same time that some saints are overly tolerant of those who deserve ecclesiastical discipline, others are taking their brothers to court to be judged by the unbelievers. (6:1-8.) Paul tells them that most of these disputes are over issues so trivial that they should be overlooked, and in the more serious cases they should be solved within the jurisdiction of the church. Finally he exhorts the Corinthians to refrain from any sexual immorality (6:9-20), because such sin defiles the body, which is the "temple of the Holy Ghost" (6:19).

III. Paul's Response to Questions Posed by the Corinthians

The introductory verses in chapters 7, 8, and 12 indicate that Paul's teachings in chapters 7 through 15 are responses to questions posed by the Corinthians in a previous letter concerning marriage (7); idol sacrifices (8–11:1); proper worship—including questions about the place of women, the administration of the sacrament and spiritual gifts (11:2–14:40); and the resurrection (15). Apparently many of these issues had contributed to the contention among the saints.

Questions on Marriage

The Joseph Smith Translation is an invaluable aid in helping us to understand the perplexing passage contained in chapter 7. On the surface it appears that Paul is telling the Corinthians that celibacy is preferable to marriage. The Joseph Smith Translation changes the first verse—"It is good for a man not to touch a woman"—into a statement made in the letter from the Corinthians rather than a statement of Paul, so that verses 2 through 5 are Paul's response to this statement. This simple clarification radically changes the tone of Paul's response, from the implication that the institution of marriage is a concession made to mortals in order to avoid immorality, to a defense of marriage as an essential part of the gospel, one in which sexual relations are essential.

Because Paul claims to have fulfilled all of the religious requirements of Jewish law (Philip. 3:6; Gal. 1:14), which included marriage, many scholars accept the fact that Paul must have been married at some point in his life.[8] In light of this fact, Paul's apparently positive attitude toward celibacy and his disparagement of marriage in this passage seem odd. Paul himself says that these instructions are given not as doctrine ("commandment of the Lord") but as his own personal opinion (1 Cor. 7:25), and that his approval of the unmarried state is a temporary injunction "good for the present distress" (7:26). Many interpret this "distress" (Gr. *anágkē*) to be reference to Paul's belief that the end of the world and the Second Coming were imminent and therefore the commandment of marriage was suspended for a time. This assumption, however, contradicts other statements made by Paul himself (i.e., 2 Thes. 2) where it is clear that he understood that the apostasy and restoration (and therefore a considerable period of time) must precede the return of the Savior.[9]

The Joseph Smith Translation confirms that indeed this counsel is a temporary injunction and explains that it is given specifically to those who are involved in missionary work, rendering 1 Corinthians 7:29: "But I speak unto you who are called unto the ministry. For this I say, brethren, the time that remaineth is but short, that ye shall be sent forth unto the ministry. Even they who have wives, shall be as though they had none; for ye are called and chosen to do the Lord's work."

Sacrifice to Idols

The second question that Paul addresses is whether it is permissible for the saints to eat meat that had been sacrificed to idols. This was a problem commonly faced by Christians in many Hellenistic and Roman cities. Much of the meat sold in the markets had originally been sacrificial offerings in the local temples. Partially burned as offerings to the idols of the pagan deities, the remainder of the meat belonged to the priests, who sold and distributed it to the butchers in the area. Furthermore, festive meals held in the homes of pagans, often social events to which they would invite their Christian neighbors, consisted of sacrificial animals that were dedicated to the gods on those occasions.

In chapters 8 through 11:1, Paul discusses the complexities of this difficult issue and gives counsel. In chapter 8 he begins his argument, identifying the relevant principles. First he recognizes that many of the saints have the knowledge that there is only one God and that "an idol is nothing in the world" (8:4-6), and because of this knowledge they are not bothered by eating idol sacrifices. This knowledge, however, "puffeth up" and makes those who are not bothered proud. (8:1.) On the other hand, some saints do not enjoy this knowledge, and when they eat meat offered to idols, "their conscience being weak is defiled." (8:7.) Under the circumstances Paul reminds them that "charity edifieth." (8:1.) It is true that many have the knowledge that eating such meat neither commends nor condemns (8:8), but charity dictates that all members of the church be sensitive to those with less understanding, lest eating meat sacrificed to idols becomes "a stumblingblock to them that are weak" (8:9). The first priority is unity, and while the eating of idol sacrifice may be in and of itself of no import, if it affects the fellowship of the saints it is an important issue. Paul reminds the Corinthians, who would eat such meat in the pride of their knowledge, "When ye sin so against the brethren, and wound their weak conscience, ye sin against Christ." (8:12.)

Divine Worship and the New Covenant

Paul's teachings throughout the New Testament are enriched by frequent references to the Old Testament. In his letters he introduces direct quotations from scripture by the phrase "for it is written" (see, for example, the citation of Isa. 29:14 in 1 Cor. 1:19 and Isa. 64:4 in 2:9). At other times he makes general reference to Old Testament history and imagery to illustrate and more effectively communicate a point. When he makes his plea to the Corinthians to remain pure from the impure "leaven" of fornicators, he compares it to the fastidious purging of leaven necessary for the feast of Unleavened Bread associated with Passover. From a concrete example well understood from the law of Moses, he teaches the spiritual principle that the saints should "keep the feast, not with old leaven, neither with the leaven of malice and wickedness; but with the unleavened bread of sincerity and truth." (1 Cor. 5:7-8.)

In his appeal for chastity Paul declares, "Your body is the temple of the Holy Ghost which is in you, which ye have of God, and ye are not your own." (6:19.) Giving the reason that the body belongs in part to deity, he cites the Old Testament imagery of God redeeming Israel from slavery by means of the miraculous deliverance at the Red Sea and quotes Exodus 15:16: "For ye are bought with a price." (1 Cor. 6:20.) The image, well known in Israel, is that they were slaves ransomed ("redeemed") from their owners in Egypt by a mighty act of divine intervention and thus became the property of their new master—the Lord God of Israel.[10]

In chapter 10 Paul builds on this image of Israel's miraculous preservation in the wilderness and compares the present saints with their physical, if not spiritual (in the case of the Gentiles), forefathers. They, just as their forefathers, had been baptized, had "passed through the sea," and had eaten the spiritual meat and drink from the Rock that guided them in the wilderness. (10:1-4.) The author of the old covenant as well as the new is the same—Jesus Christ. Through this comparison, Paul shows the miracles in the desert to be a type of the new covenant instituted by Jesus, made efficacious through baptism and the partaking of the spiritual meat and drink of the sacrament. At the same time, the sacred history of the Old Testament is a foreshadowing of the mighty act of redemption, also a mighty act of divine intervention, accomplished by the Atonement. The point of Paul's masterful sermon is to remind the Corinthians of the darker side of the story of the children of Israel in the wilderness—that they, just as the covenant people of old, were capable of murmuring, idolatry, fornication, and blasphemy. (10:5-12.)

In chapters 12 through 14, Paul turns to the problem of spiritual gifts that had also apparently become a source of contention in the congregation at Corinth. He explains that while unity in the church depends on oneness of purpose, it does not dictate a uniformity of the different manifestations of the Spirit among the individual members. There is a diversity of gifts—wisdom, knowledge, faith, healing, working of miracles, prophecy, discerning of spirits, gift of tongues—all manifestations of the same Spirit. (12:4-10.) Paul illustrates his point with the apt metaphor of the body. Just as there are different offices and callings in the church (12:28-30), so the various spiritual gifts are given to different individuals and must function together like the different members of the human body. Every part of the body is necessary for its proper function, and no part can claim independence from any other part. While this metaphor delineates the proper function of spiritual gifts and offices in the church, at the same time it speaks to the larger issue of unity in the church. This oneness is characterized by a recognition of the importance of each individual as well as a spirit of mutual empathy that makes the saints as one—suffering and rejoicing with the fortunes of each member of the "body of Christ." (1 Cor. 12:27.) In short, unity is achieved only through love. Joseph Smith recognized this and quoted, in part, Paul's metaphor of the body in an editorial appearing in the April 2, 1842, issue of the *Times and Seasons* encouraging the Saints in their efforts to build the Nauvoo Temple:

> The advancement of the cause of God and the building up of Zion is as much one man's business as another's. The only difference is, that one is called to fulfill one duty, and another another duty; "but if one member suffers, all the members suffer with it, and if one member is honored all the rest rejoice with it, and the eye cannot say to the ear, I have no need of thee, nor the head to the foot, I have no need of thee;" [1 Cor. 12:25-26] party feelings, separate interests, exclusive designs should be lost sight of in the one common cause, in the interest of the whole.[11]

The crowning gift of the Spirit is charity—"the pure love of Christ" (Moro. 7:47)—which every Saint should seek (1 Cor. 14:1), for without love one is "as sounding brass, or a tinkling cymbal" (13:1).[12] Paul's discourse on love has been immortalized in the traditional language of the King James Version and incorporated in part into the thirteenth Article of Faith. Echoing the themes found throughout the letter, Paul identifies charity as that which "rejoiceth not in iniquity, but rejoiceth in the truth; beareth all things, believeth all things, hopeth all things, endureth all things." (13:6-7.) Of all of the enduring gifts of God—faith, hope, and charity—"the greatest of these is charity." (13:13.) Charity is the answer to many of the problems among the saints in Corinth and is ultimately the most important ingredient in the unity of the church.

Resurrection in 1 Corinthians

The final problem that Paul addresses in 1 Corinthians is resurrection. In response to those who apparently doubt the resurrection of the dead (15:12), he presents to the Corinthians in chapter 15 one of the most explicit and complete doctrinal expositions of resurrection found anywhere in the New Testament. He reaffirms the historical reality of Christ's crucifixion and resurrection and cites the witnesses of the scriptures: Peter, the Twelve, and the five hundred. (15:3-7.) Last of all he adds his own personal witness, as the "least of the apostles" (15:8-9), that He who once was dead lives. The victory over death is universal, "for as in Adam all die, even so in Christ shall all be made alive." (15:22.) But while resurrection will be enjoyed by all, Paul reminds the Corinthians that in the hereafter there are three glories to be gained (15:40-41), according to one's performance in mortality. The doctrine of resurrection and judgment reminds the saints that the relevance of Paul's letter transcends the cause of local tranquillity and extends to the eternities.

IV. Conclusion: Exhortations and Salutation

In conclusion, Paul mentions the collection for the poor saints in Palestine according to the request of the Jerusalem council. (Acts 11:29.) He then outlines his travel plans to pass through Macedonia and come to Corinth in the near future and adds a touching request in behalf of Timothy that "he may be with you without fear: for he worketh the work of the Lord, as I also do." (16:10.) His final exhortation sums up the whole letter: "Let all your things be done with charity." (16:14.)

Paul sends greetings from the churches of Asia, from Aquila and Priscilla, and from all of the brethren (16:19-20), and then adds his greeting "with [his] own hand," perhaps a reference to his own signature as in Colossians 4:18 and 2 Thessalonians 3:17. Just as he began his letter, Paul closes with the repetition of the name of the focal point of the gospel—the Lord Jesus Christ (three times in verses 22-24). He looks forward to the return of the resurrected Lord with the Aramaic exclamation *Maran-atha* (KJV) divided *māran 'athā*: "The Lord comes" (or "has come"), or *māranā'thā'* "Come, O Lord!" (16:22), and seals the letter with the blessing of "the grace of our Lord Jesus Christ." Last but not least, he adds his personal prayer: "My love be with you all in Christ Jesus. Amen." (16:24.)

2 Corinthians: Historical Background

The events leading up to the writing of 2 Corinthians must be reconstructed from scattered references in the epistles to the Corinthians. After writing 1 Corinthians in Ephesus in the early summer of A.D. 57 (shortly before Pentecost, 1 Cor. 16:8), Paul had sent Timothy to Corinth to see how his letter was received and if the situation there had improved (1 Cor. 16:10-11). Evidence in 2 Corinthians suggests that initially the situation in Corinth got worse rather than better. There are allusions to a second visit by Paul to Corinth (2 Cor. 2:1; 12:14; and 13:1-2) to help rectify the situation; this visit was made "in heaviness" (2 Cor. 2:1). There are also references to a stern letter (2 Cor. 2:4; 7:8-12) sent by Paul. These references may be to 1 Corinthians or perhaps to another letter, now lost, sent in the interim between 1 and 2 Corinthians. Eventually, after his visit the letter, whether 1 Corinthians or another letter, got positive results that Paul later acknowledged: "For though I made you sorry with a letter, . . . I perceive that the same epistle hath made you sorry." (2 Cor. 7:8.)

Meanwhile, still concerned about the Corinthians, Paul sent Titus and another unnamed brother to Corinth (2 Cor. 12:17-18), probably in connection with the collection for the Saints in Palestine. He had evidently prearranged to meet Titus returning from Corinth in Troas, and when Titus did not appear at Troas, he went to Macedonia to meet him there. (2 Cor. 2:12-13.) Paul's anxiety about the affairs at Corinth were finally relieved when Titus arrived and informed him that the Corinthians had mourned and repented of their past behavior. (2 Cor. 7:6-7.) Probably sometime in the fall of A.D. 57, the same year in which he had previously written 1 Corinthians, Paul wrote the epistle preserved in 2 Corinthians (actually his third or fourth letter to the Corinthians) to express his love and concern for the saints at Corinth and his relief and joy that they had responded to his rebuke, and to further encourage those who had remained rebellious to repent.

2 Corinthians: Structure and Contents

The epistle in 2 Corinthians is a personal and emotional letter and gives us much insight into the person of Paul. Most of the material in the letter is relevant to his relief at the repentance of many Corinthians and an explanation and defense of his ministry, directed toward those who have not yet repented. Thus there are passages reflecting many emotions, ranging from love and joy to impatience and anger. Perhaps due to its emotional nature, the letter does not contain a clear-cut structure as does 1 Corinthians, and much of the material can be divided many different ways. The following should be considered only as a general guide to the major themes and not as a comprehensive outline:

    I. Introduction (1:1-14)
      A. Salutation (1:1-2)
      B. Thanksgiving/blessing (1:3-11)
    II. Paul's apostolic ministry (1:15–9:15)
      A. Paul's recent relations with the Church (1:15–2:13)
      B. Paul's apostolic ministry (2:14–5:9)
      C. Appeal for reconciliation (5:10–7:16)
      D. The collection for Jerusalem (8:1–9:15)
    III. Paul's defense of his ministry and call to repentance (10:1–13:10)
      A. Initial appeal for obedience (10:1-18)
      B. Paul replies to charges (11:1–12:13)
      C. Concerns and warnings (12:14–13:10)
    IV. Conclusion (13:11-14)

Following the formal introduction (1:1-14), the body of the letter is a loosely organized collection of material. In the first half of the letter Paul expresses his concern for the church at Corinth; explains his apostolic ministry; makes a plea for reconciliation of the saints with him, with each other, and with God; and makes an extended appeal for generous contributions to the relief fund to be sent to the saints in Palestine. (1:15–9:15.) In chapters 10 through 13 he makes a detailed defense of his apostolic calling and ministry, which had apparently been called into question by some in Corinth; replies to specific charges leveled at him; and ends with warnings directed at those who have not yet repented of their dissension. (10:1–13:10.) The letter ends, as do all of Paul's letters, with a formal conclusion and benediction. (13:11-14.)

I. Introduction: Salutation and Thanksgiving

It is apparent that Timothy had returned to Paul from Corinth, as he is included in Paul's salutation. (1:1-2.) As always in his letters, Paul addresses his thanksgiving to God, here referred to as "Father of our Lord Jesus Christ." (1:3.) The object of his gratitude is the comfort that proceeds from "the Father of mercies, and the God of all comfort; who comforteth us in all our tribulation." (1:3-4.) Paul sees fit to remind the saints at Corinth of the great afflictions and sufferings he has been called to bear in his missionary labors in Asia. Even though his trials were so great that at one point he says he "despaired even of life" (1:8), he has trust in the "God which raiseth the dead" (1:9)—probably a reference to the detailed exposition he had already sent them on resurrection in 1 Corinthians 15. Paul has experienced God's deliverance from death as a mortal and furthermore has the assurance that God will ultimately deliver him when he finally does succumb to death in the future. Trust in God's eventual deliverance from suffering provides comfort to all persons faced with affliction. Referring to the trials endured by many of the saints at Corinth, Paul assures them that just as the victory over death was wrought by Christ through suffering, so too it is through suffering that mortals can receive consolation and salvation: "For as the sufferings of Christ abound in us, so our consolation also aboundeth by Christ." (1:5-7.)

II. Paul's Apostolic Ministry

The epistle in 2 Corinthians demonstrates that Paul understood well, as a priesthood leader, the eternal principle outlined by the Prophet Joseph Smith in the Liberty Jail that "no power or influence can or ought to be maintained by virtue of the priesthood, only by persuasion, by long-suffering, by gentleness and meekness, and by love unfeigned; . . . reproving betimes with sharpness, when moved upon by the Holy Ghost; and then showing forth afterwards an increase of love toward him whom thou hast reproved." (D&C 121:41-43.) In a previous letter, and by his visit, Paul had sharply rebuked the saints at Corinth. In this letter he assures them that the letter was written "out of much affliction and anguish of heart" and was motivated solely by the love he had for them. (2:4.) Throughout 2 Corinthians he expresses an increasing love and concern for them.

Increased love should be exercised by the saints toward each other as well. In 2:5-11 Paul refers to a specific individual who had apparently been involved in a serious act of rebellion and who had subsequently repented. He advises the saints that they ought to "forgive him [the individual] and comfort him, lest perhaps such a one should be swallowed up with overmuch sorrow." (2:7.) Paul is teaching the principle that after he, representing the church, has forgiven someone, the members of the congregation must also find the capacity to forgive as well, "lest Satan should get an advantage." (2:11.)

Paul rejoices in his missionary labors and describes them as a "triumph in Christ." (2:14.) In chapter 3 he eloquently teaches how the new covenant instituted by Christ replaces the old covenant embodied in the law of Moses. The ancient prophets Jeremiah and Ezekiel had witnessed the destruction of Jerusalem and the scattering of her people, which were the disastrous results of centuries of Israel's disobedience (systematically recorded in the Old Testament) to the old covenant inscribed on tables of stone. They must have wondered if mortals could ever be obedient to the conditions of the covenant. To both of these prophets the Lord gave a vision of hope for the future. The Lord promised Jeremiah that he would establish a "new covenant," which he described thus: "I will put my law in their inward parts, and write it in their hearts." He then echoed the same promise attached to the Mosaic covenant: "And [I] will be their God, and they shall be my people." (Jer. 31:31-33.) To Ezekiel came the word of the Lord couched in similar language: "I will give them one heart, and I will put a new spirit within you; and I will take the stony heart out of their flesh, and will give them an heart of flesh: that they may walk in my statutes, and keep mine ordinances, and do them: and they shall be my people, and I will be their God." (Ezek. 11:19; 36:26-27.)

Paul declares that Christ has now established this new covenant, and, building on the prophetic metaphor of stone and flesh, he describes it as a covenant "written . . . not in tables of stone, but in fleshy tables of the heart." (2 Cor. 3:3.) He adds that ultimately we look through Christ to God the Father, and it is he who has "made us able ministers of the new testament [covenant]." (3:4, 6.)[13] Continuing with the imagery of stone and flesh, he teaches that the power of the new covenant—which makes it possible to fulfill its conditions—is found "not of the letter, but of the spirit: for the letter killeth, but the spirit giveth life." (3:6.)

Paul explains that the manifestation of God to Moses in the revelation of the old covenant was so glorious that Moses had to "put a vail over his face, that the children of Israel could not steadfastly look." (3:13.) He then expands on the Old Testament passage with an allegory, noting ironically that there remain some "even unto this day, when Moses is read, the vail is upon their heart." (3:15.) In other words, they are not able to see that the old covenant was transitory ("the end of that which is abolished," 3:13), and the "vail is [now] done away in Christ." (3:14.) Whereas once the law was written with letters on stone, now it is the Spirit that giveth life, and "the Lord is that Spirit: and where the Spirit of the Lord is, there is liberty"—freedom from the death of the old law. (3:17.)

Paul reveals that it is through the Spirit that the covenant becomes internalized (written on the "fleshy tables of the heart"), and this internalization is a process by which a mortal, gradually becoming more like God, can acquire the power to comprehend and obey the conditions of the new covenant: "But we all, with open face beholding as in a glass the glory of the Lord, are changed into the same image from glory to glory, even as by the Spirit of the Lord." (3:18.)

In the next section Paul explains the reconciliation of fallen man to God made possible through the gospel. (5:11–7:16.) It is God who has initiated this process, "who hath reconciled us to himself by Jesus Christ." (5:18.) An individual who enters into the new covenant in Christ becomes a "new creature" (5:17), and the Atonement makes it possible for that person to repent of "trespasses" and achieve reconciliation with God the Father (5:19). Paul links this concept to his defense of the divine authority of his apostleship that follows, noting to the Corinthians: "Now then we are ambassadors for Christ, as though God did beseech you by us." (5:20.) His role as their priesthood leader has been a painful one, and he has had the unpleasant task of calling them to repentance. (7:4-9.) He is relieved that finally they have humbled themselves and that they "sorrowed to repentance." (7:9.) While God has initiated the possibility of reconciliation, it is the duty of the individual saints to finally make it effective in each of their lives by repentance and righteous living.

Years earlier, probably around A.D. 44, the council in Jerusalem had decided that a collection would be made from the church to send to the impoverished saints in Palestine, and Paul and Barnabas were put in charge of the project. (Acts 11:29-30.) Now, thirteen years later, Paul is still carrying out his assignment. Elsewhere in his epistles he briefly mentions this undertaking (1 Cor. 16:1-4; Rom. 15:24-29), but in chapters 8 and 9 in 2 Corinthians, he gives an extended exposition on the subject. He begins his long and tactful appeal for contributions from the Corinthians, giving as an example the generosity of the Macedonians, who, in spite of their "deep poverty," had given abundantly. (8:1-5.) He does not exert his authority to command compliance or prescribe an amount, but wishes it to be a voluntary contribution "to prove the sincerity" of their love. (8:8.) He gently attempts to persuade the Corinthians, comparing the gift to "the grace of our Lord Jesus Christ, that, though he was rich, yet for your sakes he became poor, that ye through his poverty might be rich." (8:9.) Paul goes to great lengths to attest the honesty and trustworthiness of the two unnamed messengers that have been sent to collect the funds (8:16–9:5) and then enumerates the blessings promised for generosity (9:6-15). He compares charitable contributions to the law of the harvest, writing that "he which soweth sparingly shall reap also sparingly; and he which soweth bountifully shall reap also bountifully." (9:6.)

III. Paul's Defense of His Ministry and Call to Repentance

At the heart of the contention in the church at Corinth are those who have ridiculed Paul and denied his authority. His necessary response is a bold and vigorous defense of his apostolic authority and his work in the ministry. (10:1–13:10.) Some had accused him of "walk[ing] according to the flesh" (10:2), and others had ridiculed his physical appearance and his inelegant speech (10:10). Elsewhere in the same letter he addressed the charges that he was vacillating and indecisive. (2 Cor. 1:17-18; 4:1-2.)

Paul acknowledges that such charges against him, or any of the authorities of the church, are a sure sign of apostasy and therefore a very serious matter. He fears that the saints in Corinth will be beguiled by false apostles, "transforming themselves into the apostles of Christ" (11:13) and preaching another Christ, another spirit, and another gospel. The kingdom of God is a house of order, and to work in the ministry "a man must be called of God" (Article of Faith 5) for "not he that commendeth himself is approved, but whom the Lord commendeth" (10:18).

In his defense, Paul gives a detailed account of his ministry. (11:1–12:13.) Employing the Old Testament imagery of Israel as the bride of the Lord, he portrays himself as the father (founder) of the church at Corinth who has betrothed his daughter (the church) as a chaste virgin to her husband, Christ. (11:2.) In spite of his weaknesses of body and speech—he sarcastically refers to himself as a fool—Paul has given all of his time and energy to building up the church. He recounts at length some of the great persecutions, dangers, and afflictions he has endured (11:24-33) as a witness to his dedication, and he also refers to the great visions and revelations he has enjoyed. (12:1-7.) He declares, "I take pleasure in infirmities, in reproaches, in necessities, in persecutions, in distresses for Christ's sake: for when I am weak, then am I strong." (12:10.)

Paul then solemnly warns the Saints, "Truly the signs of an apostle were wrought among you in all patience, in signs, and wonders, and mighty deeds." (12:12.) He informs them of his plans for another visit (12:14–13:10), reminding them once again, "We do all things, dearly beloved, for your edifying (12:19). He also includes a warning against continued dissension, contention, and immorality, expressing the fear that when he returns, he will find "debates, envyings, wraths, strifes, backbitings, whisperings, swellings, tumults," and those who "have sinned already, and have not repented of the uncleanness and fornication and lasciviousness which they have committed." (12:20-21.)

IV. Conclusion

Paul's conclusion to 2 Corinthians is short and to the point. Echoing the theme of love and unity well-known from his letter in 1 Corinthians, and with great emotion, he sums up the totality of his ministry to the Corinthians in the final four verses. He bids the Saints farewell and exhorts them, "Be perfect, be of good comfort, be of one mind, live in peace; and the God of love and peace shall be with you." (13:11.) Whereas Paul included salutations from numerous individuals in his conclusion to 1 Corinthians (16:19-20), here he sends the greetings of "all the saints," presumably the members of the church in Macedonia to whom he has "boasted" of the Corinthians. (See 2 Cor. 9:2.)

His final succinct benediction includes a special blessing from each member of the Godhead: "The grace of the Lord Jesus Christ, and the love of God, and the communion of the Holy Ghost, be with you all. Amen." (13:14.) He may have been describing a process here whereby through the atonement of Christ and the gift of love from God, the Saints may enjoy fellowship with each other and "communion with the Holy Ghost."[14] In light of the emphasis on love, brotherhood, and unity prevalent in Paul's two surviving letters to the Corinthians, it is a fitting blessing for the saints there—and for that matter for the saints everywhere.

Joseph Smith, in a letter dated October 19, 1840, to the Twelve laboring in the mission field in England, repeated to the saints in the last dispensation the challenge of brotherhood and love that Paul gave to the infant church at Corinth. The Prophet reminded the Latter-day Saints of the importance of love and unity in the church. Like Paul, he looked back to the past, referring to the "oneness of heart" realized as Zion by the City of Enoch and prophesied by Ezekiel (11:19) as a sign of the new covenant. Then, quoting Paul from the opening verses of 1 Corinthians, the Prophet looked forward to the future return of the Savior:

> Let the Saints remember that great things depend on their individual exertion, and that they are called to be co-workers with us and the Holy Spirit in accomplishing the great work of the last days; and in consideration of the extent, the blessings

and glories of the same, let every selfish feeling be not only buried, but annihilated; and let love to God and man predominate, and reign triumphant in every mind, that their hearts may become like unto Enoch's of old, and comprehend all things, present, past and future, and "come behind in no gift, waiting for the coming of the Lord Jesus Christ." [1 Cor. 1:7.][15]

In the introductory section of the Doctrine and Covenants, the Lord has revealed, just as Paul wrote to the Corinthians (1 Cor. 1:27), that "the weak things of the world shall come forth and break down the mighty and strong ones." (D&C 1:19.) The source of the power of the weak is unity, and great is the power of love, brotherhood, and friendship through which the saints become one. Jesus taught that love among mortals is patterned after the divine and is an expected fruit of the gospel: "A new commandment I give unto you, That ye love one another; as I have loved you. . . . By this shall all men know that ye are my disciples, if ye have love one to another." (John 13:34-35.) The Lord has strongly reemphasized this injunction in our dispensation: "I say unto you, be one; and if ye are not one ye are not mine." (D&C 38:27.)

But the greater power of the weak is found in a higher oneness to which mortal unity is but a prerequisite. Jesus prayed to his Father for his disciples "that they all may be one; as thou, Father, art in me, and I in thee, that they also may be one in us." (John 17:21.) As Latter-day Saints, we—just as the Corinthians—can begin to comprehend (though as mortals "we see through a glass, darkly"—1 Cor. 13:12) and receive that power which derives from this divine unity, by first loving each other.

Notes

1. The exact chronology of Paul's life and the order of his epistles present many problems for the historian. For the most part this study follows the reconstruction found in Richard Lloyd Anderson, *Understanding Paul* (Salt Lake City: Deseret Book, 1983). See especially his discussion in pages 390-98.

2. Richard Kugelman, "The First Letter to the Corinthians," in *The Jerome Biblical Commentary: Volume II The New Testament,* ed. Raymond E. Brown, Joseph A. Fitzmyer, and Roland E. Murphy (Englewood Cliffs, New Jersey: Prentice-Hall Inc., 1968), p. 254. The meaning of *korinthiázomai* "to practice fornication" was known in Classical Greek as well; see Aristophanes Fr. 354, *Liddell, Scott, and Jones Greek-English Lexicon,* p. 981.

3. Paul's arrival at Corinth can be dated with some confidence to A.D. 50 because of an inscription found at Delphi that dates the beginning of Gallio's term as governor of Achaia in A.D. 51. Assuming that Paul was brought before Gallio in the first year of his rule, we can count back a year and a half and date his arrival in A.D. 50. For a complete discussion, see Anderson, *Understanding Paul,* pp. 390-92.

4. Aquila and Priscilla may have been among those Jews expelled from Rome by edict of Claudius. Dated by some scholars to A.D. 49, this edict is attested by Suetonius, *Claudius* 25: "Since the Jews constantly made disturbances at the instigation of Chrestus (Christ?), he [Claudius] expelled them from Rome." See Hans Conzelmann, *1 Corinthians* (Philadelphia: Fortress Press, 1975), p. 13.

5. 1 Corinthians 12:2 suggests that the majority of the members were Gentiles.

6. See discussion in David R. Seely, "From Unprofitable Servant to Beloved Brother in Christ," chapter 11 in this volume. See also William F. Orr and James A. Walther, *1 Corinthians,* Anchor Bible Series 32 (Garden City, New York: Doubleday & Co., 1976), p. 143.

7. Kugelman, "The First Letter to the Corinthians," p. 256.

8. For further discussion of Paul and marriage see Anderson, *Understanding Paul,* pp. 24-25, 104-6.

9. Ibid., p. 106.

10. Peter, like Paul, portrays the imagery of Israel being redeemed from slavery as a type of the atonement by which mankind is redeemed "with the precious blood of Christ." (1 Pet. 1:17-21.)

11. *Teachings of the Prophet Joseph Smith,* comp. Joseph Fielding Smith (Salt Lake City: Deseret Book, 1976), p. 231.

12. For a more complete discussion of 1 Corinthians 13, see Richard Lloyd Anderson's excellent treatment in *Understanding Paul,* pp. 117-25.

13. The Greek translators of the Old Testament translated the Hebrew term for covenant (*běrît*) as *diathékē,* a term in a broad sense referring to an arrangement made between two parties, but specifically referring to a legal will. This is the term used in the New Testament for *covenant.* From the legal connotation of *diathékē* derived the Vulgate *testamentum* and the English

testament. Therefore "the new testament" in 2 Corinthians 3:6 refers to "the new covenant," as opposed to the "old" Mosaic covenant.

14. "Communion with the Holy Ghost" = *hē koinōnía toû hagíou pneúmatos. Koinōnía* is the word often translated as *fellowship* that denotes a close relationship between human beings, often used in Greek in referring to the intimate relationship of marriage. The genitive "the Holy Ghost," *toû hagíou pneúmatos,* can be taken with *koinōnía* to mean "communion (or fellowship) *with* the Holy Ghost" or it may be understood as a subjective genitive or a genitive of quality meaning "fellowship *brought about by* the Holy Spirit." See Walter Bauer, *A Greek-English Lexicon of the New Testament,* rev. and ed. by F. Wilbur Gingrich and Frederick W. Danker, 2nd ed. (Chicago: University of Chicago Press, 1979), pp. 438-39. Often such grammatical ambiguity purposely suggests both interpretations. The context linking it with grace and love indicates that in either case, unity of the saints is directly related to "communion of the Holy Ghost." Joseph Smith taught that "through the love of the Father, the mediation of Jesus Christ, and the gift of the Holy Spirit, [the Saints] are to be heirs of God, and joint heirs with Jesus Christ." (*Lectures on Faith* [Salt Lake City: Deseret Book, 1985], 5:3.)

15. *Teachings of the Prophet Joseph Smith,* pp. 178-79.

6

CONCERN, CORRECTION, AND COUNSEL FOR CONVERTS
(Galatians)

GEORGE A. HORTON, JR.

A missionary receives the latest report from his field of labor with excitement, hears about the spiritual growth of faithful converts with joy, and is pained with the news of inactivity and apostasy. Such feelings are borne of deep desires for the eternal welfare of loved ones in the bonds of the new and everlasting covenant. Converts become loved by missionaries as if they were members of their immediate families.

In his letter to the Galatians, the Apostle Paul poured out his heart and soul upon receiving disturbing reports that large numbers of his converts were being led astray by a few misguided members of the church who were attempting to dissuade them from the simple gospel by questioning Paul's authority and doctrine. The shocked apostle, worried and anxious to correct the false doctrines these vulnerable converts were being fed, wrote, "I marvel that ye are so soon removed from him that called you into the grace of Christ unto another gospel." (Gal. 1:6.) He assured them that the gospel he preached was true: "I certify you, brethren, that the gospel which was preached of me is not after man. For I neither received it of man, neither was I taught it, but by the revelation of Jesus Christ." (Gal. 1:11-12.) He also defended his authority, reviewed the factors relating to his own conversion after

---

George A. Horton, Jr., is associate professor and chairman of the Department of Ancient Scripture at Brigham Young University.

having been a destroyer of the church (Gal. 1:13), and clarified his motives as bringing these converts, the Gentiles of Galatia, into the covenant of Abraham through baptism, to be one with the Lord and Savior Jesus Christ (Gal. 3:27, 29).

The Galatian saints were no ordinary converts—they were among the first congregations of Gentiles successfully brought into the bonds of the gospel of Jesus Christ. They were pioneers in an antagonistic world and needed to be protected, instructed, nurtured, and preserved with all diligence so that spiritual wolves might not enter their flock. As with most missionaries, Paul condemned the bearers of the damnable heresies and distorted practices and raised the specter of judgment for those who would try to draw away fledgling saints by preaching perversions. (Gal. 1:7-9.)

No one can doubt the depth of love and devotion that Paul and his companions had shown for these converted Gentiles. He had been mercilessly beaten with thirty-nine stripes, threatened, stoned, cast out of the cities to which he was now addressing his letter, and dragged out of one city and left for dead. (2 Cor. 11:24-25; Acts 14:19.) The Jews in the synagogues of these Galatian cities had violently rejected him and his companions (Acts 13:45-46), but fortunately they had found some Gentiles who believed and responded to the message of salvation in the gospel of Jesus Christ (Acts 13:48). These new Christians had great faith the Lord could show forth signs and wonders, and they allowed the missionaries to perform priesthood healings among them. (Acts 14:8-10.) How could such converts fall prey so soon to those who would pull them from the precious gospel that had been delivered? What could prove such a successful wedge in turning hearts from pure love and faith in Christ?

Missionary Work in Galatia

Barnabas and Paul had not left the cities of Derbe, Lystra, Iconium, and Antioch of Pisidia,[1] the areas of their first journey, without "confirming the souls of the disciples, and exhorting them to continue in the faith." (Acts 14:22.) They had also "ordained them elders in every church, and had prayed with fasting" (Acts 14:23), and commended them to the Lord.

Shortly after their return to Antioch of Syria, "Certain men which came down from Judaea [to Antioch] taught the brethren, and said, Except ye be circumcised after the manner of Moses, ye cannot be saved." (Acts 15:1.) This caused such an uproar that Paul and Barnabas quickly started for Jerusalem to meet with the apostles and elders over the issue. Part of the result was the great Jerusalem Council, which included Peter, James the Lord's brother,[2] and other important leaders in the church. The question was not whether the Gentiles should receive the gospel, but whether it was also necessary for them to keep the performances of the law of Moses.

The debate was very emotional, and "there rose up certain of the sect of the Pharisees which believed [i.e., they were now Christians], saying, That it was needful to circumcise them [Gentiles], and to command them to keep the law of Moses." (Acts 15:5.) Peter, Paul, and Barnabas shared a completely opposite view. Peter quickly explained what the Lord had done for such Gentiles as the household of Cornelius. He challenged, "Why tempt ye God, to put a yoke [the law of Moses] upon the neck of the disciples, which neither our fathers nor we were able to bear?" (Acts 15:10.) Paul and Barnabas supported Peter's view and declared the miracles God had permitted them to perform in behalf of the Gentiles. Finally, the decision was pronounced by James, the Lord's brother: the Gentile converts need not be troubled with the law of Moses in general. Exceptions noted had to do with "meats offered to idols, . . . blood, . . . things strangled, and . . . fornication," all of which they were to avoid. (Acts 15:29.)

If Paul's letter to the Galatians was written after the council, which it very likely was, it clearly demonstrates that the question debated in that important and unique meeting had not really been put to rest by the decision. Either way, certain Christian Jews, commonly called Judaizers, had followed Paul and Barnabas to the area of the Galatian branches and had begun to counteract their efforts with the Gentiles by persuading these converts that they must keep the law of Moses and be circumcised. The result was disastrous to the new and growing church, for apostasy from the pure and unadulterated gospel of Jesus Christ began to set in. (Gal. 1:6.) If unchecked, it would completely destroy the branches and nullify the hard-earned missionary success of Paul and his companions. It is in this context of anxious feelings that Paul penned his pointed and powerful letter to the Galatians.

Background on the Epistle

Knowing to whom and from where this letter was written is not critical in order for us to profit from its message. In fact, we know little that sheds light on these questions. Opinions continue to be sharply divided among scholars on such details.

The questions of when and from where this epistle was written are closely tied—the answer to one helps answer the other. Rome, Ephesus, Antioch of Syria, and Corinth have all been put forth as the point of its origin. The time of its writing could range from prior to the Jerusalem Council to the time of Paul's imprisonment in Rome. The answer one selects as the correct site will largely set the time for the letter. Therefore, the date could range from A.D. 48 to 58.[3]

The question of those to whom Paul was writing is not as difficult because the general area is well defined. Only the details are unclear. Galatia in general was the territory in the central part of Asia Minor (modern Turkey) stretching in a northwesterly direction.[4] In the north-central area was the ancient city of Ancyra (modern Ankara), and to the south were the cities visited on Paul's first missionary journey—Derbe, Lystra, Iconium, and Antioch. Three possible answers to the question of exactly who were the objects of his writing include:

1. The branches of the church that he and Barnabas had set up on their first missionary journey (i.e., Pisidia, Antioch, Iconium, Lystra, and Derbe—all in the southern part of Galatia).

2. The people converted in the more northerly part of Galatia around the city of Ancyra, which served as its capital.

3. All the organized branches and isolated members in the entire Roman province of Galatia.

Those who subscribe to the idea that the letter was written to the branches organized on the first missionary journey generally believe that it was written from Antioch before the Jerusalem Council. Those who believe it was being written to the northern part, which includes the city of Ancyra, most often opt for Ephesus as its point of origin on the third missionary journey. A majority of those who believe it was sent to all the branches and members of the province generally set its origin in Corinth during the second or third missionary journey. A statement in the epistle itself may give some reason to believe that it was after a second visit: "Ye know how through infirmity of the flesh I preached the gospel unto you at the first." (Gal. 4:13.) On the other hand, some believe that since Paul made a swing down and back on the first journey, the allusion is simply to the first visit on the same journey. One point that could be argued from the letter itself is that Paul would most likely have wanted it addressed to all of those who had been influenced by the Judaizers.

What Brought the Letter Forth?

Did a Gentile convert to the gospel of Jesus Christ have to be circumcised and live the law of Moses before he could be baptized unto salvation? (Acts 15:1.) Some who took an affirmative stand on this position were influential in the church. This was a time of transition, with the gospel being preached to the Gentiles for the first time after more than a millennium of the Jews looking at the Gentiles as inferior people—declared unclean by the standard of the law of Moses. The matter of how to treat Gentiles had not been completely clarified in the minds of many Christian Jews, particularly the Judaizers.

This is not surprising. Remember Peter's resistance to the idea of eating the unclean meats. In order to prepare him for the giving of the gospel to the Gentiles, the voice said, "What God hath cleansed, that call not thou common." (Acts 10:14-15.) Cornelius and his household were of the "unclean" Gentiles, but as a result of his vision Peter had a change of mind and proceeded to perform the baptisms. His reluctance reflected the feelings of many of the Jews when Gentiles were first converted to the church. The Jews were, after all, a "chosen" people; therefore, they concluded, they should have certain prerogatives. From this view, it was easy to assume that Gentiles could not come into the church without first submitting to the token of circumcision and living the sacred laws given by God to Moses.

The token of circumcision was not only part of the law of Moses that, they could mistakenly reason, preceded the gospel; it was also given as the token of the covenant of Abraham even before the law of Moses was instituted. Since converts were entering the covenant of Abraham through baptism (cf. Gal. 3:27, 29), it was easy to imagine that they must be circumcised first.[5] Paul knew, however, that this was a damnable distortion of the truth, a perversion that, if not terminated, would cause the people to fall into serious apostasy. Such a false doctrine failed to fully recognize the saving power of Jesus Christ. It failed to recognize that the law was to help Israel rise to a point of faith in Christ such that the Atonement could become effective in their behalf. If they did not turn from the false teachings immediately, serious spiritual penalties would result. (Gal. 1:8-9.)

The Major Message of Galatians

The major message of the letter to the Galatians centers around the relationship of the law of Moses to the gospel and the importance of living so that one is worthy to receive the blessings that come from obedience to gospel covenants. Paul appeals for these converts to "stand fast . . . in the liberty wherewith Christ hath made us free." (Gal. 5:1.) He counsels them to throw off the shackles of false philosophies and practices and not to allow perverted understanding of the doctrines to cause distortions and apostasy. He warns that now that they have received the true light and way to salvation, they must not slip back and become entangled again in the sins of the flesh.

Issue One: How Is a Person Justified?

One of the main themes of this epistle has to do with justification. This theme is introduced by the statement "a man is not justified by the works of the law" (Gal. 2:16), a warning to those who were being swayed by the efforts of the Judaizers. Before pursuing the argument, let us consider the basic principle.

The Greek meaning underlying the word *justify* is to "make righteous," to declare righteous, or to acquit.[6] The implication is that when individuals are justified, they are looked upon as righteous and as though they had committed no sin. In order for us to receive salvation, we must be able to stand before the Lord as *just* persons—as righteous individuals, not as sinners. To understand this concept, consider the following principles:

1. There are laws given. (D&C 88:36.)

2. There are certain bounds and conditions to all laws. (D&C 88:38.)

3. If we violate the conditions, we are no longer *just*—we are not justified. (D&C 88:39.)

4. All persons sin, break the law. (Rom. 3:10, 23; 1 Jn. 1:8; Eccl. 7:20.)

5. Payment must be made for broken law. (Alma 42:25.)

There are two ways that payment can be made.

Alternative One: The sinner can pay the penalty or make whatever restitution is possible. However, even after it is paid, the person is still looked upon as one who broke the law. In a spiritual sense, it is much the same when a person takes all the steps possible to repent and pay for his or her sins; that person is still one who broke the law and therefore is not seen as a righteous or completely just person. The only way one can be looked upon as totally just before the law is never to break the law. Only one person has ever qualified in this way: the Lord Jesus Christ, who is referred to as the Just One. It is only he who has been totally righteous and therefore is justified before the law. (Heb. 4:15.) Once we have fallen into transgression, "by the deeds of the law there shall no flesh be justified" (Rom. 3:20), for the broken law then stands to bear testimony against us.

Alternative Two: The sinner can exercise faith in Jesus Christ, repent, be obedient to the covenant, and then be justified through the Atonement, "being justified only by [God's] grace through the redemption that is in Christ Jesus." (JST, Rom. 3:24.) "He cometh into the world that he may save all men if they will hearken unto his voice; for behold, he suffereth the pains of all men, yea, the pains of every living creature, both men, women, and children, who belong to the family of Adam." (2 Ne. 9:21.) With his suffering, Christ brought about the plan of mercy so that the demands of justice can be met when we fully repent. (Alma 42:14-15.)

When we truly exercise faith in the Lord Jesus Christ, repent, are baptized by immersion for the remission of sins, and receive the gift of the Holy Ghost, then the Spirit—the Holy Spirit of Promise—seals or ratifies these actions, and we are justified by having our guilt transferred to the Savior, who made an infinite atonement for us,[7] and he now looks upon us again as just persons, or as having never committed sin. (D&C 58:42.) Having done the foregoing, under the influence of the Holy Ghost, we continue on in faithful observance of our covenants to sanctify our lives so that we will be prepared to enter into the celestial kingdom of God. (3 Ne. 27:19-20.)

Throughout Paul's writings, whenever he refers to "the law" it is almost always the law of Moses that is intended.[8] Therefore, when he says that "a man is not justified by the works of the law," we can safely assume that he is referring to the works of the law of Moses. However, when we consider the principle of justification in the eyes of God, we will also realize that works alone in *any* context are not sufficient for a person to become justified. It takes the grace of Christ through the Atonement to bring this about "after all we can do." (2 Ne. 25:23.)

Since a person cannot, once he or she is a lawbreaker, be completely justified by the works of the law—the law of Moses or any other law—the second alternative is really the only practical way by which the Lord will look at us as justified. We desire to be justified; this goes beyond simply paying the penalty for our transgressions, for we want to be viewed as having never committed transgressions in the first place. "Therefore ye are justified of faith and works, through grace, to the end the promise [given to Abraham] might be sure to all the seed; not to them only who are of the law, but to them also who are of the faith of Abraham." (JST, Rom. 4:16.) This promise includes receiving the blessings of the gospel, priesthood, and life eternal. (Abr. 2:11.)

Does this mean that since we cannot be justified by works, works play no role? Certainly not, for we must do all that we are able to do in righteousness—do good works and keep the commandments; then the saving grace of the Lord takes over and does that which only *he* can do. Therefore it is important for us to keep the law, which for us is the law of the gospel. "That which is governed by law is also preserved by law and perfected and sanctified by the same. That which breaketh a law, and abideth not by law, but seeketh to become a law unto itself, and willeth to abide in sin, and altogether abideth in sin, cannot be sanctified by law, neither by mercy, justice, nor judgment. Therefore, they must remain filthy still." (D&C 88:34-35.)

Since the Galatian saints were now being hoodwinked by Judaizers into believing that they must keep the performances of the law of Moses, the apostle was very clear: "By the works of the law shall no flesh be justified." (Gal. 2:16.) Justification comes only by faith in Jesus Christ and keeping the commandments embodied in the gospel.

A subtle implication emerging out of this letter is that Abraham was justified. Paul says, "Even as Abraham believed God, and it was accounted to him for righteousness." (Gal. 3:6.) This quotation from Genesis 15:6 is probably another way of saying that because of his faithfulness before the Lord, Abraham was justified. In so saying, the apostle tells the Galatians that it is not necessary to have the law of Moses in order to obtain salvation. In other words, Abraham was justified even before the law of Moses was instituted. So why should Christians allow themselves to believe they must also keep the law of Moses? (In order to pursue this question further, consider what is said in Galatians 3:7-8, 11, and 24, and Romans 4:1-9, and in the broader context of Romans 3:20-28; 4:25; 5:1-21.)

Issue Two: What Is the Relationship of the Law of Moses to the Covenant of Abraham?

Paul makes a major point about the historical relationship between "the covenant" of Abraham and "the law" of Moses. (Gal. 3:17.) There are things implicit in his reasoning that must be understood in order to more fully understand this message to the Galatians. Some of these he undoubtedly taught them on his first mission, plus he is writing out of a historical context wherein the Jews had been dealing with the law of Moses for generations.

Although it may not be totally clear in the biblical record, we have adequate scripture to show that the Abrahamic covenant, the new and everlasting covenant, and the fullness of the gospel are all one and the same. The fullness of the gospel is referred to in scripture as the "everlasting covenant." (D&C 1:22-23; 39:11; 45:9; 66:2; 101:39; 133:57.)

Abraham received the gospel by baptism, had the Melchizedek Priesthood conferred upon him, and entered into celestial marriage.[9] This gave the prospect of eternal increase, and coupled with it was the promise that these same blessings would be available to his mortal posterity. (Abr. 2:6-11; D&C 132:29-50.) He was also taught that from his lineage would be born the Messiah and that his posterity would have other choice blessings pertaining to land and inheritance. (Abr. 2; Gen. 17; 22:15-18; Gal. 3.) Bruce R. McConkie wrote: "All of these promises lumped together are called the *Abrahamic Covenant.* This covenant was renewed with Isaac (Gen. 24:60; 26:1-4, 24) and again with Jacob. (Gen. 28; 35:9-13; 48:3-4.) *Those portions of it which per-*

tain to personal exaltation and eternal increase are renewed with each member of the house of Israel who enters the order of celestial marriage; through that order the participating parties become inheritors of all the blessings of Abraham, Isaac, and Jacob. (D&C 132; Rom. 9:4; Gal. 3:4.)"[10]

The covenant and its associated promises were first given to Adam and Eve. That being the case, it has sometimes been asked, "Why is it called the Abrahamic covenant?" It is probably safe to assume that the covenant was named after Abraham in a manner similar to how the "Holy Priesthood, after the Order of the Son of God" was named after Melchizedek. (D&C 107:3.) It too had been given long before Melchizedek's time. In Abraham's case, there was also something unique: the responsibility was specifically given to his posterity down through Isaac and Jacob to be the ministers of the covenant and its blessings to the rest of mankind. Today, only those who have received the gospel, entered into covenants, and become spiritually the children of Abraham have the responsibility to do missionary work and take the promises of Abraham to the rest of the Lord's children.

The relationship between the gospel, the covenant of Abraham, and the law of Moses is brought into much better focus for understanding the letter to the Galatians when we put the matter into a chronological context.

Paul makes passing reference in several of his letters to the fact that the gospel and the covenant of Abraham preceded the law of Moses. This point had been made generations earlier by Moses, who said, "The Gospel began to be preached, from the beginning, being declared by holy angels sent forth from the presence of God, and by his own voice, and by the gift of the Holy Ghost. And thus all things were confirmed unto Adam, by an holy ordinance, and the Gospel preached." (Moses 5:58-59.)

Paul mentioned that Moses knew of Christ (Heb. 11:24-26), and it was Christ who was the "spiritual Rock" (1 Cor. 10:4) that Israel drank from in the wilderness. Also setting a context for the apostle's instruction to the Galatians is the mention in one of his epistles that the Israelites had the gospel preached to them: "For unto us was the gospel preached, as well as unto them [Israelites]: but the word preached did not profit them, not being mixed with faith in them that heard it." (Heb. 4:2.)

With the foregoing in mind, it is easier to understand Paul's reference to Abraham: "And the scripture, foreseeing that God would justify the heathen through faith, preached before the gospel unto Abraham, saying, In thee shall all nations be blessed." (Gal. 3:8.) The Apostle to the Gentiles was thoroughly familiar with the details of Abraham's covenant with the Lord and is commenting out of that context. To the great patriarch the Lord said, "I will make of thee a great nation, and I will bless thee above measure, and make thy name great among all nations, and thou shalt be a blessing unto thy seed after thee, that in their hands they shall bear this ministry and Priesthood. . . . And I will bless them through thy name; for as many as receive this Gospel shall be called after thy name, and shall be accounted thy seed, and shall rise up and bless thee, as their father; . . . and in thee (that is, in thy Priesthood) . . . shall all the families of the earth be blessed, even with the blessings of the Gospel, which are the blessings of salvation, even of life eternal." (Abr. 2:9-11.)

In summary, the gospel was available in each previous dispensation—with Adam (Moses 5:58), Enoch (Moses 6:52-62), Noah (Moses 8:19, 24), Abraham (Gal. 3:8), and Moses (Heb. 4:2)—but it was not equally well received by the people living in each of them. With this perspective, we return to Paul's letter.

Israel had the fullness of the gospel before the performances and ordinances of the law of Moses were given. (Heb. 3:14-19; 4:1-2.) This is dramatically demonstrated by what was on the second set of tablets received by Moses on the mount. "It shall not be according to the first [tablets], for I will take away the priesthood out of their midst; therefore my holy order, and the ordinances thereof, shall not go before them." (JST, Ex. 34:1.) Because "they hardened their hearts and could not endure [the Lord's] presence," the Lord "took Moses out of their midst, and the Holy Priesthood also." (D&C 84:24-25.)

With this perspective we can appreciate Paul's assertion to the Galatians: "And this I say, that the covenant [of Abraham], that was confirmed before of God in Christ, the law [of Moses], which was four hundred and thirty years after, cannot disannul, that it should make the promise [to Abraham] of none effect." (Gal. 3:17.) His statement raises a question which he first asks and then answers: "Wherefore then serveth the law? It was added because of transgressions, till the seed should come to whom the promise was made." (Gal. 3:19.) What seed? "Specifically, Christ, the preeminent descendant of Abraham; generally, all of the descendants of Abraham who keep the commandments, plus those adopted into his lineage, who are thus made heirs with his natural descendants."[11] If the overzealous Judaizers would only receive this, the law of Moses would be in force for only a limited time.

By emphasizing that the law did not precede the gospel or Abrahamic covenant, does that mean that the law is in opposition to the covenant? "Is the law then against the promises of God [made to Abraham and his seed]?" (Gal. 3:21.) No, "the law was our schoolmaster to bring us unto Christ, that we might be justified by faith." (Gal. 3:24.) The schoolmaster (from the Greek word *pedagogue*) is a servant who has the care of children and of leading them to and from school or a tutor who is responsible for their training. This law was intended to teach the people that obedience would bring the people back to their faith in Christ so they could be justified through his atoning blood and stand innocent once again in the eyes of God.

In its time, Moses' law was a high standard compared to other worldly codes of law, but this law could not in itself save the people. As Abinadi said, "Salvation doth not come by the law alone." (Mosiah 13:28.) The children of Israel "were a stiffnecked people, quick to do iniquity, and slow to remember the Lord their God; therefore there was a law given them . . . of performances and of ordinances, a law which they were to observe strictly from day to day, to keep them in remembrance of God and their duty towards him." (Mosiah 13:29-30.) It pointed their souls to Christ. (Jacob 4:5.) Its intent was to "persuad[e] them to look forward unto the Messiah." (Jarom 1:11.) It served to "strengthen their faith in Christ." (Alma 25:16.)

It was intended that when Christ had offered the Great and Last Sacrifice, the performances, ordinances, and carnal commandments of the law would no longer be necessary—they would be fulfilled. (Matt. 5:18; 3 Ne. 15:4-5.) So also the token of circumcision would no longer be required. (Moro. 8:8.)

94

Since one who enters and is obedient to the Abrahamic covenant will receive eternal life, how do we enter? The Galatian saints were reminded, "As many of you as have been baptized into Christ have put on Christ. . . . And if ye be Christ's, then are ye Abraham's seed, and heirs according to the promise." (Gal. 3:27, 29.) That is, whether we are children of Abraham by blood lineage or not, when we enter the waters of baptism and are baptized by an authorized bearer of the holy priesthood, we are adopted into the family of Abraham and become his spiritual sons and daughters and thus heirs of the covenant. Then we can go on and receive the covenants and ordinances that will qualify us to receive all of the blessings the Lord has in store for his faithful and obedient children.

It seems as if Paul is saying to the Galatians, "You do not have to be circumcised. You do not have to keep the law of Moses. If you have faith, repent, and are baptized into the Church of Jesus Christ, you have taken the fundamental steps toward being justified before the Lord. So exercise more faith, keep the commandments, and seek to be worthy of the higher ordinances that lead to salvation and exaltation in the celestial kingdom."

Paul uses an allegory to demonstrate the significant advantage of being subject to the gospel over being under the demands of the law of Moses. These two covenants are symbolically identified—the law is referred to as Mount Sinai and the covenant as the heavenly or new Jerusalem. From the first comes bondage under the law of performances and ordinances, but from the second comes freedom through the fullness of the gospel. The allegory is extended by using the family of Abraham. The Mosaic law is likened unto Ishmael, son of the bondwoman, who persecuted Isaac. The Abrahamic covenant is like the son of the freewoman, and consequently the first (the law of Moses) was cast out. But Sarah's son came under the Abrahamic covenant and was to inherit all the blessings promised to Abraham. (Gen. 26:1-4.)

So it is that those who are under the law of Moses cannot obtain their complete blessings until they rise to the heights of the gospel and accept the fullness of the covenant responsibilities, thereby qualifying for the fullness of the covenant's blessings. In essence, Paul is saying: "So, you foolish Galatians, do not take a step back and jeopardize your greatest blessings." After all, "in Jesus Christ neither circumcision availeth any thing, nor uncircumcision; but faith which work-eth by love." (Gal. 5:6; 6:15.)

Although Paul does not discuss in this epistle the fact that the blood lineage of Abraham, Isaac, and Jacob alone is not sufficient, he makes a major point of it in his letter to the Romans. One must enter into the covenant and bring forth the proper fruits of repentance and righteous living to be considered a child and heir of the promise. (Rom. 9:6-8; 11:17-25; cf. 2 Ne. 30:1-2.)

Freedom Does Not Give License

Having clarified the relationship between the law of Moses, the covenant of Abraham, and the gospel of Jesus Christ, Paul turns to the Galatians' manner of living as covenant Christians. It is true that the gospel frees them from the obligations of the law of Moses, but it also puts them under other, loftier responsibilities. Several related points are stressed in the latter part of this letter, including:

1. If individuals give heed to the prescriptions of the law of Moses, then they are unwittingly nullifying the power of the gospel of Christ. (Gal. 5:4.)

2. Faith in Christ, not circumcision, is the power that promotes the proper kind of godly love. (Gal. 5:6.)

3. If the people continue to keep the law of Moses, the crucifixion and resurrection of Christ are of no effect in their lives. (Gal. 5:11.)

4. Those who militantly teach false doctrines should be excommunicated. (Gal. 5:12.)

5. The carnal desires of the flesh, to which all people are subject, work against the Spirit. (Gal. 5:17.)

6. One can overcome the desires of the flesh by walking in the Spirit. (Gal. 5:16.)

7. The fruits of the Spirit are love, joy, peace, longsuffering, gentleness, goodness, faith, meekness, and temperance. (Gal. 5:22-23.)

As we consider the works of the flesh apparent in the days of Paul, ponder on those that would have to be added to the list today. In his time there was "adultery, fornication, uncleanness, lasciviousness [debauchery], idolatry [worshipping false gods], witchcraft [spiritualism], hatred, variance [quarreling], emulations [jealousies], wrath, strife [conflict], seditions, heresies [false doctrines], envyings, murders, drunkenness, revellings, and such like." (Gal. 5:19-21.) Our list would have to include homosexuality, pornography, habit-forming harmful drugs, X-rated movies, embezzlement, and a multitude of other spiritually destructive practices. As Paul reminds the Galatians, those who indulge in such things are on a course that will lead them to damnation rather than salvation in the kingdom of God. (Gal. 5:21.)

True disciples of Christ must seek to put all forms of sin and transgression out of their lives and live worthy of the Spirit. It is the Spirit that helps us achieve justification and sanctification and leads to the presence of God.

Paul's Final Appeal

The missionary apostle's final soul-searching appeal is something like this: "Now, dear Galatian saints, brothers and sisters in the covenant, if there are those of you who have resisted the false doctrines and remained worthy of the Spirit, do not look down upon those who have been otherwise affected. Forgive those who are erring, lift them up, and help them overcome their faults. Do all you can for the less fortunate, and it will help you personally to resist temptation. Bear one another's burdens, and in this way you will be fulfilling some of the major requirements of the law of Christ." (See Gal. 6:1-5.)

Though we are free to choose what we will do, we cannot avoid the consequences of our own acts. "Whatsoever a man soweth, that shall he also reap." (Gal. 6:7.) "One may do as he pleases, but he cannot evade responsibility. He may break laws, but he cannot avoid penalties. One gets away with nothing. No one ever gets anything for nothing. God is just."[12] If we choose the lesser life, we will reap corruption and spiritual destruction. But if we choose the influence of the Spirit, we will reap life everlasting in the kingdom of God. We will each become a new creature—changed and spiritually born of God. (Gal. 6:15; cf. Alma 5:14.)

As a brother in Christ, Paul makes his final appeal in words like these: "Don't be like the Judaizers who are trying to get you to keep the law of Moses when they don't even keep the law themselves. It would be to your destruction, but being faithful in the cause of Christ will bring you peace and eternal life."

Commentary on Selected Verses

1:1. Since there is no direct mention of an apostolic ordination, the question has been raised as to whether Paul filled one of the vacancies in the Quorum of the Twelve or whether the title generally refers to something like that of the Seventy. It has been pointed out that he was called and set apart for his first mission by "prophets and teachers" (Acts 13:1-4) at Antioch without direct mention of a member of the Twelve. On the other hand, Paul and Barnabas are referred to as apostles more than once in Luke's account. (Cf. Acts 14:4, 14.) Paul also refers to his apostolic authority in the first verse of many of his epistles. (Rom. 1:1; 1 Cor. 1:1; 2 Cor. 1:1; Gal. 1:1; Eph. 1:1; Col. 1:1; 1 Tim. 1:1; 2 Tim. 1:1; Titus 1:1; compare 1 Pet. 1:1; 2 Pet. 1:1. See also 1 Cor. 9:1-2; 15:7-9.) The nature of his mission and associated events tend to support the fact that he was one of the Twelve. According to Joseph Fielding Smith, "This quorum was continued for a time, and other apostles were ordained when vacancies occurred."[13] (Acts 1:23-26; 14:14; Gal. 1:1.)

1:3. "God the Father" refers to Elohim, the father of our spirits.

1:4. The reference to "evil world" means people who are not living in righteousness.

1:6-9. Harold B. Lee declared: "Today those warnings are just as applicable as they were in that day in which they were given. There are some as wolves among . . . our own membership, men are arising speaking perverse things. Now perverse means diverting from the right or correct, and being obstinate in the wrong, willfully, in order to draw the weak and unwary members of the Church away after them."[14]

1:12. This revelation came at least in two ways: first, through the actual appearance of Jesus Christ to Paul on the road to Damascus (Acts 9:3-7; 22:6-11; 26:13-15), and second, by inspiration through the Holy Spirit, some of which apparently came during the time spent in Arabia (cf. vs. 17).

1:13. Compare Acts 9:1-2; 22:4, "I persecuted this way unto the death."

1:14. "Profited" means he was above others in advancing knowledge as one of the Pharisees, which Paul calls "the most straitest sect of our religion." (Acts 26:5.)

1:16. "Flesh and blood" here is an idiom meaning human being.

1:17. Two questions are raised: (1) Which area of Arabia is referred to and what was Paul's motivation? Though Damascus was now part of the Roman province of Syria, at the time of Paul it was under the influence of the Nabatean King Aretas IV who ruled from Petra—identified as Sela in Edom on map number 7 in the LDS edition of the King James Version. (Cf. 2 Cor. 11:32.) The reference could mean that this new convert simply went into the desert a short distance from Damascus, or, as some speculate, he may have gone as far as the red rock city of Petra itself. (2) Did he go to escape the opposition of the Jews of Damascus who would have been irate over his conversion, or did he go for contemplation and to commune with the Lord? Both reasons are likely. Surely he needed time to restructure his thinking about the relationship of the gospel of Jesus Christ with the law of Moses, which he had learned to venerate.

1:19. See note 2 at the end of the chapter.

1:21. Paul was originally from the city of Tarsus in the province of Cilicia, near the northeastern tip of the Mediterranean Sea.

2:2. The reference to fourteen years probably puts Paul, Barnabas, and Titus in Jerusalem at the time the Jerusalem Council settled the question of circumcision and the law of Moses. (Acts 15:4ff.) Another possibility might be the trip to bring provisions for the poor of Jerusalem (Acts 11:29-30), but the chapter is couched in the context of the controversy over circumcision, which suggests that the first possibility is more likely.

2:2. Paul's first discussion took place privately with some church leaders.

2:3. As an outgrowth of the private discussion, it was determined that Paul's companion Titus, a Greek who had joined the church, would not be compelled to be circumcised. This is in contrast to Paul's later willingness to have a Jewish disciple, Timothy, circumcised. Timothy's mother was a Jewess and his father a Greek, making Timothy Jewish under Jewish law. Paul did not suggest that Jews should give up circumcision, only that Gentiles need not practice it. (Acts 16:1-3.)

2:7. Paul was to preach to the Gentiles, while Peter would preach unto the Jews. (Cf. 2:9.) This decision came despite the fact that Peter, head of the church at this time, turned the key that opened the gospel to the Gentiles when he baptized the household of Cornelius. (Acts 10:44-48.)

2:9. This James is most likely the Lord's brother, since James the brother of John had been put to death by Herod Agrippa I sometime earlier. (Acts 12:1-2.) Cephas is the Aramaic name corresponding to the Greek Petros or Peter. (Cf. John 1:42.) "The right hands of fellowship" means he was extended complete acceptance and brotherhood with the saints and was entitled to all the privileges and blessings of the gospel with the community of believers.

2:11-12. Whether his assumption was right or wrong, Paul felt that Peter was hypocritical because Peter got up and left the Gentiles' table when Jews from Jerusalem entered the room where he was eating. This caused others to do the same. The action made Paul so angry that he "withstood him [Peter] to the face"—meaning Peter was scolded for his seeming hypocrisy.

2:14. Bruce R. McConkie declared: "Peter and Paul—both of whom were apostles, both of whom received revelations, saw angels, and were approved of the Lord, and both of whom shall inherit the fulness of the Father's kingdom—these same righteous and mighty preachers disagreed on a basic matter of church policy. Peter was the President of the Church; Paul, an apostle and Peter's junior in the Church hierarchy, was subject to the direction of the chief apostle. But Paul was right and Peter was wrong. Paul stood firm, determined that they should walk 'uprightly according to the truth of the gospel;' Peter temporized [i.e., temporarily compromised] for fear of offending Jewish semi-converts who still kept the law of Moses."[15]

2:15. "Jews by nature" includes not only those born of the lineage of Judah, but also those who are politically Jews. (Acts 22:3.) Paul, for example, was of the lineage of Benjamin. (Philip. 3:5.)

2:19. Being "dead to the law" means that a person has nothing to do with it or is totally separated from it.[16]

2:20. "Crucified with Christ" is a figurative way of saying he has crucified the old man of sin and lusts of the flesh and is now living a life of faith.

3:1. Brigham Young said: "Now, let us help the poor, bring them here, place them in good, comfortable circumstances, so that they can strut up and say, 'I guess I am somebody, and I ask no odds of the Lord.'

O, fools! When I hear such expressions, or see such a disposition manifested, I think, 'O, foolish Galatians, who hath bewitched you?' Who
has turned your brain and made you believe that you are independent
of that Being who bought you and all the human family on the earth?
Who has instructed you to believe that God has nothing to do with us,
that everything that is by the providence of chance, or no providence
at all, and that man is all there is?"[17]

3:3. According to Brigham Young, "We often find persons among
us who have borne testimony of the truth of their religion by the gift
and power of the Holy Ghost, who again fall backwards into darkness
by beginning to express doubts whether their religion be true or false;
they begin to exchange the substance for the shadow—the reality for
a phantom."[18]

3:7. Those who exercise faith in Jesus Christ and enter the waters
of baptism thereby enter into the Abrahamic covenant, becoming the
children of Abraham by spiritual adoption, and are legal heirs to Abraham's blessings.

3:8. According to John Taylor, "It was through the medium of the
Gospel that Abraham obtained these promises."[19]

3:10. Review Deuteronomy 27:15-26.

3:13. "Being made a curse for us" means that Christ paid the penalty for sins, and symbolically the curse or punishment was laid on
him.

3:14. The "blessing of Abraham" specifically refers to Abraham's
being justified, and generally to the promises of the gospel, priesthood, posterity, and eternal life. (Cf. Abr. 2:11.)

3:16-29. Details are discussed in the body of the text.

3:17. The word *disannul* means the same thing as annul or make
void.

3:19. "What, we ask, was this law added to, if it was not added to
the Gospel?" the Prophet Joseph Smith asked. "It must be plain that it
was added to the Gospel, since we learn that they had the Gospel
preached to them."[20]

3:28-29. "We witnessed something wonderful in the great
Munich conference," President Harold B. Lee reported. "They were
members from countries whose political differences had caused war
and bloodshed. And yet we brought them all together in one congre-

gation with a peaceful, sweet spirit! I was moved to repeat what the apostle Paul said to the Galatians. . . . I paraphrased to them, 'You are neither German, nor Austrian, nor French nor Italian, nor Dutch, nor Spanish, nor English, but you and I are all one in The Church of Jesus Christ of Latter-day Saints."[21]

4:1-2. The heir is the one who inherits something. Though the Jews were literal descendants of Abraham, as long as they were under the law of Moses they were likened unto an heir who had not yet come of age. That is, they could not exercise their prerogatives as the lord and master or executor of the estate until they came of age and entered into the covenant. As explained in the preceding verses, this was done by exercising faith in Jesus Christ and entering into the waters of baptism. It is in this sense that Paul said, "For they are not all Israel, which are of Israel: neither, because they are the seed of Abraham, are they all children. . . . They which are the children of the flesh, these are not the children of God: but the children of the promise are counted for the seed." (Rom. 9:6-8.) As in the allegory of the tame olive tree, only those branches which produce good fruit will be preserved; the others will be cut off and in their place will be grafted others (e.g., the Gentiles) who will produce good fruit.

4:4. Jesus' coming to earth made it the "fulness of the time," which should be distinguished from the "fulness of times" referring to the last dispensation.

4:5-6. The adoption of sons refers to becoming sons and daughters of God by being "born again; yea, born of God, changed from their carnal and fallen state, to a state of righteousness, being redeemed of God, becoming his sons and daughters." (Mosiah 27:25.)

4:7. Joseph Fielding Smith explained: "As sons and daughters then, we are heirs of his kingdom and shall receive by right the fulness of the glory and be entitled to the great blessings and privileges which the Lord in his mercy has revealed to us in the dispensation of the fulness of times."[22]

4:9. Cf. 5:1.

4:10. This is partly an allusion to the fasts, feasts, festivals, and other days of celebration under the law of Moses. It might be something like modern saints continuing to observe the feast of the Passover, which Christ fulfilled. (Cf. 1 Cor. 5:7.) To keep him in our remembrance, we partake of the emblems of his flesh and blood in the sacrament.

4:12. "Brethren, I beseech you to be perfect as I am perfect; for I am persuaded as ye have a knowledge of me, ye have not injured me at all by your sayings." (JST, Gal. 4:12.) Paul sees perfection in this life as a process of total dedication to living the commandments. The person who is so living is perfect. (Cf. Philip. 3:12-15.) In this regard we must distinguish between finite perfection here and now and the infinite perfection possible in the eternities to come.[23]

4:13-15. Apparently Paul was suffering some kind of physical affliction, which he referred to as a "thorn in the flesh." (2 Cor. 12:7.) He told the Corinthians some would say that his "bodily presence is weak." (2 Cor. 10:10.) However, the Galatians received him wholeheartedly and would have given their all for him.

4:19. Paul is laboring with concern and anxiety for the spiritual rebirth of those converts who are going astray as a result of the false doctrine relating to the law of Moses.

4:20. The expression "desire . . . to change my voice," judging by what follows, means that Paul was now going to be very pointed and employ strong language in challenging the new views the Galatian saints were accepting from the Judaizers.

4:22-26. This is discussed in the text.

4:27. The allusion here is to Isaiah 54:1, which refers to the "married wife." The concept is that of Israel married to Jehovah by the covenant. The Gentiles are referred to as coming from the "desolate" wife. There is a lament that because of transgression and ignoring the covenant, the married wife cannot claim many true children—faithful in the covenant—but there are "many more children" coming from the wife (Gentiles) without any husband.

5:1. The gospel is the "perfect law of liberty." (Cf. James 1:25.)

5:3. That is, Paul has made himself responsible to keep all of the laws given to Moses.

5:7. That is, "You Galatians did so well when you first accepted the gospel, but what have you allowed to happen to you?"

5:13. That is, do not use your freedom from the demands of the law of Moses to exercise license in fulfilling the worldly lusts of the flesh.

5:14. It is ironic that the greatest commandments are to be found in the law of Moses: Deuteronomy 6:5, "Love the Lord thy God with all thine heart, and with all thy soul, and with all thy might" and Leviticus 19:18, "Love thy neighbour as thyself." If we would completely live the latter commandment, we would fulfill the spirit of the law of Moses.

5:16-26. David O. McKay explained: "Man is a dual being, and his life a plan of God. That is the first fundamental fact to keep in mind. Man has a *natural* body and a spiritual body. . . . Man's body, therefore, is but the tabernacle in which his spirit dwells. *Too many, far too many, are prone to regard the body as the man, and consequently to direct their efforts to the gratifying of the body's pleasures, its appetites, its passions."*[24]

5:17. Brigham Young commented: "It is a constant warfare. . . . The spirit that is put into man is pure and holy; but through the power of evil with the flesh, it is more or less contaminated, influenced, seduced, and brought into bondage by the evil that exists upon the earth. Let the spirit overcome and come off conqueror."[25]

6:1. Joseph Smith said, "I charged the Saints not to follow the example of the adversary in accusing the brethren, and said, 'If you do not accuse each other, God will not accuse you. If you have no accuser you will enter heaven, and if you will follow the revelations and instructions which God gives you through me, I will take you into heaven as my back load. If you will not accuse me, I will not accuse you. If you will throw a cloak of charity over my sins, I will over yours—for charity covereth a multitude of sins.'"[26]

6:8. David O. McKay told the Saints: "In their yearning for a good time, young people are often tempted to indulge in the things which appeal only to the baser side of humanity, five of the most common of which are: First, vulgarity and obscenity; second, drinking and petting parties; third, unchastity; fourth, disloyalty; and fifth, irreverence."[27]

6:9. We must never put a timetable on the Lord. He is the Lord of the harvest, and in due time he will pay those who labor. It is only for us to know that we will be fully rewarded for what we do.

6:12. In other words, "those who want to make a good impression want to compel you to be circumcised so that they will not have to suffer any persecution for their allegiance to Christ."

6:15. The important thing is to be born again. "Because of the covenant which ye have made ye shall be called the children of Christ, his sons, and his daughters; for behold, this day he hath spiritually begotten you; for ye say that your hearts are changed through faith on his name; therefore, ye are born of him and have become his sons and his daughters." (Mosiah 5:7.)

6:17. This is probably an allusion to the scars in Paul's flesh received during persecution, attesting to his faithfulness in testifying to the gospel of Jesus Christ even in the face of death.

Notes

1. See Map no. 19 in LDS edition of the King James Version.

2. The James referred to is not the brother of John whom Herod Agrippa I had killed earlier (Acts 12), but is thought to be the brother of Jesus who, tradition says, became the Bishop of Jerusalem. The latter may explain his key role in the Jerusalem Council. Compare James's role in giving the "sentence" (Acts 15:13-19) to instances in the history of the restored church when someone other than the person holding the directing power (i.e., the prophet) was appointed to act as president pro tem and presided over a conference. (Cf. *History of the Church* 4:146.)

3. Consult the chronology in the Bible Dictionary of the LDS edition of the King James Version or any other good Bible chronology.

4. A look at Map no. 2 in the back of the LDS edition of the King James Version reveals this area—the central portion of Asia Minor.

5. The need for circumcision was fulfilled by Christ. (Moro. 8:8.)

6. "The Greeks used 'justify' of judges giving a decision of innocence, so Paul testifies that God through Christ holds his children guiltless. So to 'justify' is to award forgiveness through Christ's sacrifice. One is justified when his sins are canceled through Christ's atonement." (Richard L. Anderson, *Understanding Paul* [Salt Lake City: Deseret Book, 1983], p. 159.)

7. Jesus commanded baptism for the remission of sins. (Acts 2:38.) Paul did not argue for baptism, since he was writing to those who were already baptized, but he does mention that it was through baptism that we become heirs to the promises of Abraham. (Gal. 3:27, 29.)

8. Exceptions to this will be found in Romans 7:22-23, 25; 8:2, 7.

9. Bruce R. McConkie, *Mormon Doctrine,* 2nd ed. (Salt Lake City: Bookcraft, 1966), p. 13.

10. Ibid. Italics in original.

11. Bruce R. McConkie, *Doctrinal New Testament Commentary,* 3 vols. (Salt Lake City: Bookcraft, 1965-73), 2:470.

12. Spencer W. Kimball, *Speeches of the Year,* May 1954 (Provo: Brigham Young University Press), p. 4.

13. Joseph Fielding Smith, *Answers to Gospel Questions,* 5 vols. (Salt Lake City: Deseret Book, 1965-75), 5:176.

14. Harold B. Lee, *Conference Report,* October 1972, p. 125.

15. McConkie, *Doctrinal New Testament Commentary* 2:463.

16. Cf. Roman 6:2 and Clarke's *The Holy Bible ... with Commentary and Critical Notes,* 6 vols. (Nashville: Abingdon Press, n.d.), 6:76.

17. Brigham Young, *Journal of Discourses* 14:82.

18. Brigham Young, *Journal of Discourses* 10:266.

19. John Taylor, *Journal of Discourses* 13:18.

20. Joseph Smith, *Teachings of the Prophet Joseph Smith,* comp. Joseph Fielding Smith (Salt Lake City: Deseret Book, 1976), p. 60.

21. Harold B. Lee, *BYU Speeches of the Year,* September 1973, pp. 102-3.

22. Joseph Fielding Smith, *Doctrines of Salvation,* comp. Bruce R. McConkie, 3 vols. (Salt Lake City: Bookcraft, 1954-56), 2:38.

23. Cf. McConkie, *Mormon Doctrine,* p. 512.

24. David O. McKay, *Improvement Era,* September 1949, p. 558; emphasis added.

25. Brigham Young, *Journal of Discourses* 7:268.

26. Joseph Smith, *History of the Church* 4:445.

27. David O. McKay, *Conference Report,* April 1949, p. 14.

7

GRACE, MYSTERIES, AND EXALTATION
(Ephesians)

RODNEY TURNER

Paul was an aged man. (Philem. 1:9.) Nearly thirty years of un-wearying labor for Christ had taken its toll. Now Paul was in Rome under house arrest, awaiting the outcome of his "appeal unto Caesar." (Acts 25:11.) Nero was that Caesar; he had ruled since A.D. 54 and would commit suicide in 68, about six years hence. Paul would precede him in a martyr's death by a year or two (66-67).

In the meantime there was still much to do: the Gentile branches scattered throughout Greece and Asia Minor continued to require the apostle's steadying hand. Persecution, heresy, apostasy, and apathy were ongoing realities; instruction and admonition had to be relent-less. Such was the background of the so-called "letters of imprison-ment" written by Paul from Rome between the years 61 and 62.[1]

Of the four, and indeed of all of Paul's fourteen extant letters, Ephesians is the broadest in scope and loftiest in conception.[2] It is Paul's climactic summation of the plan of salvation, encompassing the premortal, mortal, and postmortal estates of man. Time is swallowed up in eternity as Paul declares the ultimate destiny of the saints to be nothing less than union with the Father and the Son in nature, pur-pose, knowledge, power, glory, and dominion.

The theme of Ephesians is summed up in a famous passage: "There

---

Rodney Turner is professor of ancient scripture at Brigham Young Univer-sity.

is one body, and one Spirit, even as ye are called in one hope of your calling; one Lord, one faith, one baptism, one God and Father of all." (Eph. 4:4-6.) The achievement of this oneness in all things via God's grace and man's foreordained works is the heart of the message of Ephesians.

While unity is the keyword in Ephesians, it is multifaceted in that it involves the unity of peoples, doctrines, ordinances, dispensations, the church, and, above all, the Father with his eternal family.

Saints Foreordained

Paul writes his fellow saints that the Father "hath chosen us in him before the foundation of the world." (Eph. 1:4.) The truly converted among these Gentiles were part of the "elect of God" of whom Peter also spoke. (1 Pet. 1:2.) They were noble spirits who, because of their commitment to Christ in their premortal (first) estate, had been elected or foreordained by the Father to be identified with Christ's church on earth.

Having received the principles and ordinances of the gospel as administered by the earthly priesthood, they had been *born again* into the Father's heavenly family through Christ, his *Firstborn* Son. (Eph. 1:5, 11; compare D&C 93:22; Moses 6:59.) They possessed a "hope of eternal life, which God, that cannot lie, promised [them] before the world began." (Titus 1:2.) Their election to membership in the Lord's church constituted a foreordained opportunity, not a guarantee, of realizing that hope.[3]

In an earlier letter Paul had written: "Eye hath not seen, nor ear heard, neither have entered into the heart of man, the things which God hath prepared for them that love him." (1 Cor. 2:9.) Only the Holy Spirit, which "searcheth all things, yea, the deep things of God" (1 Cor. 2:10), could make them known to any mortal. Therefore, Paul's prayer for the Gentile saints was that they would be granted "the spirit of wisdom and revelation" so that they might more fully comprehend the true nature of that eternal life for which they hoped. (Eph. 1:15-18.)

Like Israel itself (Deut. 32:8), Christ's church was first organized in the premortal world ages before it was organized on earth in the time of Adam. It is an eternal principle that all things are first organized in a spirit state before they are organized temporally. (D&C 29:30-32.)

The divine Shepherd knows his sheep "by name" and they "know his voice," having become familiar with it in the premortal world. (John 10:3-5, 27; compare Mosiah 26:21.) Jesus told the Jews: "I am the good shepherd, and know my sheep, and am known of mine." (John 10:14; compare 1 Ne. 22:25.) He told the Nephites: "I know my sheep, and they are numbered." (3 Ne. 18:31.) And he told the Latter-day Saints: "You are of them that my Father hath given me; and none of them that my Father hath given me shall be lost." (D&C 50:41-42; compare D&C 27:14; 84:63.)[4] These souls were doubtless "given" to Christ in those councils of heaven in which they personally participated before the physical earth was organized. (Abr. 3:22.) All was done without compulsion on the Father's part; his children acted as free agents in the matter.

The doctrine of election has been distorted by post-apostolic Christians who, in affirming the immateriality of God, deny the premortal existence of man. Prominent theologians have compounded these errors with another: the doctrine of unconditional election or predestination to salvation or damnation as touted by Augustine in the fourth century and later by John Calvin in the sixteenth.[5]

It is argued that since fallen man, being depraved, can be saved only by divine grace, it logically follows that God must determine who will and who will not partake of that grace. One is numbered among "God's elect," not for any act of his, but by God's good pleasure.

This view of predestination is based on a highly selective (sectarian) interpretation of Paul's theology.[6] It robs God of his indispensable attribute of justice, rendering him a respecter of persons who, contrary to his own disavowals (Acts 10:34; D&C 1:35), overwhelms and negates the agency of mankind by his sovereign will. But what father worthy of the name would capriciously consign one child to wealth and another to poverty? (D&C 38:26.)

If God functions as an absolutely omnipotent being as viewed by sectarian religions (which he does not), he has the power to predestine all mankind to salvation. On what basis does he fail to do so? Why does he choose to damn anyone? Is he vindicated by his very omnipotence on the grounds that might makes right? If so, then he is not a god of law, justice, or mercy. (Alma 42:13, 21-25.) The god of Augustine and Calvin is not the God and Father of Jesus Christ.

Grace: The Power of God

The preeminence of Jesus Christ over all things in heaven and on earth (treated in Col. 1:16-18) is reemphasized in Ephesians. "The Father of glory" displayed his awesome power in resurrecting his Son, in exalting his Son above all things, and in appointing his Son the eternal head of the eternal church—the church of the Firstborn. (Eph. 1:17, 19-23; compare Heb. 12:23; D&C 76:94.)

The power that exalted the Son is the same power that exalts God's elect. Pertaining to man, this power may be summed up in one word: *grace.* The gospel, "the power of God unto salvation" (Rom. 1:16), is the message of grace. By pure grace, mankind is redeemed from physical death. (1 Cor. 15:20-23.) By qualified grace (grace by covenant), the sinner is redeemed from his sins; he is justified. (Rom. 5:1, 9; 6:3-11.)

What then is grace? The term is derived from the Greek *charis,* which suggests condescension, kindness, generosity, charity, and so forth. In essence, divine grace consists of divine works. Broadly speaking, grace is everything the Father and the Son do to bring to pass the immortality and eternal life of man. Pertaining to man's redemption, it is centered in the atonement and resurrection of Jesus Christ.

While Paul uses the term *grace* ninety-five times in his letters, his critical passages on the subject are found in Romans 3:23–4:5 and 11:5-6, Galatians 2:21, and, most especially, in Ephesians 2:8-10, which reads: "For by grace are ye saved through faith; and that not of yourselves: it is the gift of God; not of works, lest any man should boast. For we are his workmanship, created in Christ Jesus unto good works, which God hath before ordained that we should walk in them."[7]

Paul's phrase "not of works" applies not only to the law of Moses, but to all human works, even gospel works. Ephesians was not written to Jews under the law, but to Gentiles who had been baptized into the organized church of Christ. Paul wanted these Gentiles who had come out of heathenism to understand that the ultimate source of their salvation was Jesus Christ, not their own efforts or those ordinances, however essential, they had received. Self-salvation, like self-righteousness, is an illusion for Jew and Gentile alike.

The Jew erred in seeking salvation wholly through the killing letter of a law centered in the symbolic blood of animals, rather than the redeeming blood of Christ. (2 Cor. 3:6-8; Heb. 8:12-14; 10:4.) The law, being Levitical or Aaronic in nature, was not enlivened by the gift and powers of the Holy Ghost. (See Gal. 3:2-5, 14; Jer. 31:31-34.) Then, too, the law had become irrelevant; it had been fulfilled by the One who had given it. (Matt. 5:17; Gal. 2:19; 3:13-25; 3 Ne. 15:4-5.)

Understanding this fact, Paul cites Abraham (a symbol of the saved Jew and Gentile) as one who obtained justification (remission of sins and salvation) seven centuries before the Mosaic code was instituted. (Gal. 3:5-18.) In Romans, Paul reasons that if righteousness is something men earn, then salvation is something God owes them: "Now to him who is justified by the law of works, is the reward reckoned, not of grace, but of debt." (JST, Rom. 4:4.)

But we can never put God in our debt no matter how diligently we labor. All are, at best, "unprofitable servants." (See Luke 17:7-10; Mosiah 2:21.) Consequently, eternal life is "the greatest of all the gifts of God." (D&C 14:7; compare 1 Ne. 15:36.) A gift is not a debt. Without the atonement and resurrection of Christ, all mankind would be forever lost to God, no matter how diligently his commandments were kept. (2 Ne. 9:5-9.)

The Book of Mormon is emphatic in declaring that salvation is centered in the redemptive mission of Christ. For example, Lehi told his son Jacob, "There is no flesh that can dwell in the presence of God, save it be through the merits, and mercy, and grace of the Holy Messiah." (2 Ne. 2:8.) Nephi wrote that we must rely "wholly upon the merits of him who is mighty to save." (2 Ne. 31:19; see also Alma 24:10; Hel. 14:13; Moro. 6:4; D&C 3:20.) The combined good deeds of the entire human race cannot save a single soul, for we can no more save ourselves than we can create ourselves.

Foreordained Works

Yet the fact remains that no one is saved without prescribed works any more than he is saved exclusively by them. Salvation is a joint venture between the Savior and the sinner, a truth stated in simplicity by the prophet Nephi: "We labor diligently to write, to persuade our children, and also our brethren, to believe in Christ, and to be reconciled to God; for we know that it is by grace that we are saved, *after all we can do."* (2 Ne. 25:23; emphasis added. Compare Moro. 10:32-33.)

However, in maximizing what Christ does, most Protestants (following Martin Luther's lead) minimize what man must do. The assumption seems to be that in freeing the Jews from the onerous demands of the hard-to-bear law of Moses (see Acts 15:10), Christ freed mankind from virtually all sacraments or ordinances. For example, baptism becomes purely symbolic, being but the "outward sign of an inward grace." Thus, what matters is not what one does, but what one believes. Faith *in* faith is the path to salvation. Works died on the cross.

But Paul writes: "We are his workmanship, created in Christ Jesus unto good works, which God hath before ordained that we should walk in them." (Eph. 2:10.) "Good works" are God's works, those he prescribed in mankind's first estate for mankind's salvation in the second, or mortal, estate. Contrary to Luther, James is not "an epistle full of straw." Paul saw eye to eye with James. The issue was never faith *or* works, but faith *with* works. (James 2:14-26.) More to the point, it was the *right* faith with the *right* works. The Father foreordained precisely what those right works would be for the elect when he chose the elect "before the foundation of the world." (Eph. 1:4.)

These mandated labors take several forms and consist of far more than those desirable virtues derived from Christian ethics. For as vital as these are—and they are essential—of themselves they cannot save anyone. If they were sufficient of themselves, there would be no need for apostles and prophets or for any doctrines and ordinances.

There isn't enough water in all of the baptismal fonts in eternity to put out the fires of damnation for an unrepentant sinner. (D&C 29:44;

88:35.) Consequently, the repentance of one's sins and the acknowledgment of Christ as one's Savior is the minimum requirement for any measure of salvation. God cannot save us *in* our sins, only from them. (See Alma 11:36-37; Hel. 5:10.) Paul made it abundantly clear that practicing sinners would not be saved in the kingdom of God. (Eph. 5:3-6; 1 Cor. 6:9-10; Gal. 5:19-21.)

Those works designed to exalt us in the presence of the Father begin with faith, repentance, and baptism (Mark 16:15-16; Rom. 6:3-5), and "go on unto perfection" (Heb. 6:1) in those ordinances for the living and the dead performed in holy temples. They also include all that must be done "for the perfecting of the saints, for the work of the ministry, [and] for the edifying of the body of Christ." (Eph. 4:12.)

The critical distinction between a true saint and other religious people is not morality, but truth. The saint is prepared to receive and internalize all the light and truth, the intelligence, that God reveals. For the saint, revelation is an unbound book to which new pages are added as the Lord directs. (2 Ne. 29:11-12.) On the other hand, religionists in general (like the Shakers of Joseph Smith's day) "desire to know the truth in part, but not all." (D&C 49:2.)

Practicing Christians are good men and women. However, people can be good in the normative sense of the word without belonging to any religious organization. There are many good men and women who seldom, if ever, darken the doors of a church. However, the goal of the saint is not mere goodness, but holiness. (Eph. 4:24; 1 Thes. 4:7; Heb. 12:10.) And holiness requires not only personal morality but also those doctrines and ordinances through which the saint is endowed with the holiness of the Godhead. Only those who accept and live the fullness of the gospel of Jesus Christ can be sanctified. And only the sanctified are heirs of the celestial kingdom. (D&C 88:20-21.) They alone are members of the heavenly church, the Church of the Firstborn. They alone partake of a fullness of the grace of God.

Heirs of exaltation are those "who overcome by faith, and are sealed by the Holy Spirit of promise, which the Father sheds forth upon all those who are just and true." (D&C 76:53.) Paul assured the elect Gentiles that they had been "sealed with that Holy Spirit of promise, which is the earnest [guarantee] of our inheritance until the redemption [claiming] of the purchased possession." (Eph. 1:13-14; compare 2 Cor. 1:22; 5:5; D&C 88:3-4.) The "possession" is eternal life, "purchased" by the atonement.

The seal of the Holy Spirit is initially conditional in that its retention is dependent upon one's faithfulness. But as long as it remains unbroken, it is conclusive proof that we have God's immutable promise of eternal life (the "inheritance"). Our "hope of the glory of God" (Rom. 5:2) is fully justified.

The Church on Earth

The chief cornerstone of the church is Jesus Christ; apostles and prophets constitute the remainder of its authorized foundation. (Eph. 2:20; 1 Cor. 12:28.) The superstructure of lesser authorities cannot viably rest upon any other foundation. When God removed that foundation, the edifice collapsed and its debris was used to build the many churches now dotting the Christian landscape.

Paul knew that the church was destined to become much more than a human enterprise, however elaborate, clothed in clerical robes. When finally completed, the "building"—and each man and woman in it—would be nothing less than a holy temple in which God, through the Holy Ghost, would dwell. (Eph. 2:21.) It was for this reason that the church had to be built upon the solid foundation of apostles and prophets, who would not only teach correct principles and administer correct ordinances, but who would also *safeguard* those principles and ordinances against heresy. In addition to apostles and prophets, Christ provided evangelists (patriarchs), pastors (bishops), and teachers in his church "for the perfecting of the saints, for the work of the ministry, for the edifying [upbuilding] of the body of Christ." (Eph. 4:11-12.) The word *perfecting* implies oneness. A divided church, much less a fragmented Christianity, can never become perfect. Christ declared: "I say unto you, be one; and if ye are not one ye are not mine." (D&C 38:27.) The hallmark of the true church is unity.

Mystery: Salvation of the Gentiles

Paul employs the term *mystery* twenty times in his letters in discussing Christ, the gospel, the resurrection, Israel, the Gentiles, speaking in tongues, iniquity, and godliness. A mystery is a divine secret or unknown truth. Three mysteries are discussed in Ephesians.

The first mystery pertains to a process that began in the days of the apostolic church. For the first time since the Flood, the non-Israelitish nations (Gentiles) were to be given the opportunity to receive the gospel and be adopted into immortal Israel. (Rom. 11:11-26; 1 Ne. 10:12-14.) In doing so, they would partake of "the unsearchable riches of Christ." (Eph. 3:2-8.)[8] This proselytizing period is called "the times of the Gentiles." (Luke 21:24; D&C 45:25-30.)

Paul reminded the Gentile converts of their pre-grace condition when they were spiritually dead, "children of disobedience," ruled by Satan, and gratifying "the desires of the flesh and of the mind." (Eph. 2:1-3; compare Col. 1:21.) In that lost state, they were "separate from Christ, excluded from citizenship in Israel and foreigners to the covenants of promise, without hope and without God in the world." (Eph. 2:12, New International Version [NIV].)

But now, "by the blood of Christ," the dividing wall that separated the Gentiles from Israel, and the sinner from God, had been "broken down." The "iron curtain" of the Mosaic law of carnal commandments—"the letter [that] killeth"—was no more. It had been replaced by the unifying law of Christ—"the spirit [that] giveth life." (2 Cor. 3:6; compare Gal. 3:2.) Jeremiah's prophecy had been fulfilled; the Lord had made a new covenant with Israel, one in which the Gentiles could fully participate. (Jer. 31:31-34; compare Heb. 8:8-13.) The Prince of Peace had reconciled Jew and Gentile to God and to one another. The two had become one. The Gentiles were "no more strangers and foreigners, but fellowcitizens with the saints, and of the household of God." (Eph. 2:13-19.)

Mystery: "The Dispensation of the Fulness of Times"

Paul looked far down the corridors of time and prophesied: "In the dispensation of the fulness of times" the Father would "gather together in one all things in Christ, both which are in heaven, and which are on earth." (Eph. 1:10.)[9] Paul understood that his own dispensation (the meridian of time—D&C 20:26) would end in a general apostasy (Acts 20:28-31; 2 Thes. 2:1-12; 2 Tim. 3:1–4:4). The fullness of the

115

gospel would then be restored in a subsequent, all-encompassing dispensation that would be the sum of all previous dispensations.

The finest description of this culminating dispensation was given by its president, Joseph Smith. It consists, he stated, of "a whole and complete and perfect union, and welding together of dispensations, and keys, and powers, and glories . . . from the days of Adam even to the present time. . . . [Also] things which never have been revealed from the foundation of the world . . . shall be revealed unto babes and sucklings in this, the dispensation of the fulness of times." (D&C 128:18; compare 27:13.) This is what is meant by the restitution or restoration of all things. (Acts 3:21; D&C 27:6; 86:10.) Christ is the focal point, the magnetic center, around which all things, including the worthy living and dead, will assemble in this last dispensation. As God of the terrestrial order (D&C 76:71, 77-78), the Son of Man will come to the redeemed earth, which will have been renewed with paradisiacal (terrestrial) glory, and will rule as king and lawgiver for a thousand years (D&C 29:11; 45:59).

Thus all dispensations under the jurisdiction of Jesus Christ will be welded together in "a whole and complete and perfect union." This will bring to pass the perfection of "the dispensation of the fulness of times," or, in other words, the perfection of Zion. (Moses 7:31.)

Mystery: Marriage and the Church

In Ephesians, Paul expands upon those human relationships discussed in Colossians: husband and wife, parent and child, master and slave. Pertaining to the latter, he reminds the Christian slave and owner alike that they are first and foremost followers of Christ, seeking the same reward. "There is neither Jew nor Greek, there is neither bond nor free, there is neither male nor female: for ye are all one in Christ Jesus." (Gal. 3:28.) Such was the underlying principle that should dictate all interpersonal relationships within the body of Christ. Master and slave were expected to be guided by that principle. (Eph. 6:5-9; compare Col. 3:22—4:1; 1 Pet. 2:18-23.) The important thing was not their transitory situations in life, but their conduct toward one another in those situations. The same principle applies in the parent-child relationship, where one is also temporarily subordinate to another. It is right for children to obey their parents "in the Lord." It is wrong for fathers to be overbearing and to provoke their children to anger and rebellion. (Eph. 6:1-4.)

Paul is accused of being a misogynist who had little regard for marriage.[10] Nothing could be further from the truth. Nowhere in scripture is the marriage relationship defined so beautifully as in Ephesians. As with masters and slaves, parents and children, he applies the principle of stewardship to marriage. The wife in Christ (meaning, a gospel covenant wife) is to follow her husband as she would follow the Lord himself. (Eph. 5:22-24.)

To put the principle in proper perspective, Paul draws an analogy between the relationship of a priesthood husband to his wife and of Christ to the church. Christ and the husband "in Christ" constitute the "head" in their respective callings. For marriage is more than a partnership; it is also a priesthood stewardship. Since every steward is accountable for his stewardship, he must be able to exercise righteous dominion over it. There can be no legitimate responsibility without legitimate authority.

Historically, arbitrary domination has been exercised by countless supposedly Christian husbands who defended their conduct by citing Ephesians 5:22-23. However, husbands do not derive their authority from their sex, but from Christ. They are the "head" of their wives because Christ is their "head." A man's authority and the right to exercise that authority in righteousness originate in Christ, not in the man. Consequently, a wife's commitment to her husband imposes a profound obligation on him to be worthy of her commitment. To justify the wife's commitment, Paul commands: "Husbands, love your wives, *even* as Christ also loved the church, and gave himself for it. . . . So ought men to love their wives as their own bodies. He that loveth his wife loveth himself. For no man ever yet hated his own flesh; but nourisheth and cherisheth it, *even* as the Lord the church. . . . Let every one of you in particular so love his wife even as himself; and the wife see that she reverence her husband." (Eph. 5:25, 28-29, 33; emphasis added.)

Obviously, a wife's righteous submission to her husband should stem from her husband's righteous submission to Christ. When this occurs, a divine triangle exists with Christ at its apex. Husband and

117

wife are one flesh with each other because they have become one flesh with Christ. This is the foundation of all eternal unions. Paul had such a union in mind when he wrote: "Neither is the man without the woman, neither the woman without the man, in the Lord." (1 Cor. 11:11.) To be *in the Lord* is to be eternally one with him and, therefore, with one another. Only through this three-way union can men and women achieve exaltation in the celestial kingdom. (D&C 131:1-4; 132:19-25.)

In summary, just as the saints become "members of his body, of his flesh, and of his bones," so those married for eternity "in the Lord" become "one flesh" with each other. (Eph. 5:30-31.) Consequently, the union of man and woman is meant to be as eternal as the Church of the Firstborn (D&C 76:54-59, 94) of which exalted men and women will be immortal "members."

Celestial marriage is the key to a fullness of divinity. In declaring the preeminence of the Son of God over all things in heaven and on earth, Paul wrote: "For it pleased the Father that in him should all fulness dwell. . . . For in him dwelleth all the fulness of the Godhead bodily." (Col. 1:19; 2:9.) In other words, the attributes and powers of the Father, Son, and Holy Ghost are possessed by the risen Christ.

These same attributes and powers will be possessed by those who become one with the Father and the Son. (John 17:20-23.) Consequently, the process of perfecting the Saints must continue "till we, in the unity of the faith, all come to the knowledge of the Son of God, unto a perfect man, unto the measure of the stature of the fulness of Christ." (JST, Eph. 4:13.) Knowledge *of* the Son of God is more than knowledge *about* him; it is knowledge *of* him. And knowledge of him is acquired only as we partake of his divine nature and thereby become spiritually one with him. Only in doing so can we obtain a fullness of eternal life. Hence, Jesus' prayer: "This is life eternal, that they might know thee the only true God, and Jesus Christ, whom thou hast sent." (John 17:3.)

It is only when the *human* spirit is baptized by the *Holy* Spirit (John 3:5-8) that one is born again as a son or daughter of God and empowered to attain "the stature of the fulness of Christ" (Eph. 4:13; compare 1 Jn. 3:1-3). To be so baptized is to have "Christ in you" (Col.

1:27; compare Gal. 2:20), not literally, but as the sanctifying power (or companionship) of the Holy Ghost.

In attaining the spiritual stature of Christ, the saints will, perforce, become one with him and also "be filled with all the fulness of God." (Eph. 3:19.) Acquiring a celestial fullness of the Father's nature means that they will become exalted even as he is exalted. They will be Gods.[11] Christ confirmed this doctrine in a modern revelation: "For if you keep my commandments you shall receive of his fulness, and be glorified in me as I am in the Father." (D&C 93:20; compare Rev. 3:21.) This doctrine, once lost but now restored, was the crowning revelation of the Prophet Joseph Smith to the Church. He sealed it with his blood.

While it may seem incredible to the rational mind that fallen mortals with all of their weaknesses could dare hope to attain the moral and spiritual stature of the very Son of God, yet this is precisely what must occur if the saints are to become "joint-heirs with Christ" (Rom. 8:17) to the riches of eternity. Hence the indispensable need for divine grace as primarily manifest in the atonement, the resurrection, and the sanctifying gift of the Holy Ghost. (Alma 5:54; 3 Ne. 27:20.)

The Pursuit of Perfection

Ultimate perfection is unobtainable in this fallen world. The ascent to oneness with the Father was begun in eternity past and will not be achieved until eternity future. Salvation is not achieved in one effortless moment of fervent commitment; it is a matter of climbing step by step from one level of exaltation to another. Said Joseph Smith: "It is not all to be comprehended in this world; it will be a great work to learn our salvation and exaltation even beyond the grave."[12]

Even though he had seen the risen Christ and beheld the "third [celestial] heaven" (2 Cor. 12:1-4),[13] Paul did not presume to be saved. He knew the difference between a man's testimony of God and God's testimony of the man. As Joseph Smith observed: "Though they might hear the voice of God and know that Jesus was the Son of God, this would be no evidence that their election and calling was made sure, that they had part with Christ, and were joint heirs with Him."[14]

Paul was well aware of this principle. He knew that accepting Christ was but the beginning of the long race for eternal life. Over twenty years after his conversion he wrote: "Everyone who competes in the games goes into strict training. They do it to get a crown of laurel that will not last; but we do it to get a crown that will last forever. Therefore, I do not run like a man running aimlessly; I do not fight like a man shadow boxing. No, I beat my body and make it my slave so that after I have preached to others, I myself will not be disqualified for the prize." (1 Cor. 9:25-27, NIV.)

About five years later he wrote the Philippians: "Continue to work out your salvation with fear and trembling. . . . Brothers, I do not consider myself yet to have taken hold of it [salvation]. But one thing I do: Forgetting what is behind and straining toward what is ahead, I press on toward the goal to win the prize for which God has called me heavenward in Christ Jesus." (Philip. 2:12; 3:13-14, NIV; compare 2 Ne. 31:20.) Only when facing certain death did Paul finally write: "I have fought the good fight, I have finished the race, I have kept the faith. Henceforth there is laid up for me the crown of righteousness, which the Lord, the righteous judge, will award to me." (2 Tim. 4:7-8.) Paul then knew that his calling and election into the eternal church and kingdom of God was, at last, made sure.[15]

The Whole Armor of God

Having shown the saints the heights the Father would have them attain, Paul, as he was wont to do, closed his letter with practical counsel designed to safeguard them against "the god of this world." (2 Cor. 4:4.) Because that god is yet to be dethroned, our modern world is an astonishing replay of the Roman world of the first century. The vices that ail us ailed them. The things living prophets warn against today are the same things Paul denounced in Ephesians.

He admonished the Gentile converts to forsake the corrupt ways of their unregenerated neighbors and then proceeded to catalogue the more blatant of those ways: lying, theft, idleness, anger, rage, brawling, slander, obscenities, coarse humor, lightmindedness, greed, and licentiousness or sexual impurity in all of its manifestations. (Eph. 4:25–5:4.) "Be sure of this, that no immoral or impure man, or one who is covetous (that is, an idolater), has any inheritance in the kingdom of Christ and of God." (Eph. 5:5, Revised Standard Version.)

The very body of a truly repentant soul is transformed into a spiritual temple wherein dwells the influence of the Holy Spirit. But that Spirit cannot dwell in an unclean house. (1 Cor. 3:16-17; Alma 7:21.) Therefore, should that temple become defiled by unrepented sins, the Spirit is forced to forsake it. It is a temple no longer; it is destroyed. (D&C 93:35.) If the offenses are grievous enough, the body that once housed the Spirit of God becomes the habitation of devils. (JST, Matt. 12:37-39.) To prevent such a tragedy, Ephesians ends with Paul's resounding call to "put on the whole armour of God." (Eph. 6:11.) The spiritual war that began in the premortal world continues to rage on earth. The enemy that the spirit children of God once confronted face to face is no longer visible; he has become the "prince of the power of the air" (Eph. 2:2), meaning the invisible or unseen ruler of this fallen world. Nevertheless, he and his cohorts are very real and very deadly. They must be faced and vanquished. Being spiritual enemies, they must be fought with spiritual weapons.

Like the gladiator of the Roman arena, the saint must be fully armed (the panoply), both offensively and defensively. The wide belt to which the gladiator fastened all of his equipment symbolizes eternal truth. The heart-protecting breastplate is personal righteousness. The hobnailed sandals (for sure footing) represent the gospel of Jesus Christ. The movable shield of faith protects the spiritual gladiator from Satan's fiery arrows, regardless of their origin. A firm-minded hope of salvation is represented by the gladiator's helmet, protecting against any fatal blows the enemy might attempt to strike. But the spiritual gladiator's offensive power lies in "the sword of the Spirit"— the directing, sustaining word of God provided to the saint day by day. As the Spirit is God's means of communicating wisdom and power to the saint, so is the prayer of faith the saint's means of assuring that that divine support will be forthcoming. (Compare D&C 27:15-18.)

Victory is possible only when the spiritual gladiator puts on the *whole* armor of God. Failure to be fully armed may make the saint, like Achilles, fatally vulnerable. The "whole armour of God" had enabled Paul to win his own victory. He had, indeed, "fought a good fight." (2 Tim. 4:7.) He prayed a like victory for those he left behind.

Gracious Paul closed Ephesians with a characteristic expression of affection: "Peace to the brothers, and love with faith from God the Father and the Lord Jesus Christ. Grace to all who love our Lord Jesus Christ with an undying love." (Eph. 6:23-24, NIV.)

At the present time, we do not know the specific outcome of his appeal to Caesar. But one thing we do know: he faced his uncertain future with faith, hope, and love. "These three" were his constant companions in those long years of unwearying labor he had known since he first beheld his Redeemer that foreordained noonday on the road to Damascus.

Notes

1. The four letters are Ephesians, Philippians, Colossians, and Philemon.

2. Ephesians, Colossians, and Philemon were written in the same time period and delivered by Paul's companion, Tychicus. (Eph. 6:21; Col. 4:7.) Colossians and Ephesians are much alike in subject matter and phraseology. Ephesians builds upon ideas found in Colossians, being an elaboration on the doctrine of Christ's preeminence and its implications for the saints. Some scholars believe that Ephesians is actually the missing letter to Laodicea. (Col. 4:16.) Others regard Ephesians as encyclical in nature. Paul headquartered in Ephesus for about three years (A.D. 54-57) and was well-known there. (Acts 19.) This fact has led some scholars to doubt that Ephesians was written to the church in Ephesus because the formality of the letter suggests a Gentile audience with whom Paul was personally unacquainted. (1:13, 15; 3:3-4.) However, his impersonal approach may simply reflect his concentration on the profound message he wanted to impress upon his Gentile audience.

3. Joseph Smith said: "Unconditional election of individuals to eternal life was not taught by the Apostles." (*Teachings of the Prophet Joseph Smith*, p. 189.)

4. In arguing that the early Christians believed in the doctrine of a premortal Church, Richard L. Anderson cited a portion of the "Shepherd of Hermas," dating from the late first century: "Hermas saw the Church in the form of an old woman because, as his messenger [an angel] said, 'She was created

the first of all things. . . . God . . . created the world . . . and by his own wisdom and forethought created his holy Church . . . and everything is becoming level for his elect in order that he might keep for them the promise which he made with great glory and joy, if they keep the commandments of God, which they received in great faith.'" (Richard L. Anderson, *Understanding Paul* [Salt Lake City: Deseret Book, 1983], pp. 275-76.)

5. *Predestinate* appears only in Romans 8:29-30 and Ephesians 1:5, 11, where the more correct translation of the Greek *proorizo* would be *foreordained.* Some modern translations render the word *destined, planned, chosen,* and so forth. *Foreordained,* referring to Christ, appears but once in the King James version: 1 Peter 1:20.

6. The primary scriptural basis for this doctrine is Romans 9:8-21, wherein Paul defends the justice of God in choosing Jacob over Esau before either was born, and in granting or withholding mercy according to His will: "Hath not the potter power over the clay, of the same lump to make one vessel unto honour, and another unto dishonour?" Throughout the entire chapter Paul is defending God's righteous sovereignty, his divine agency. He fails to explain that the determining factor in how God expresses his sovereignty is how men exercise their own agency both before and after entering mortality. While God wills as he pleases, he wills only that which is just. He can be merciful only when people are obedient—not because he is arbitrary, but because his commitment to eternal law dictates his varying responses regarding mankind. (See Alma 42:21-25.)

7. For an extended treatment of Paul's teachings on grace, see the writer's article, "Paul: Apostle of Grace," in the *Sidney B. Sperry Symposium,* Brigham Young University, Provo, Utah, January 1983, pp. 113-24.

8. The term *Gentiles* (meaning "the nations") first appears in connection with events following the Flood. (Gen. 10:5.) Israel, the covenant people, descend from Shem; Japheth's posterity constitute the Gentiles. Noah prophesied: "God shall enlarge Japheth, and he shall dwell in the tents of Shem." (Gen. 9:27.) The adoption of Gentiles into Israel via the gospel covenant fulfills this prophecy. (See Rom. 11:13-26; 1 Ne. 10:12-14.)

9. A dispensation is a presentation of saving truths and a delegation of priesthood authority to one or more agents of God and the labors accomplished by those so authorized.

10. Paul's seemingly reluctant approval of marriage in 1 Corinthians 7 must be understood in context. He was deeply concerned for the spiritual welfare of the Corinthians and believed, rightly or wrongly, that they were in a crisis situation calling for singleness of purpose. (1 Cor. 7:29-31.) His statements on the relationship of women vis-à-vis men (1 Tim. 2:9-15) probably

reflect his awareness of growing tensions within Gentile branches over the ecclesiastical roles of women and, to an extent, his own cultural background. The Joseph Smith Translation of 1 Corinthians 7 also helps to show that the "present crisis" pertains to the pressing need for single-minded, unhindered missionaries.

11. For an extended treatment of this doctrine, see the writer's article, "The Doctrine of Godhood in the New Testament," *The Principles of the Gospel in Practice* (Sandy, Utah: Randall Book, 1985), pp. 21-37.

12. See *Teachings of the Prophet Joseph Smith,* pp. 346-48.

13. Ibid., pp. 305-6.

14. Ibid., p. 298.

15. Ibid., pp. 149-50; 2 Pet. 1:10.

8

"WORK OUT YOUR OWN SALVATION"
(Philippians)

H. Dean Garrett

Philippi, located in eastern Macedonia on the east-west Egnation Highway, which linked Rome with Asia, was a Roman military colony. Luke described Philippi as "the chief city of that part of Macedonia." (Acts 16:12.) It was there that Paul was able to establish the first branch in Europe. He had the privilege of visiting Philippi on both his second and his third missionary journeys.

To Paul, Philippi was a city of challenge and opportunity. Events transpired there that allowed the church to expand into Europe. Paul had the occasion to cast out the evil spirits from a woman who was used by the soothsayers to get gain. (Acts 16:16-40.) The soothsayers charged Paul, as a Jew, with rabble rousing, and he and Silas, his companion, were beaten and thrown into jail. Their miraculous release from jail allowed Paul to testify of Christ and to proclaim his Roman citizenship. He used this occasion to teach what the Christians believed, and thus was able to show that Christianity was not just another Jewish religion. It is of interest that most of the converts to the church in Philippi were Gentiles.

Paul's experiences in Philippi helped to develop a close bond between him and the members. Thus, when he wrote to the Philippians, he was writing to a people who were his first converts in Europe. This

---

H. Dean Garrett is assistant professor of Church history and doctrine at Brigham Young University.

epistle was one of "friendship, full of affection, confidence, good counsel, and good cheer," according to Dummelow. "It is the happiest of all St. Paul's writings, for the Philippians were the dearest of his children in the faith."[1]

The epistle also gives us some insight into Paul's own spiritual life. Dummelow explains that it "reveals the spring of his inward peace and strength. It admits us to St. Paul's prison meditations and communions with his Master. We watch his spirit ripening through the autumn hours when patience fulfilled in him its perfect work."[2] The saints at Philippi loved Paul as an apostle and were faithful to the gospel. Thus, he wrote this epistle as a letter of encouragement. He taught them concerning the sacrifice that they must make for Christ and challenged them to be united and one with Christ. He instructed them how to work out their salvation and how peace could come to them. This epistle is the best example of what he taught on the requirements for salvation.

Paul the Prisoner

After his third missionary journey, Paul was arrested in Jerusalem by the Romans in an effort to protect him from the Jewish mobs. He insisted that he be tried before a Roman tribunal and thus was transported to Rome. After a long, difficult trip there, he was imprisoned in a house, which gave him much freedom. With him was Timothy, his beloved companion.

The Philippian saints, hearing of Paul's struggles, sent Epaphroditus with supplies that had "an odour of a sweet smell, a sacrifice acceptable, wellpleasing to God." (Philip. 4:18.) "It was doubtless the liberality of the Philippians that made this favorable arrangement possible," Goodspeed writes. "Certainly Paul could no longer earn his living as he had done when he was at liberty, and the Philippians were sending him money to lighten the hardships of his imprisonment and if possible secure his acquittal. So they constituted themselves in effect a kind of ancient Red Cross or Prisoner's Aid for Paul's benefit."[3] Paul's letter to the Philippians was a letter of love and appreciation. He thanked God "upon every remembrance" of them (Philip. 1:3) and

126

prayed that their love "may abound yet more and more in knowledge and in all judgment" (Philip. 1:9).

Paul's imprisonment was not a deterrent to his mission. He told the Philippians, "The things which happened unto me have fallen out rather unto the furtherance of the gospel." (Philip. 1:12.) Because of his imprisonment, his testimony of Christ was heard in the "palace, and in all other places." (Philip. 1:13.) The saints gained courage because of his example and spoke out without fear and with much boldness. (Philip. 1:13-14.) He felt that some, perhaps, taught Christ for the wrong reasons, but Christ was preached. This all would turn to Paul's salvation. (Philip. 1:17-19.)

Paul's desires put him in a bind. He had a "desire to depart, and to be with Christ," but he knew that it was best for him to stay in the flesh, for that was "more needful" for the Philippians. There was still work to be done and a witness to be borne. Paul was still needed by the church members for the "furtherance and joy of faith." (Philip. 1:23-25.) Perhaps he understood that his life and struggles would be a faith-builder for them. President Spencer W. Kimball taught: "To see the forbearance and fortitude of Paul when he was giving his life to his ministry is to give courage to those who feel they have been injured and tried. He was beaten many times, imprisoned frequently for the cause, stoned near to death, shipwrecked three times, robbed, nearly drowned, the victim of false and disloyal brethren. While starving, choking, freezing, poorly clothed, Paul was yet consistent in his service. He never wavered once after the testimony came to him following his supernatural experience."[4]

Oneness with God

The apostle's own experiences had taught him that whatever was required by the Lord was sufficient. It was really nothing to be imprisoned for the sake of Christ. His counsel to the saints was to "stand fast in one spirit, with one mind striving together for the faith of the gospel." (Philip. 1:27.) It was Paul's having "one mind," striving for the gospel of Christ, that led to the arrest and imprisonment in which he found himself. He also understood that if the Philippian saints remained saints, they would face the rewards of those who "reject the gospel, which bringeth on them destruction." (JST, Philip. 1:28.) Therefore, the saints must understand the following principle: "For unto you it is given in the behalf of Christ, not only to believe on him, but also to suffer for his sake." (Philip. 1:29.) The time would come, he said, when they would have "the same conflict which ye saw in me, and now hear to be in me." (Philip. 1:30.) According to Bruce R. McConkie, the saints would learn that "when the saints suffer persecution for righteousness' sake, they stand in the place and stead of Christ and are receiving what the ungodly would heap upon the Son of God were he personally present."[5]

For the saints to stand steadfast, they must be able to stand together. The Master has taught, "If ye are not one ye are not mine." (D&C 38:27.) Paul desperately wanted them to fulfill his joy, "that ye be like-minded, having the same love, being of one accord, of one mind." He was concerned that there be "comfort of love," "fellowship of the Spirit," tender affections of the heart, and compassion and mercy among them. They were not to allow "strife or vainglory" to be part of their society. (Philip. 2:1-3.) Paul understood that if they were living the commandments, the result would be a unity among the saints that would make them one with the Father and the Son. Christ had prayed that the saints would be one (John 17:20-22), and that they might be sanctified and made perfect. As Elder Francis M. Lyman commented: "We may be thousands of miles apart, yet we are in unison, because [we are] bound together and inspired by the one Spirit. It is the same Spirit which binds the Father and the Son and makes them one.... This is accomplished through our faith, repenting of our sins, cleansing our hearts, and living lives of purity before Him."[6]

It was in this setting of oneness that Paul taught a very important doctrine. He told the Philippians to let this oneness "be in [them], which was also in Christ Jesus: Who, being in the *form of God,* thought it not robbery to be *equal with God.*" (2:5-6; emphasis added.) Paul understood the Savior's teaching, "My Father is greater than I" (John 14:28), and that He called the Father "my God, and your God" (John 20:17). Yet, he still taught that Christ was "in the form of" and "equal with" God the Father. Paul understood the heirship of Christ (Rom. 8:17), and that he did "inherit the same power, the same glory and the same exaltation"[7] as the Father. Through his humility, he "became obedient unto death. . . . God also hath highly exalted him, and given him a name which is above every name." (Philip. 2:8-9.)

The Prophet Joseph Smith understood this principle when he taught: "God himself was once as we are now, and is an exalted man, and sits enthroned in yonder heavens!"[8] He also taught that "God himself, the Father of us all, dwelt on an earth, the same as Jesus Christ himself did."[9] He continued: "Here, then, is eternal life—to know the only wise and true God; and you have got to learn how to be Gods yourselves, and to be kings and priests to God, the same as all Gods have done before you, namely, by going from one small degree to another, and from a small capacity to a great one; from grace to grace, from exaltation to exaltation, until you attain to the resurrection of the dead, and are able to dwell in everlasting burnings, and to sit in glory, as do those who sit enthroned in everlasting power."[10] Lorenzo Snow, a later prophet of this dispensation, having read Paul, John (1 Jn. 3:1-3), and Joseph Smith, felt inspired to respond to Paul this way:

Dear Brother:
Hast thou not been unwisely bold,
Man's destiny to thus unfold?
To raise, promote such high desire,
Such vast ambition thus inspire?

Still, 'tis no phantom that we trace
Man's ultimatum in life's race;
This royal path has long been trod
By righteous men, each now a God:

As Abra'm, Isaac, Jacob, too,
First babes, then men—to gods they grew.
As man now is, our God once was;
As now God is, so man may be,—
Which doth unfold man's destiny.

For John declares: When Christ we see
Like unto him we'll truly be.
And he who has this hope within,
Will purify himself from sin.

Who keep this object grand in view,
To folly, sin, will bid adieu,
Nor wallow in the mire anew;

Nor ever seek to carve his name
High on the shaft of worldly fame;
But here his ultimatum trace:
The head of all his spirit-race.

Ah, well: that taught by you, dear Paul,
'Though much amazed, we see it all;
Our Father God, has ope'd our eyes,
We cannot view it otherwise.

The boy, like to his father grown,
Has but attained unto his own;
To grow to sire from state of son,
Is not 'gainst Nature's course to run.

A son of God, like God to be,
Would not be robbing Deity;
And he who has this hope within,
Will purify himself from sin.

You're right, St. John, supremely right:
Whoe'er essays to climb this height,
Will cleanse himself of sin entire—
Or else 'twere needless to aspire.[11]

Each of these prophets understood that as men "overcome all things," they shall become "gods, even the sons of God—wherefore, all things are theirs, whether life or death, or things present, or things to come, all are theirs and they are Christ's, and Christ is God's." (D&C 76:58-60; compare D&C 88:29; 132:20.)

Because of Christ's exaltation, "every knee should bow... and ... every tongue should confess that Jesus Christ is Lord, to the glory of God the Father." (Philip. 2:10-11.) Elder Bruce R. McConkie indicated that the timing of this is dependent on the timing of Christ himself:

Since Christ is the Savior, since all things pertaining to life and salvation center in him, since he is God—it follows that all men must turn to him and his gospel for salvation, and that in his own due time he shall receive the worship and adoration of all men. Indeed, to all men, by the mouth of Isaiah, Israel's Jehovah said: "Look unto me, and be ye saved, all the ends of the earth: for I am God, and there is none else. I have sworn by myself, the word is gone out of my mouth in righteousness, and shall not return, That unto me every knee shall bow, every tongue shall swear" (Isa. 45:22-23).[12]

Working Out Our Own Salvation

Because Christ has set the pattern by working out his salvation, it now becomes necessary and possible for all individuals to work out their own salvation. This, according to Paul, should be done "with fear and trembling." (Philip. 2:12.) In the "midst of a crooked and perverse nation," the saints are to be a light in the world. No matter how challenging and overpowering the world will become, it will be through God, "which worketh in [them] both to will and to do of his good pleasure" (Philip. 2:13), that their perfection will come. Therefore, they should "do all things without murmurings and disputings." (Philip. 2:14.) If they do this, they will know that they have not served in vain.

Paul understood this principle. He indicated, "I have not run in vain, neither laboured in vain." (Philip. 2:16.) He had assurance that all the sacrifice and persecution that he had experienced was for the glory of God. The Philippians' own example of sacrifice was Epaphroditus, who left his home to travel to Rome to minister to Paul. He drew "nigh unto death, not regarding his life, to supply [his] lack of service" toward Paul. (Philip. 2:30.) Paul had to send Epaphroditus back home with the instructions that the Philippians "receive him therefore in the Lord with all gladness; and hold such in reputation." (Philip. 2:29.)

In Paul's life, he had lost everything that he once thought was important and instead gained a special witness of Christ. When he was known as Saul, he was circumcised on the eighth day of life as a member of the tribe of Benjamin. He studied the law and became a Pharisee. He lived that law and life to the point of zealously fighting against that which he saw as a threat to it. Thus, the Christians became his target, and as a result of his conversion, he lost it all. He probably lost close friendships and maybe even family. He definitely lost social and political positions. Yet, he said, he counted "all things but loss for the excellency of the knowledge of Christ Jesus my Lord: for whom I have suffered the loss of all things, and do count them but dung, that I may win Christ." (Philip. 3:8.)

Paul gained so much more than he lost. He came to realize that it was not through the law of the Pharisees, which he so strongly defended, that salvation comes, but rather "through the faith of Christ, the righteousness which is of God by faith." (Philip. 3:9.) He, through that faith, had now come to the knowledge of the "power of his resurrection, and the fellowship of his sufferings, being made conformable unto his death." (Philip. 3:10.) Paul realized that he had not yet arrived at his exalted station, but he did commit to the Philippians that he would "press toward the mark for the prize of the high calling of God in Christ Jesus." (Philip. 3:14.) He invited the Philippians to "be followers together" of him (Philip. 3:17) in working out their salvation.

Paul recognized the difficulties of the challenge. To have to "press" meant that there would be resistance from the world. Yet, with "our conversation . . . in heaven" (Philip. 3:20), he said, it could be done. "It is true that we each have imperfections to overcome," Elder Theodore M. Burton observed. "Life is a constant series of challenges and trials. Notwithstanding, we should never fail to strive for that perfection of life which can bring us closer into harmony with God."[13] Paul understood that it was through the suffering of Christ that all "might attain unto the resurrection of the dead." (Philip. 3:11.)

The result of the struggle for perfection will be a desire for things that are good and uplifting. Paul counseled the saints to seek after those things which are true, honest, just, pure, lovely, virtuous, and of good report. In fact, he instructed them to "think on these things." In other words, such things should be a part of a saint's being. (Philip. 4:8.) This will be a direct result of the feeling of testimony and commitment to the doctrine of the gospel that the behavior of righteous living will take place. "It is only when gospel ethics are tied to gospel doctrines that they rest on a sure and enduring foundation and gain full operation in the lives of the saints," Elder McConkie wrote.[14] Joseph Smith understood the same principle when he wrote the thirteenth article of faith based on Paul's writings. At another time, Paul taught that "the fruit of the Spirit is love, joy, peace, longsuffering, gentleness, goodness, faith, meekness, temperance." (Gal. 5:22-23.) To live a good life just because it is the ethical thing to do is not enough. There must be a spiritual power behind the act. As Elder McConkie explained:

> Conformity to the highest ethical standards is the natural outgrowth of believing the eternal truths that save. Morality, chastity, virtue, benevolence—all that is "virtuous, lovely, or of good report or praiseworthy"—these are the fruits of the gospel. It follows that the saints of God conform to the Word of Wisdom; honor the Sabbath day and keep it holy; pay their tithes and offerings gladly and not grudgingly; provide for the poor among them (currently through the great Welfare Program of the kingdom); identify their dead ancestors and perform the ordinances of salvation and exaltation for them in the temples of the Most High; labor freely and anxiously in the missionary cause; consecrate their time and talents freely and willingly for the furtherance of the Lord's work; endure persecution without flinching; and face martyrdom without fear—all because they know of the truth and divinity of the doctrines of salvation they have received.[15]

If the saints are willing to sacrifice for Christ, they will also be willing to live for Christ.

Paul knew the results that would come from living a life patterned after Christ. He knew that a firm foundation of testimony based on the knowledge of gospel doctrine would lead to desirable results. He knew Christ. He had a strong testimony of his divine mission. He understood the doctrines of the gospel and how they applied to daily living. He had lived for Christ, preached for Christ, suffered for Christ. He now sat as a prisoner waiting for what would eventually be a death sentence. Yet he was able to promise the Philippian saints, and all saints, that if they would follow the doctrines of Christ, "the peace of God, which passeth all understanding, shall keep [their] hearts and minds through Christ Jesus." (Philip. 4:7.) After all, Christ is the Prince of Peace. His promise to his disciples was: "Peace I leave with you, my peace I give unto you: not as the world giveth, give I unto you. Let not your heart be troubled, neither let it be afraid." (John 14:27.) He is, therefore, the "founder of peace." (Mosiah 15:18.) Paul understood, as he sat as a prisoner, that the peace promised would be internal and not external. A latter-day apostle, John Taylor, understood the full meaning of this type of peace when he said:

> Some in speaking of war and troubles, will say are you not afraid? No, I am a servant of God, and this is enough, for Father is at the helm. It is for me to be as clay in the hands of the potter, to be pliable and walk in the light of the countenance of the Spirit of the Lord, and then no matter what comes. Let the lightnings flash and the earthquakes bellow, God is at the helm, and I feel like saying but little, for the Lord God Omnipotent reigneth and will continue his work until he has put all enemies under his feet and his kingdom extends from the rivers to the ends of the earth.[16]

With this type of faith and commitment, a person will know that "he who doeth the works of righteousness shall receive his reward, even peace in this world, and eternal life in the world to come." (D&C 59:23.)

Paul was able to promise the saints, "Those things, which ye have both learned, and received, and heard, and seen in me, *do*: and the God of peace shall be with you." (4:9; emphasis added.) Paul was at peace. He had learned, "In whatsoever state I am, therewith to be content." (4:11.) No matter what happened to Paul, whether it be hunger, imprisonment, or suffering, he would "do all things through Christ which strengtheneth" him. (4:13.) He knew that he would achieve his eternal goal. We, too, must have the same patience and faith.

The Philippian saints, as they read this epistle, probably responded as a latter-day apostle, Spencer W. Kimball, did when he thought of Paul:

> I have a great admiration and affection for our brother Paul, our fellow apostle. He was so dedicated, so humble, so straightforward. He was so eager, so interested, so consecrated. He must have been personable in spite of his problems, for the people hung onto him with great affection when he was about to leave them.
>
> I love Paul, for he spoke the truth. He leveled with people. He was interested in them. I love Paul for his steadfastness,

even unto death and martyrdom. I am always fascinated with his recounting of the perils through which he passed to teach the gospel to member and nonmember.[17]

Notes

1. J. R. Dummelow, *A Commentary on the Holy Bible* (New York: Macmillan Co., 1930), p. 969.

2. Ibid., p. 969.

3. Edgar J. Goodspeed, *Paul* (Philadelphia: The John C. Winston Co., 1947), pp. 199-200.

4. *Teachings of Spencer W. Kimball,* ed. Edward L. Kimball (Salt Lake City: Bookcraft, 1982), p. 132.

5. Bruce R. McConkie, *Doctrinal New Testament Commentary,* 3 vols. (Salt Lake City: Bookcraft, 1965-70): 2:530.

6. Francis M. Lyman, *Conference Report,* April 1904, p. 11.

7. *Teachings of the Prophet Joseph Smith,* comp. Joseph Fielding Smith (Salt Lake City: Deseret Book, 1976), p. 347.

8. Ibid., p. 345.

9. Ibid., p. 346.

10. Ibid., pp. 346-47.

11. *Improvement Era* 22 (June 1919): 660-61.

12. McConkie, *Doctrinal New Testament Commentary* 2:534.

13. *Conference Report,* October 1973, p. 151.

14. Bruce R. McConkie, *A New Witness for the Articles of Faith* (Salt Lake City: Deseret Book, 1985), p. 700.

15. Ibid., pp. 701-2.

16. John Taylor, *Journal of Discourses* 10:58.

17. *Teachings of Spencer W. Kimball,* p. 483.

9

THE PREEMINENCE OF CHRIST
(Colossians)

CLYDE J. WILLIAMS

In the fourth and fifth centuries B.C., the community of Colossae was described as a "populous city, prosperous and great." By the first century A.D., however, it had declined in size and importance. Located approximately twelve miles east of Laodicea in a volcanic region of western Turkey, Colossae was the site of a growing branch of the church. Little is known of this branch other than what we can ascertain from the letter written to the Colossians and the letter to Philemon, who was a member residing in Colossae at the time.

Though it is difficult to determine the date and the precise location of Paul's whereabouts, it is likely that Colossians was written from Rome in about A.D. 60 while Paul was imprisoned there. It would appear that Paul had not visited Colossae prior to his writing this letter. (See 1:4; 2:1.) We do know that he had a strong desire to visit this community, as he expressed in his letter to Philemon. (Philem. 1:22.) Not many years later, according to one writer, "the town was ruined by an earthquake, and its site was not excavated until the nineteenth century."[1]

To understand the message and reason for this Pauline epistle, it will be helpful to identify some of the key characters mentioned in the text. Epaphras was apparently Paul's representative in Colossae (Col. 1:7-8), the person who probably brought word to Paul that false doc-

---

Clyde J. Williams is assistant professor of ancient scripture at Brigham Young University.

trines of serious proportion were creeping in among the Colossian saints. It was not Epaphras, however, who would deliver the letter to the Colossians. This was done by Tychicus and Onesimus, who were returning to Colossae. (Col. 4:7-9.) Onesimus was a fugitive slave of Philemon, who was returning at the suggestion of Paul.[2] Tychicus had been associated with Paul for some time, having accompanied him, as a representative of the churches in Asia, on Paul's journey to Jerusalem. (Acts 20:4.) He was also well known to the saints at Ephesus. (Eph. 6:21-22 and 2 Tim. 4:12.)

From a careful reading of the Colossian letter, one can readily observe Paul's concern and reaction to perverted doctrines that were creeping in among the church members. (Col. 2:4, 8.) For Latter-day Saints, this letter is one additional evidence of the impending apostasy that would engulf the Christian church after the death of the apostles. Even many Christian commentators refer to the problems alluded to by Paul as the Colossian "heresy."[3] We cannot determine with certainty the exact origin of the subversive teachings in Colossae. However, it would appear that a combination of influences was beginning to undermine this branch of the church. As one writer said, "The trouble of Colossae was 'syncretism'—that tendency to introduce ideas from other philosophies and religions on a level with Christian truth."[4] Judging by Paul's response, the most serious doctrinal departure in Colossae had to do with the doctrine of Christ: his nature, his mission, and his preeminence. Worldly philosophies and doctrines were challenging the position of Christ as head of the church and kingdom of God. (Col. 2:8, 18-19.)

The message to the Colossians can be summarized in three major topics: the preeminence of Christ, false doctrines that seek to undermine the doctrine of Christ, and principles that will help us become like Christ.

The Preeminence of Christ

The Lord and Savior Jesus Christ surpassed all other beings who have lived and will live on this earth. He is the literal son of God the Father (Col. 1:3), and because of his life and atoning sacrifice, we have a hope of obtaining eternal life with our Father in heaven (Col. 1:5). This hope has been made known to prophets in all generations of the world. (1:6.) As we endeavor to live worthily and to attain eternal life, we must be filled with a knowledge of what our Heavenly Father expects of us. This kind of knowledge comes only through the Spirit. (1:9.) Elder Bruce R. McConkie wrote that it is this spiritual understanding or knowledge that "sets the saints apart from the world. Others may equal or excel them in scientific knowledge, in philosophical comprehension, or in any of the things of the world, but only the saints of God do or can understand the things of God, for these come by revelation. For instance, only the saints understand the atonement, comprehend the doctrines of salvation, enjoy the gifts of the Spirit, receive the spiritual rebirth, exercise faith unto life and salvation, and have a sure hope of eternal life."[5] It is revelation and a knowledge of God's will that can spur us on to be fruitful in doing righteous works. (Col. 1:10-11.)

In our day as well as Paul's, spiritual darkness reigns. Our Heavenly Father provided the means whereby we could escape the darkness by sending his Son. Through Christ's redemption we can gain forgiveness and be transformed from a carnal nature to a divine nature, a point at which we are entitled to an inheritance in the celestial kingdom. (Col. 1:12-14.)

Paul refers to Christ as the firstborn in two different passages in chapter one of Colossians. A review of the scriptures reveals that Jesus is the firstborn in three very significant ways. (1) He is the firstborn spirit son of God, the firstborn of all creation. (Col. 1:15.) "His is the eternal birthright and the everlasting right of presidency," wrote Elder McConkie.[6] As the firstborn, it was Jehovah's right to be chosen and foreordained as the Savior. It would also be his right, under the direction of the Father, to create worlds without number. (Col. 1:16; see also Moses 1:33.) (2) Jesus Christ is the literal son of God the Father. (1:3.) He is the Only Begotten or firstborn of the Father in the flesh. (See John 1:14.) Because of his divine birth, both in the spirit and in the flesh, it is particularly appropriate to refer to him as being in the image of his Father, whom we have not seen. (Col. 1:15; see also Heb. 1:3.) (3) The Savior is the firstborn from the dead. (1:18.) Because of his unique birth, he had power over death and was able to rise from the dead.

These three qualities give Christ preeminence over all things. Because of his unique mortal birth and his resurrected body, he could possess the fullness of the Godhead. (Col. 1:19; 2:9.) In clarifying this concept, Elder McConkie wrote: "In other words, in Christ is found every godly attribute in its perfection, which means that the Father dwells in him and he in the Father."[7] This same promise—that the Father can dwell in us—is offered to all people. As we perfect our lives, we can become one with the Father and the Son. Concerning this principle the Prophet Joseph Smith explained: "All those who keep his commandments shall grow up from grace to grace, and become heirs of the heavenly kingdom, and joint heirs with Jesus Christ; possessing the same mind, being transformed into the same image or likeness, even the express image of him who fills all in all; being filled with the fullness of his glory, and become one in him, even as the Father, Son and Holy Spirit are one."[8]

The mission of Jesus Christ, as the firstborn Son of God, was to offer himself as a ransom for the sins of all mankind. In this way he was able to help us be reconciled to God even though we have all committed sins and have thus been enemies to God. (Col. 1:20-22.) Furthermore, as we are reconciled to God we also become reconciled to Christ and join those who the Father promised would be given unto the Son. (John 17:11, 20.) This process of being reconciled or having Christ atone for our sins places certain conditions on us, as Paul explained to the Colossian saints. We must seek to become holy by removing sin from our lives, so we can stand blameless before God (Col. 1:22), which requires that we be firmly rooted or established in the principles of the gospel. (Col. 1:22-23.)

Paul's indication that the gospel has been preached to every creature under heaven must refer to its being preached in the pre-earth life (Col. 1:23), for only in that setting had all of our Father's children heard it preached.

There are mysteries that God has not seen fit to reveal, nor will he do so until after the coming of the Son of Man. (See D&C 101:32-34.) There are also mysteries that we may call the mysteries of godliness, which are made known by revelation to those who demonstrate maturity and obedience and who diligently seek them from the scriptures. The mystery about which Paul speaks to the Colossians is one of the mysteries of godliness. (1:26-27.) This mystery, which, if understood by modern Christians, would reveal to them the true nature and oneness of the Godhead, has been explained by Elder McConkie: "It is that Christ dwells in the hearts of those who have crucified the old man of sin, and that as a consequence they have a hope of eternal glory!"[9] It is a key to understanding why the scriptures speak of the oneness of the Godhead and yet maintain that they are also three separate and distinct individuals, and why we can become one with Christ in the same manner that Christ is one with his Father. (3 Ne. 19:23, 29.)

Among the Colossian saints, ideas of mysticism and hidden knowledge were apparently flourishing. Judging by the concerns voiced by Paul in the second chapter of Colossians, the saints were entertaining, as one writer described it, "the germs of later Gnosticism."[10] The Gnostics were followers of many religious movements in the early history of Christianity. They believed that people were saved through a secret or esoteric knowledge, and that the physical creation was evil. Many did not believe the physical body was necessary, and thus they often practiced one of two extremes: either complete self-denial toward physical matters, particularly sex and marriage, or total promiscuity, since in their view the body could not affect the spirit and would be destroyed forever at death.[11]

Perhaps it was the emphasis on secret knowledge and mysteries that caused Paul to declare that real wisdom and knowledge are known only through the Son of God. (Col. 2:2-3.) This knowledge comes by revelation.

Avoiding False Doctrine

Today and in all ages there are those who use the power of persuasive speech and the philosophies and wisdom of the world to try to dissuade the faithful from the strait and narrow path. (Col. 2:4, 8.) Paul's unwavering response is to remember that it is in Jesus Christ, whose mission and role he reaffirms, that we must build our faith if we hope to be saved. (Col. 2:6-7.) False philosophies and supposed secret knowledge appear to have been challenging the very position and status of the Son of God. Paul reaffirms that Christ possesses the fullness of the Godhead *bodily.* (Col. 2:9.) Some pre-Gnostic Christians at

Colossae may have been denying, as many Christians do today, that Christ needed or yet possesses his physical body. (Compare 1 Jn. 4:2; 2 Jn. 1:7.) Concerning Colossians 2:9 Richard L. Anderson has written: "Many commentators sidestep the [word *bodily*] by claiming that it can mean essentially or really. But Paul used *sōmatikôs,* formed from *sôma,* the Greek word for body, which Paul uses equally for man's earthly body and Christ's resurrected body. Thus, Paul testifies that Christ possesses godhood *physically.*"[12]

Paul declares the corporeal nature of the Godhead. Jesus Christ is the head, the chief cornerstone upon which the kingdom of God on earth is built. (Col. 2:19; Eph. 2:20.) It is in Christ that we can find complete fulfillment or perfection (Col. 2:10), not in the law of man and all its warnings, ordinances, holy days, or Sabbath days (Col. 2:14-16). All of these were a mere shadow, a type of things to come. The real substance, the real message is that we can be perfected only in and through Jesus Christ. (Col. 2:17.)

Paul warns of other dangerous teachings that were apparently gaining acceptance in Colossae. There were those who were becoming puffed up in their false humility, declaring marvelous things they claimed to have witnessed and turning themselves to worshiping angels rather than Christ. (Col. 2:18-19.) According to Richard L. Anderson, "Paul warns them not to be led astray from Christ by anyone who gives himself over to 'worship of the angels' or various ascetical practices connected with this. Paul could also have been thinking of some kind of imitation of pagan mystery rites where the aspirant was introduced into membership through alleged 'visions of angels.'"[13]

These detractors pride themselves on what they perceive is their superior intellect and self-made system of worship. (Col. 2:18, 23.) Moreover, their Gnostic attitude of neglecting the body and its passions and subjecting themselves to meaningless man-made rules has given them a false sense of superiority. (Col. 2:20, 23.) Though the diabolical approaches may differ, every dispensation is challenged by false philosophical and doctrinal ideas fostered by those who "when they are learned . . . think they are wise, and they hearken not unto the counsel of God, for they set it aside, supposing they know of themselves, wherefore, their wisdom is foolishness and it profiteth them not. And they shall perish." (2 Ne. 9:28.)

Becoming Like Christ

To raise the Colossian saints from the grasp of apostate practices, Paul reminds them that through baptism they have each buried their former sins and worldly teachings, and through the power of God they have been raised to a new life of faith and understanding. (Col. 2:12, 20; 3:1.) Those who accept and live the gospel of Jesus Christ are spiritually circumcised, with their carnal natures or desires removed, and they become completely open and receptive to the influence of the Holy Ghost. (Col. 2:11.) When this occurs, Paul says, they will seek the things of a better life. Obtaining a celestial glory and exaltation requires that the heart and mind be set firmly on spiritual things. We must become dead to sin and ultimately have our callings and elections made sure in order to appear with Christ at his coming. (Col. 3:1-4.)[14]

In order to reach that lofty goal, Paul explains that we must progress toward perfection by putting off the "old man," the carnal man, and putting on the "new man," the spiritual man, with all the attributes that must accompany this new birth. (Col. 3:9-10.) The process requires mortifying or subduing our physical bodies, thus avoiding sins of commission. Fornication, lust, idolatry, anger, profanity, and lying are among the sins that must be overcome if we are to continue the new birth process. (Col. 3:5-9.)

Next Paul turns to principles that are sometimes neglected by the saints, thus preventing them from approaching perfection and having their callings and elections made sure. These qualities are among the attributes of godliness: meekness, longsuffering, forgiveness, and charity (which binds all the other principles together). (Col. 3:12-15.) Persons who possess these virtues will no longer see themselves divided by nationality, ideology, or social classes; all will be one with Christ. (Col. 3:11.)

In this process of becoming like Christ, Paul reminds us of the powerful impact of spiritual hymns and songs sung from the heart. All who have experienced the exultation that comes from meaningful words and inspiring music know why Paul includes this encouragement to those who are seeking to become one with Christ. (Col. 3:16.) Commenting on the power of music, President J. Reuben Clark said: "Sometimes I feel that we get nearer to the Lord through music than perhaps through any other thing except prayer."[15]

Recognizing that many interactions in this life are done in the home, Paul counsels the Colossians in their relationships as husbands, wives, and children. (3:18-21.) In emphasizing this point, President Spencer W. Kimball declared: "God established families. The Lord organized the whole program in the beginning with a father who procreates, provides, and loves and directs, and a mother who conceives and bears and nurtures and feeds and trains . . . [and] where children train and discipline each other and come to love, honor, and appreciate each other. The family is the great plan of life as conceived and organized by our Father in Heaven."[16] President Kimball taught on another occasion: "Family life is the best method for achieving happiness in this world, and it is a clear pattern . . . of what is to be in the next world."[17]

The final counsel Paul gives pertains to the missionary responsibilities of those who possess the mystery of Christ. We are to use wisdom in watching for the opportunities to share the gospel with nonmembers (Col. 4:3-5), and if we set a proper example, others will see the benefit of having the gospel in their lives. We are also counseled to study and prepare ourselves so that we may know how to answer investigators without giving them advanced doctrine when they are only prepared for the basic principles. (Col. 4:6.) This principle was important for the Colossians, for they were receiving much advanced doctrine in this letter from Paul. It was not to be shared indiscriminately with those who had no foundation in the gospel. To do so would likely place stumbling blocks in the path of those who were investigating the faith.

Colossians Today

The message to the Colossians is both timely and relevant for us. Many persons in the Christian world today deny the preeminence of Christ, both in his mortal mission and in his divine Sonship. Unfortunately many also rely upon what they perceive as their superior learning. In their wisdom, they feel no need to become like Christ or to conform to those principles which lead to perfection. The sins and diversions found at Colossae were in principle the same as those that we face today. The process of becoming like Christ has been and always will be the same. Paul's epistle to the Colossians contains the true doctrine of Christ, doctrine that, when understood and applied in our lives, will move us toward exaltation in the kingdom of God.

Notes

1. G. H. P. Thompson, *The Letters of Paul to the Ephesians, to the Colossians and to Philemon*, The Cambridge Bible Commentary (London: Cambridge University Press, 1967), p. 112.

2. See David R. Seely, "From Unprofitable Servant to Beloved Brother in Christ," chapter 11, in this volume.

3. See *The New Bible Commentary*, D. Guthrie, et al., ed. (Grand Rapids, Michigan: William B. Eerdmans Publishing Co., 1970), p. 1140; *The Interpreter's Bible*, 12 vols. (Nashville, Tennessee: Abingdon Press, 1955), 11:137; J. R. Dummelow, *A Commentary on the Holy Bible* (New York: Macmillan, 1936), p. 980.

4. David and Pat Alexander, ed., *Eerdmans' Handbook to the Bible* (Grand Rapids, Michigan: William B. Eerdmans Publishing Co., 1973), p. 611.

5. Bruce R. McConkie, *Doctrinal New Testament Commentary*, 3 vols. (Salt Lake City: Bookcraft, 1966-73), 3:23-24.

6. Bruce R. McConkie, *A New Witness for the Articles of Faith* (Salt Lake City: Deseret Book, 1985), p. 66.

7. Bruce R. McConkie, *The Promised Messiah: The First Coming of Christ* (Salt Lake City: Deseret Book, 1978), p. 128.

8. *Lectures on Faith* (Salt Lake City: Deseret Book, 1985), 5:2.

9. McConkie, *The Promised Messiah*, p. 124.

10. Marvin R. Vincent, *Word Studies in the New Testament*, 4 vols. (McLean, Virginia: McDonald Publishing Co., n.d.), 3: xxxv.

11. Edwin M. Yamauch, "The Gnostics," in *Eerdmans' Handbook to the History of Christianity* (Carmel, New York: Guideposts, 1977), pp. 98-103.

12. Richard Lloyd Anderson, *Understanding Paul* (Salt Lake City: Deseret Book, 1983), p. 254.

13. Joseph A. Grassi, "The Letter to the Colossians," in *The Jerome Biblical Commentary*, 2 vols., ed. Raymond E. Brown, et al. (Englewood Cliffs, New Jersey: Prentice Hall, 1968), 2:339.

14. McConkie, *Doctrinal New Testament Commentary* 3:35.

15. *Conference Report,* October 1936, p. 111.

16. *The Teachings of Spencer W. Kimball,* ed. Edward L. Kimball (Salt Lake City: Bookcraft, 1982), p. 324.

17. *Ensign,* November 1978, p. 103.

10

HOPE FOR THE "CHILDREN OF LIGHT"
AS THE DARKNESS DESCENDS
(1, 2 Thessalonians)

JO ANN H. SEELY

The glorious Second Coming of the Lord Jesus Christ was anticipated by Paul and the Thessalonian converts with hope and joy. Paul
mentions this great event many times as he exhorts the saints in righteous living and instructs them concerning the dark events of the
great apostasy. It is this sustaining hope that enables them to endure
persecution and continue in faithfulness when left alone as a new
branch of the church. The Lord prepared the people of Thessalonica
for the visit of Paul and to receive this marvelous message, and Paul
himself was guided to them by inspiration. "And a vision appeared to
Paul in the night; there stood a man of Macedonia, and prayed him,
saying, Come over into Macedonia, and help us. And after he had seen
the vision, immediately we endeavoured to go into Macedonia, as-
suredly gathering that the Lord had called us for to preach the gospel
unto them." (Acts 16:9-10.)

Following the direction of the Spirit, Paul and his companions left
Asia Minor from Troas and sailed across the Aegean Sea to
Macedonia—a small part of a missionary journey, yet this one small
trip opened the door for the gospel of Jesus Christ to go beyond its
Asian home and enter a new continent. The missionaries were very
successful in their efforts in these first European cities and established

Jo Ann H. Seely has a master of arts degree in Near Eastern studies at Brigham
Young University.

churches at Philippi, Thessalonica, and Corinth, to which Paul later wrote several of his letters. The two letters to the Thessalonians are full of tender concern and further instruction for the new converts and provide us with an invaluable window into the development of the early church.

Paul began his second missionary journey with the intention of visiting the cities where he had previously taught. (Acts 15:36.) After a disagreement with Barnabas, he chose Silas (Silvanus in Thessalonians) to accompany him, "confirming the churches" through Syria and Cilicia. (Acts 15:41.) Silas, a member of the church in Jerusalem, had been sent by the apostles along with Judas (surnamed Barsabas) to carry the news of the Jerusalem Conference to Antioch both by letter and by word of mouth. (Acts 15:22-23, 27.) He is also noted as a prophet who exhorted the brethren there. (Acts 15:32.) Paul and Silas were joined by Timothy (Timotheus in Thessalonians), a convert from Galatia who became a trusted companion of Paul. Timothy was sent by Paul on several ecclesiastical errands to new converts and was liaison between the converts when Paul was unable to visit. (1 Thes. 3:2, 6; 1 Cor. 4:17; 16:10; Philip. 2:19.) Paul commended him to the Philippians, saying, "For I have no man likeminded, who will naturally care for your state. . . . As a son with the father, he hath served with me in the gospel." (Philip. 2:20, 22.)

Twice the Spirit altered the paths of Paul and his companions, first directing their path away from Bithynia (Acts 16:7), and then through Paul's vision to come to Macedonia (Acts 16:9). They left Troas and went through Neapolis to Philippi, where they spent some time teaching the gospel, and then continued about ninety miles along the Via Egnatia—the major Roman road through Macedonia—to Thessalonica.

Thessalonica was a major city in Macedonia. Founded by the Macedonian king Cassander in 315 B.C., it was named after his wife, who was the daughter of Philip and half-sister of Alexander the Great. It became the seat of Roman administration when Macedonia was made a Roman province in 146 B.C. and was declared a free city by the Romans, which meant that it enjoyed a status free from taxation or military occupation, and the privilege of self-government.[1] Because of its location on the Via Egnatia, which ran from the western side of

Greece all the way through Macedonia, it was a center of commerce, as demonstrated by its prolific coinage; being situated on the coast, it was the chief seaport of the area.

Two inscriptions found at Thessalonica have significance for the scriptural record. The Vardar Gate inscription from a Roman arch spanning the Via Egnatia, dating to the period of Paul (between 30 B.C. and A.D. 143), notes city officials called "politarchs." These officials were responsible for the autonomous rule enjoyed at Thessalonica. Acts 17:6 refers to these officials as "the rulers of the city." Other occurrences of this term have been found epigraphically at Thessalonica, but it had otherwise been unknown in Greek literature.[2] Although no remains of the synagogue mentioned in Acts 17:1 have been found, another inscription with a Greek translation of Numbers 6:22-27 (the Aaronic benediction) and other Hebrew phrases attest to the diaspora community at Thessalonica.[3] As noted by one scholar, "Meletius long ago said, 'So long as nature does not change, Thessalonica will remain wealthy and fortunate.'"[4] It remains a large and prosperous city to this day.

At Thessalonica there was a synagogue, indicating a population with a substantial number of Jews, and Paul first went there to "reason" for three sabbath days. (Acts 17:1-2.) The scriptures record that he went right to the heart of the matter. He taught that the Messiah must suffer and be resurrected, "and that this Jesus, whom I preach unto you, is Christ." (Acts 17:3.) The simple truth of these words had a powerful yet divisive effect.

Paul's testimony converted Jews, a great multitude of Greeks, and many of the chief women. (Acts 17:4.) The Greeks are described as "devout," probably referring to the Gentile "god-fearers" who attached themselves to the synagogues of the diaspora because they preferred the worship of Israel to pagan practice. These believers were the early members of the church at Thessalonica who became examples "to all that believe in Macedonia and Achaia." (1 Thes. 1:7.)

Those who did not believe were so incensed that they not only forced the departure of the missionaries from Thessalonica and Berea, their next stopping point (Acts 17:10, 13-14), but they also persecuted the Thessalonian converts as they struggled to get established. There are many references to these afflictions in Paul's letters to this branch. (1 Thes. 1:6; 2 Thes. 1:4.) One of these incidents involved Jason, a convert who had offered hospitality and perhaps a kinsman of Paul. (Rom. 16:21.) The Jews in the city who "believed not" gathered an unruly mob and assaulted his house, searching for Paul and his companions. Unable to find the missionaries there, they seized Jason and took him before the "rulers of the city"—politarchs. (Acts 17:5-9.) There they charged him with harboring those who were guilty of treason, who proclaimed another king, "contrary to the decrees of Caesar." (Acts 17:7.) The other king was "one Jesus," and the charge was a serious problem in the Roman Empire at the time. Such rioting among the Jews over a certain "Chrestus" (probably a reference to Christ) had caused Claudius to expel them from Rome about this same time.[5] One writer comments: "The trouble in Rome had not been spontaneously generated there; it had been carried by visitors from the east. It was from the east, too, that these alleged trouble-makers had come to Thessalonica, carriers of what the emperor himself had described a few years earlier as 'a general plague which infests the whole world.'"[6] It is clear from Paul's letters that the Thessalonian saints had been somewhat confused concerning his teachings about the Second Coming of Jesus, and perhaps their overanxious enthusiasm had contributed to this problem.

The politarchs resolved the issue by making Jason responsible for the behavior of the missionaries, which in effect meant they must leave the city. Paul left and went to Athens and then on to Corinth, where he wrote his two letters to the Thessalonians. Timothy apparently accompanied him to Athens and then returned to Thessalonica. (1 Thes. 3:1-6.)

Paul passed through Macedonia on a few other occasions, but there are no specific details of other visits to Thessalonica. (Acts 19:21; 20:1-3.) References to the Thessalonian saints found in other letters by Paul are positive reflections of his joy in their faithfulness and their generosity in sending gifts and support to other members of the church. (2 Cor. 8:1-5; 11:9; Rom. 15:26.)

The Letters

Paul's letters to the Thessalonians were written shortly after his visit there. (1 Thes. 2:17.) Timothy joined him in Corinth after visiting in Thessalonica, where he had been sent to see about the welfare of the young branch, and bore good tidings concerning the converts there. (1 Thes. 3:1-2, 6-7; Acts 18:5.) This report prompted Paul's first communication, and it appears that 2 Thessalonians was written not long after.

The record in Acts 18 of the events during Paul's visit to Corinth makes it possible to date these letters fairly accurately. Paul was arraigned before Gallio, the proconsul of Achaia, while at Corinth. An inscription from Delphi preserves a letter from the Emperor Claudius to Gallio dating his tenure from July 1 A.D. 51. According to Acts 18:11, Paul spent a total of eighteen months in Corinth, and since he had already been there a considerable time before this incident, it is generally thought that he wrote the epistles to the Thessalonians in late A.D. 50 or in A.D. 51.[7]

1 and 2 Thessalonians are considered to be the earliest of Paul's epistles, and his authorship is virtually uncontested. Their canonicity is attested in the earliest lists of scriptural works, including that of Marcion the heretic and the Muratorian Fragment.[8] The dating between A.D. 50 and 51 means these letters were written less than twenty years after the resurrection of the Savior and thus provide invaluable primary information concerning the growth and trials of the very earliest Christians.

1 Thessalonians: Structure and Content

First Thessalonians is a brief letter consisting of four parts: a formal opening; an account of the missionaries' visit to Thessalonica; exhortations to righteous living and doctrinal exposition on the Second Coming of Christ; and a formal letter closing. It is positive in tone and concerned with the development of a new branch of the church.

1. Letter Opening
   a. Salutation (1:1)
   b. Thanksgiving (1:2-10)
2. Ministry at Thessalonica
   a. Missionaries' visit (2:1-12)
   b. Reception of the gospel (2:13-16)
   c. Concern for welfare of the saints (2:17–3:8)
   d. Thanksgiving and blessing (3:9-13)

3. Exhortation
   a. Sexual purity (4:1-8)
   b. Brotherly love (4:9-12)
   c. Christ's Second Coming (4:13–5:7)
   d. Various Christian duties (5:8-22)
4. Letter Closing
   a. Blessing (5:23-24)
   b. Salutation (5:25-28)

"Remembering without ceasing your work of faith, and labour of love, and patience of hope in our Lord Jesus Christ, in the sight of God and our Father; knowing, brethren beloved, your election of God." (1 Thes. 1:3-4.) This one short verse encapsulizes the essence of Paul's feelings, aspirations, and concerns for the Thessalonian saints. In his first letter to these new converts, he demonstrates that they are present in his mind and that he is aware of their good works. He instructs them in their labors and tries to strengthen them in their trials, knowing that all will be well if they are patient and continue in hope, whether they are present or among those who "sleep" at the coming of the Lord.

The seed of the gospel has been planted in new soil in Thessalonica, and Paul instructs the believers that faith, hope, and love will nourish it so that it may grow strong and bear good fruit. Paul repeats this message several times in his letters to the Thessalonians, helping them to cultivate the characteristics of faith, to purify and sanctify their lives, to establish a firm hope in the Second Coming, and to build a foundation of brotherhood and love to enable them to overcome the tribulations they face.

1. Letter Opening

The opening of the letter, typical of first century letters, refers to the sender and the receiver and has a special salutation from Paul. Paul's greeting (1:1) carries a uniquely Christian message of grace and peace that is a variation of the usual letter of the time.[9] He next includes a formal thanksgiving (1:2-10), expressing gratitude to God for the faithfulness of the Thessalonians, and this becomes a theme throughout these two letters. Between nearly every section of his writing Paul reiterates his thanks, especially for the faith and belief of the saints, and his fond feelings for them and happiness at knowing their spiritual state. He writes of the election of his brethren, stating that they not only received the message of the missionaries, but also received the gospel through the power and confirmation of the Holy Ghost (1:4-5). The spiritual strength derived from such a manifestation of the Spirit is evident in that they have remained steady even in much affliction (1:6), they have been examples of this new faith to those around them (1:7-8), and they have been able to divorce themselves from their former life of idol worship (1:9).

The noun used here for *affliction* (Gr. *thlipsis*) means tribulation caused by outward circumstances, and in extra-biblical Greek it takes the sense of pressing or pressure.[10] One scholar explains, "The corresponding verb, for example, was used of pressing the grapes in winemaking till they burst asunder, and so metaphorically came to mean very great trouble."[11] The persecution of the saints was a major challenge, as evidenced by the repeated references Paul made to it in his letters to the Thessalonians.

The converts not only set an example for believers, as noted in verse 7, but they also became missionaries to nonbelievers beyond the province of Macedonia and into Achaia, for Paul found their reputation had preceded him there. It is significant that among these new missionaries there were not only converted Jews and god-fearers, as one might surmise from the record in Acts, but there were also a number of Gentile converts, for Paul says they have "turned to God from idols to serve the living and true God." (1:9.) The conviction that caused these saints to turn from their false gods came through the power of the Holy Ghost and gives further assurance to the truth of the gospel and reconfirms the great conversion that had taken place here.

2. Ministry at Thessalonica

What better example of missionary service could the Thessalonians have had than that set by Paul, certainly the epitome of a virtuous minister of the gospel? And yet in the next segment of his letter he discusses the blameless behavior of him and his companions. It is possible that part of the persecution of the saints had been caused by accusations against Paul and his companions. In Thessalonica at that time were many zealous but ephemeral preachers of all sorts, persons with ulterior motives. Perhaps they had classified Paul and his companions in the same category, challenging the newly acquired belief of the saints. Dio Chrysostom (Cocceianus), an orator and philosopher of the late first and early second century, details what these religionists were like: "The normal heathen 'missionaries' . . . were itinerant apostles and miracle workers of the most varied persuasions, heralds of heathen gods, and dispensers of salvation, adroit and eloquent, ardent and evoking ardor, but also smart and conceited in extolling the mighty acts of their gods and fooling the masses."[12]

In defending the saints' missionary labor, Paul perhaps purposely points out the gulf between them and the charlatans. He reminds them of his and his companions' suffering at Philippi, and says that although they were both persecuted and insulted, they still taught the gospel without fear, "with much contention" (2:2). This last phrase is somewhat misleading in the King James Version, for here the term *contention* (Gr. *agōn*) means conflict. It has been translated in the Revised Standard Version as "in the face of great opposition." Paul and his companions taught without deceit or guile, without flattery or covetousness, and only to please God, not for the glory of men (2:3-6), he tells them. He also points out that they labored for their own support, disavowing any financial motives (2:6, 9). Yet their boldness in the gospel did not diminish their tender concern for the saints of Thessalonica. Several phrases give us a small glimpse of the intensity of their feelings: "We were gentle among you, even as a nurse cherisheth her children" (2:7); "being affectionately desirous of you" (2:8); and "we exhorted and comforted and charged every one of you, as a father doth his children" (2:11). Finally Paul calls upon both the converts (2:1) and God (2:5) as witnesses of all he and his companions said and of their irreproachable behavior. In verse 10, referring to the need to establish the truth by more than one witness, he uses familiar scriptural language, saying, "Ye are witnesses, and God also."

Following his defense of his missionary work, Paul focuses on the saints themselves. He writes of their sufferings for the second time, pointing out that they are suffering as others have, and in particular the churches established in Judea (2:14-16); both are persecuted of their own countrymen. This perhaps provides some comfort to the

Thessalonians in knowing they are not alone in their plight. Having been prevented by his enemies from visiting them again, Paul also tries to comfort the saints by rejoicing in the converts they have made and the assurance that they will be present at the return of the Lord Jesus Christ (2:19). In a beautiful and eloquent passage in the Doctrine and Covenants, the Lord describes this very feeling to Oliver Cowdery and David Whitmer. He tells them that they have been called with the same calling as "Paul mine apostle." Therefore, "remember the worth of souls is great in the sight of God. . . . And if it so be that you should labor all your days in crying repentance unto this people, and bring, save it be one soul unto me, how great shall be your joy with him in the kingdom of my Father! And now, if your joy will be great with one soul that you have brought unto me into the kingdom of my Father, how great will be your joy if you should bring many souls unto me!" (D&C 18:9-16.)

In chapter 3, Paul again notes that while he himself was not able to return to Thessalonica, he had sent Timothy, and Timothy's report had encouraged him. He again recognizes the tribulation of the saints and notes that those who are appointed to salvation (5:9) are also appointed to tribulation (3:3-4). Before continuing, he gives thanks again and prays for the privilege of seeing the Thessalonians in person. He is pleased with their faith, and prays also that brotherly love will be among them (3:9-12). He concludes this section with a petition for them to be established with "hearts unblameable in holiness," foreshadowing what he is about to say and looking again with hope toward the coming of the Lord (3:13).

3. Exhortation

The first two sections of this letter comprise an introduction to the body of the letter that follows. Paul has offered greetings, thanksgiving, and praise, and he has shown deep concern for the saints as well as defended his credibility and labor as a minister of the gospel. In the following passages he offers basic guidelines for Christian living and doctrinal explanations of particular concerns of the church at Thessalonica. He is judicious in mixing exhortations and reproofs with praises and encouragement. He also discusses unanswered questions on the Second Coming.

The first instructions are ones Paul indicates the saints have already received from him (4:1-2). He gives them with the preface, "For this is the will of God, even your sanctification" (4:3), and tells them that God has called the saints to holiness (4:7). These instructions form a short New Testament code of holiness (4:1-4), one that stresses cleanliness in body and spirit, reminiscent both in language and spirit of the much lengthier and more comprehensive code of holiness spelled out in the Mosaic law in the Old Testament (esp. Lev. 17–26). The saints must learn how to possess their "vessel" (body) in sanctification and honor (4:4),[13] in order to be worthy of the Holy Spirit of which they are now heirs, being members of the church (4:8). Fornication is specifically prohibited, to clearly separate the saints from the Gentile society, which considered continence an unreasonable demand on men (4:3-4). The Greek *porneía* here refers not only to fornication but to any illicit sexual activity. According to the mores of the time, it was acceptable to have a mistress for sexual and intellectual companionship, and, further, certain religious rites promoted sexual activity outside of marriage.[14]

An increase in brotherly love (4:9-10), peace, and industry are all extolled. "Study to be quiet" (4:11) could also be rendered "seek strenuously to be still," or in other words, avoid argument to bring about peace.[15] The advice to work with their own hands so that they may "walk honestly toward them that are without" (4:12) seems to refer to a specific problem in this community of idleness, a discussion that is expanded in Paul's second letter to the Thessalonians. This might also be taken to mean that the believers must be good examples to others (4:9-12), or that there were idlers waiting for the imminent return of the Lord.

Next Paul addresses the questions concerning the Second Coming that apparently trouble the Thessalonians (4:13–5:7). It seems clear that he and his companions had taught about the resurrection and Second Coming while in Thessalonica, since in both of his letters he continually writes of this event. The initial question that caused doubt in this first generation of converts concerned those who had already passed on. Would they experience the great happenings of the Lord's return?

Although Paul obviously understood that a certain sequence of occurrences was necessary before this time, as seen in 2 Thessalonians 2, apparently these converts were confused and overly anxious. He clarifies the fact that all who believe—both the dead and the living—will be caught up to meet the Lord (4:14-17). In fact, the dead shall rise first, and those who are alive shall not "prevent" (*pre* = before, plus *venio* = come) or "come before" them (4:15).[16] The Joseph Smith Translation provides a better understanding of these verses and makes Paul's meaning more precise. In verse 15 the words "we which are alive" have been changed to read "they who are alive at the coming of the Lord, shall not prevent them who remain unto the coming of the Lord, who are asleep." The same change from *we* to *they* also occurs in verse 17.

The second question that naturally follows is, "When will Christ come?" Paul responds by declaring that the saints "know perfectly that the day of the Lord so cometh as a thief in the night" (5:2). He cannot tell them the time or chronological moment; they have already been taught that the Lord's appearance will be unexpected and they must not be caught unprepared. The image of the thief was first used by Jesus, as recorded in both Matthew (24:43-44) and Luke (12:39). To allay their apprehensions, Paul reminds the Thessalonians that they need not fear, for they are "the children of light" (5:5).

This image was also used by Jesus in teaching his disciples about the imminence of his death and the preciousness of their time with him. Jesus is the Light, and to his disciples he juxtaposed the light of his presence with the darkness of his absence: "Yet a little while is the light with you. Walk while ye have the light, lest darkness come upon you: for he that walketh in darkness knoweth not whither he goeth. While ye have light, believe in the light, that ye may be the children of light." (John 12:35-36.) We become spiritually begotten of Jesus Christ through accepting the gospel, and in this sense we become his children, or "children of light." Paul reminds the saints at Thessalonica that they have already accepted the gospel and received confirmation of the Holy Ghost and are therefore children of light. They have been taught the way to go and are not left wandering in darkness (5:5). In the Doctrine and Covenants these two images of the thief in the night and the children of light are also found together in a warning that the Lord has issued for the Latter-day Saints: "The coming of the Lord draweth nigh, and it overtaketh the world as a thief in the night—therefore, gird up your loins, that you may be the children of light, and that day shall not overtake you as a thief." (D&C 106:4-5.) The same counsel is given to those who had known Jesus, to the first generation of saints after his resurrection, and to this present generation, as all must be prepared for the day of the Lord.

Those who are of darkness are associated with things of the night, such as sleep and drunkenness. "Take heed to yourselves, lest at any time your hearts be overcharged with surfeiting, and drunkenness, and cares of this life, and so that day come upon you unawares." (Luke 21:34.) Children of light are cautioned to watch and be sober and to be wary of spiritual dangers. They are to put on "the breastplate of faith and love; and for an helmet, the hope of salvation" (5:8). Paul uses his famous armor imagery in conjunction with the triad of faith, hope, and love. He mentions only defensive armor, and these three traits are the defense par excellence against the darkness.

Following these doctrinal clarifications, Paul continues his instructions and counsel. The saints are admonished to love their leaders for their work's sake, to support the weak, to rejoice and pray, and to give thanks just as Paul has done throughout his letter. They are counseled not to hinder the Spirit or prophesyings, and to abstain from all appearance of evil (5:12-22). These directions, together with Paul's earlier exhortations for holiness, will lead the way to sanctification.

4. Letter Closing

Paul aptly closes his letter with a blessing for God to sanctify the saints and a prayer that they be preserved blameless in spirit, soul, and body until the coming of the Lord Jesus Christ. In his final greeting he tells them to greet one another with "an holy kiss" (5:26; rendered in the Joseph Smith Translation "an holy salutation"), and charges them to read the letter together.

2 Thessalonians: Structure and Content

Second Thessalonians is clearly a follow-up message to 1 Thessalonians, for it covers much of the same material and is only about half as long. It is also written as a formal letter with four parts: an opening, a doctrinal discussion on the Second Coming, prayers and petitions to the saints, and a closing.

1. Letter Opening
   a. Salutation (1:1-2)
   b. Thanksgiving (1:3-4)
   c. Judgment (1:5-12)
2. The Second Coming
   a. Apostasy (2:1-3)
   b. Sons of Perdition (2:4-12)
3. Prayers and Petitions
   a. Thanksgiving (2:13-14)
   b. Blessing (2:15-17)
   c. Request for prayer (3:1-5)
   d. Instructions concerning idlers (3:6-15)
4. Letter Closing
   a. Blessing (3:16)
   b. Salutation (3:17-18)

The Thessalonian saints' continued faithfulness and enthusiasm for the gospel are evident from Paul's second letter. He is joyful at their growth and goodness. His message is brief, dealing with few problems and again acknowledging his affection and concern for the converts. Silas and Timothy are included again as senders, indicating that the letter was written only a few months after the earlier letter, while they were still at Corinth, for Silas is not mentioned with Paul after this time. Paul is aware of continued persecution of the saints, further misunderstanding about the Second Coming, and a persisting problem with idleness, but he reaffirms his confidence in the branch at Thessalonica. (2 Thes. 3:4.)

1. Letter Opening

Following the greeting, Paul expresses thanks to the saints, noting that their faith "groweth exceedingly, and the charity of every one . . . toward each other aboundeth" (1:3). He recognizes that they are developing in the most basic elements of the gospel even in the face of persecutions (1:4). He has acknowledged their tribulation several times in his first letter, and here he addresses it with two responses.

First, he calls it a "manifest token of the righteous judgment of God," a sign or indication of the Lord that they are being prepared for his kingdom: "that ye may be counted worthy of the kingdom of God, for which ye also suffer" (1:5). Second, he points out that those who are inflicting the harm will find themselves divinely recompensed (1:6).

In both letters the Second Coming of the Lord is emphasized, and here Paul discusses it in terms of the final justice the Lord will dispense at his return. Those who "know not God, and that obey not the gospel of our Lord Jesus Christ" will be faced with "everlasting destruction from the presence of the Lord, and from the glory of his power" (1:8-9). Those who "know not God" does not seem to refer to those who are ignorant or have not had an opportunity to learn, but rather to those who refuse to know God, since this phrase is parallel with the next one, "that obey not the gospel of our Lord Jesus Christ." In his letter to the Romans Paul explains what happens to those who are unwilling to know God: "Because that which may be known of God is manifest in them; for God hath shewed it unto them ... even his eternal power and Godhead; so that they are without excuse: because that, when they knew God, they glorified him not as God, neither were thankful; but became vain in their imaginations, and their foolish heart was darkened. ... And even as they did not like to retain God in their knowledge, God gave them over to a reprobate mind ... being filled with all unrighteousness, fornication, wickedness, covetousness, maliciousness; full of envy, murder, debate, deceit, malignity." (Rom. 1:19-21, 28-29.)

Eternal life is the reward of those who come to know God: "And this is life eternal, that they might know thee the only true God, and Jesus Christ, whom thou hast sent." (John 17:3.) In modern revelation the Lord has appended to this the statement, "Receive ye, therefore, my law." (D&C 132:24.) To know God is to receive his law, and to obey the gospel of Jesus Christ is to eventually gain eternal life in the presence of the Father and the Son. It follows that those who do not receive and obey the law will be cut off from eternal life to "everlasting destruction." (2 Thes. 1:9.) In the Joseph Smith Translation this verse has been altered to read "punished with destruction from the presence of the Lord," meaning they are barred from the Lord's presence. The saints will then be glorified for righteously enduring their tribulation; great is their reward in heaven. (Matt. 5:11-12; Luke 6:22-23.)

2. The Second Coming

As he ascended into heaven, the resurrected Lord promised that he would one day return in his glory. (Acts 1:11.) In Thessalonica there was much anticipation among the saints that his return was imminent. It is clear from Paul's letters to them that the focal point of the gospel for them was this eschatological event, perhaps encouraged by Paul himself, who, realizing that the Second Coming was in the distant future, continued to write with hope about the appearance of Christ. In chapter 2 he explains the sequence of things that must happen before the Second Coming in order to erase any ambiguity or false impressions that remained among the saints that the event was imminent. In the latter days the Prophet Joseph Smith made several significant changes in his translation of this passage that increase our understanding and further clarify this passage.

First, in his second letter Paul taught that the saints should remain firm in what they have already been taught and not allow themselves to be shaken by others in word, spirit, or by letter (2 Thes. 2:2). The Joseph Smith Translation renders this passage "or be troubled by letter, *except ye receive it from us.*" Perhaps a forgery was circulating that reinforced the misunderstanding. In any case it is important that teachings or instructions come from those with proper authority. In the following verse the Joseph Smith Translation emphasizes the fact that the apostasy or falling away will come first—before the day of the Lord—by placing this phrase at the beginning of the verse (2:3). Richard Lloyd Anderson has written, "In Greek, 'falling away' is *apostasía,* derived from 'standing' and 'away' in the sense of evading and opposing authority. . . . Paul, of course, means a religious departure, just as the Greek translation of the Old Testament uses *apostasía* for a hypothetical 'rebellion' of all Israel against God (Josh. 22:22)."[17]

This "falling away" comes with the "man of sin," the "son of perdition" who "sitteth in the temple of God, shewing himself that he is God" (2:3-4). In the past, commentators have tried to interpret this verse in numerous ways, shedding little light on the subject. Recently, however, Dr. Anderson has given a lucid explanation of this difficult verse as an image of the apostasy. He finds the key in Paul's use of the word *temple.* "Almost always he used it figuratively—occasionally the body is a temple for God's Spirit, but usually the Church is the temple of God.... Elsewhere Paul teaches about Christ as cornerstone, apostles as foundation, and members fitting into their places as a 'holy temple in the Lord' (Eph. 2:21)."[18] In other words, the temple here is representative of the church in which God dwells. When the "man of sin" is revealed, *he* will be in the midst of the temple; the church remains, but Satan is in the midst of it. This imagery demonstrates that the great apostasy will take place through the influence of Satan, making the restoration of the gospel and the church necessary in the latter days.

This "mystery of iniquity" was already at work at the time of Paul. The archaic form of "he who now letteth will let" found in verse 7 has been replaced in the Joseph Smith Translation by "Christ suffereth him to work, until the time is fulfilled that he shall be taken out of the way." Verse 9 of the Joseph Smith Translation summarizes the entire process: "Yea, the Lord, even Jesus, whose coming is not until after there cometh a falling away, by the working of Satan with all power, and signs and lying wonders."

Those who will fall in error after Satan are those referred to earlier (1:8) and also as those who "received not the love of the truth ... that they all might be damned ["brought to account"—see footnote in LDS edition of the Bible] who believed not the truth, but had pleasure in unrighteousness" (2:10, 12). Seven or eight years later Paul noted, in writing to the Galatians: "I marvel that ye are so soon removed from him that called you into the grace of Christ unto another gospel." (Gal. 1:6.) The great apostasy began very early and proceeded until there was only darkness, which was not pierced until the light of the First Vision.

3. Prayers and Petitions

After a serious doctrinal discussion, Paul breaks to express his continual thankfulness to God for the sanctification of the saints and the hope of the gospel (2:13-17). It is appropriate that he also asks for their prayers for the missionaries themselves, perhaps so they will not experience the difficulties that had driven them from Thessalonica.

Before some rather direct exhortations, Paul takes one more opportunity to bolster the saints' spirits by praising their obedience and praying for their welfare (3:3-5).

The admonitions in 1 Thessalonians are gentle and given in the spirit of wise counsel: the saints are to do their own business, work with their own hands, and walk honestly toward those who are not of their group (1 Thes. 4:11-12.) In contrast, the language in the second letter is strong and to the point, even while addressing the same issues. The saints had already been reminded of the missionaries' hard work and orderly conduct, so the instructions are now given in the form of commands: to withdraw from those who are disorderly and from busybodies, to work and eat their own bread, and to not be weary in doing good (3:6, 10-11, 13).

Paul also indicts those who are disobedient: "If any would not work, neither should he eat" (3:10). This does not refer to those who are poor or unable to work, but those who *would* not work or who desire not to. Idleness is something the Lord has condemned throughout the scriptures. The Lamanites in times of disobedience were called an "idle people" (2 Ne. 5:24), and in the Doctrine and Covenants there are repeated warnings for the saints of latter days to "remember their labors, inasmuch as they are appointed to labor, in all faithfulness; for the idler shall be had in remembrance before the Lord" (D&C 68:30-31; see also 56:17; 60:13; 75:29). Paul ends on a positive note, enveloping the sharp reproval in verses 6 through 13 with the confidence he expressed in the saints earlier (3:4-5) and a gentle reminder to part company with the disobedient and to admonish them as brothers rather than as enemies (3:14-15).

4. Letter Closing

Concluding with a blessing of peace, Paul's final words note his personal signature on this letter, assuring of its authenticity (3:17). Like the rest of the Pauline epistles, 2 Thessalonians was probably dictated to a scribe, perhaps to Silas or Timothy, and then signed by Paul himself. The concluding blessing of peace from the "Lord of peace" (3:16) and of the "grace of our Lord Jesus Christ" (3:18) adds an aesthetic touch—a nice chiasm to Paul's opening blessing, "grace unto you, and peace, from God our Father and the Lord Jesus Christ" (1:2).

Conclusion

The seed of the gospel found good soil in Thessalonica. The fruits of the Spirit were manifest in the faithfulness and love exhibited by the saints there. Paul rejoices affectionately and gratefully in their development. They have grown in experience as they endure the tribulations faced by the infant church, and in knowledge as they are instructed in correct doctrine by Paul. Their challenges seem in many ways similar to those of the early congregations of Latter-day Saints in New York, Ohio, Missouri, and Illinois.

Paul's wise counsel to these new converts to sanctify their lives (1 Thes. 4:3) and to make their hearts "unblameable in holiness" (1 Thes. 3:13) is equally applicable to us. President Brigham Young said, "Do not be too anxious for the Lord to hasten this work. Let our anxiety be centered upon this one thing, the sanctification of our own hearts, the purifying of our own affections, the preparing of ourselves for the approach of the events that are hastening upon us. This should be our concern, this should be our study, this should be our daily prayer. . . . Seek to have the Spirit of Christ, that we may wait patiently the time of the Lord, and prepare ourselves for the times that are coming. This is our duty."[19]

The return of the Savior was a source of inspiration to both the first generation of saints and those of the Restoration. The knowledge that Christ would one day return sustained the Thessalonian saints as they faced persecution and the encroaching darkness of apostasy wrought by "the man of sin." Likewise, we as Latter-day Saints, confronted with the challenges presented by the darkness of an increasingly wicked world, are motivated to Christlike living by the knowledge of the return of the Light. The epistles to the Thessalonians provide insight into the pursuit of faith, hope, and love that must pervade the lives of all—past, present, and future—who would be called "children of light."

Notes

1. Pliny, *Natural History* IV. 36.
2. J. Finegan, "Thessalonica," in *Interpreter's Dictionary of the Bible,* 4

vols. and Supplement (New York and Nashville: Abingdon Press, 1962-76), 4:629.

3. C. L. Thompson, "Thessalonica," in *Interpreter's Dictionary of the Bible*, Supplement, p. 902.

4. J. B. Lightfoot, in *Biblical Essays* (London, 1893), p. 255, as quoted by Leon Morris, *The First and Second Epistles to the Thessalonians*, The New International Commentary on the New Testament (Grand Rapids, Michigan: William B. Eerdmans, 1959), p. 16, n. 2.

5. Seutonius, *Claudius* 25:4; Acts 18:2.

6. F. F. Bruce, *1 & 2 Thessalonians*, Word Bible Commentary 45 (Waco, Texas: Word Books, 1982): xxiii.

7. Ibid., p. xxxv.

8. Morris, *The First and Second Epistles to the Thessalonians*, p. 27.

9. See the discussion on this greeting in David R. Seely, "From Unprofitable Servant to Beloved Brother in Christ," chapter 11 in this volume, and references cited there.

10. Walter Bauer, *A Greek-English Lexicon of the New Testament*, rev. and ed., F. Wilbur Gingrich and Frederick W. Danker, 2nd ed. (Chicago: University of Chicago Press, 1979), p. 363.

11. Morris, *The First and Second Epistles to the Thessalonians*, p. 59.

12. G. Bornkamm, *Paul*, trans. D. M. G. Stalker (London: Hodder & Stoughton; New York: Harper and Row, 1971), p. 64, as quoted in Bruce, *1 & 2 Thessalonians*, p. 26.

13. For a discussion of the term *vessel*, see Richard Lloyd Anderson, *Understanding Paul* (Salt Lake City: Deseret Book, 1983), p. 78.

14. Morris, *The First and Second Epistles to the Thessalonians*, p. 121.

15. Ibid., p. 133.

16. Anderson, *Understanding Paul*, p. 79.

17. Ibid., p. 85.

18. Ibid., p. 86.

19. *Journal of Discourses*, 26 vols. (Liverpool: F. D. Richards and Sons, 1851-86), 9:3.

11

FROM UNPROFITABLE SERVANT
TO BELOVED BROTHER IN CHRIST
(Philemon)

DAVID R. SEELY

The epistle to Philemon was sent by Paul and his companion Timothy around A.D. 61, probably from Rome, where they were imprisoned. The letter is addressed primarily to Philemon, a member of the church in Colossae, but also to Apphia, Archippus, and the members of the church in Colossae who met in Philemon's house.

We can reconstruct the historical context of the epistle from the letter itself and from the accompanying epistle to the Colossians, which was apparently written by Paul at the same time. Colossae was a small city situated on the Lycus River, a tributary of the Maeander River, in west-central Asia Minor. Originally a Phrygian town, Colossae by the time of Paul had achieved the status of a Hellenized Roman city and was known for its textile industry. The Christian community at Colossae attributed its conversion to Epaphras, a native of the city (Col. 1:7; 4:12) who was also influential in the conversion of Christians in the larger neighboring cities of Laodicea and Hierapolis (Col. 4:13).

Since there is no scriptural record that Paul ever actually visited Colossae, most believe either that his personal acquaintances with the individuals there were made elsewhere or that they were relationships carried on strictly by correspondence. Cited as evidence for this

David R. Seely is assistant professor of ancient scripture at Brigham Young University.

conclusion is Paul's statement in the epistle to the Colossians, referring to the saints at Laodicea and Colossae, that he was concerned
about "as many as have not seen my face in the flesh." (Col. 2:1.)
Nevertheless, the statement in Philemon 1:19 that Philemon owed his
"own self" to Paul suggests that Paul had been instrumental in his conversion. It is conceivable that at some point in his ministry Paul visited
Colossae or at least had personal contact with Philemon and other
Colossian saints at some other place in his travels through Asia Minor.[1]
In any case, the fact that we have two canonical epistles that Paul sent
to Colossae demonstrates Paul's genuine love and concern for the
church and the saints there.

Philemon was a prominent member of the church in Colossae.
One of his slaves, Onesimus, had run away and had been converted by
Paul to Christianity. (Philem. 1:10.) Paul, who was under house arrest
in Rome, did not wish to be guilty of harboring a fugitive, and therefore sent Onesimus back to his master in Colossae with a letter to
Philemon as well as with the epistle to the Colossians.[2] In the epistle to
Philemon, Paul makes an appeal that Philemon forgive Onesimus for
running away and accept him as a "brother" rather than as a "servant"
(v. 16)—language that suggests he is asking Philemon to free him
from slavery.

The Greek term *doûlos,* translated throughout the King James
Version as *servant,* refers to what we would consider today to be a
slave—that is, a person who is the legal property of his master. While
to modern man this concept is inhumane and reprehensible, until
very recent times slavery was a common and acceptable institution in
many societies. At the time of Paul and the rise of Christianity, it was
an essential part of the political, economic, and social structure of the
Roman Empire. The practice was widespread (some estimate that 20
to 30 percent of the population were slaves) and well-documented.[3]
While the treatment of a slave depended largely on the character and
disposition of his owner, in the first century the master had complete
legal authority over his slaves and could sell them, punish them, or put
them to death as he saw fit. Occasionally this dominion was exercised,
granting a slave his freedom and thus making him a freedman. A runaway slave was considered a fugitive, and anyone granting him refuge
would be considered as an accomplice, guilty of theft.

The status of a slave in the ancient world is often reflected in personal names. Occasionally individual slaves were called by Greek or Latin nicknames, reflecting a prominent personal trait. A few examples of these nicknames in the New Testament from the Greek are Phoebe (KJV Phebe), "radiant" (Rom. 16:1); Philologus, "talkative" (Rom. 16:15); and Tychicus, "fortunate" (Col. 4:7). Latin examples include Fortunatus, "lucky" (1 Cor. 16:17); Tryphaena (KJV Tryphena), "dainty" (Rom. 16:12); and Rufus, "red-headed" (Rom. 16:13). The Greek name Onesimus is also attested as one of these servile names and means "useful."[4]

The presence of slaves in the early church is taken for granted in the New Testament. While Paul taught that all are "one in Christ Jesus," both Jew and Gentile, bond and free, male and female (1 Cor. 12:13; Gal. 3:28; Col. 3:11), and urged humane treatment of slaves, nowhere does he ever denounce the institution of slavery as such. In fact, in several passages Paul exhorts slaves to be faithful in fulfilling their duties to their masters. (Col. 3:22-23; 1 Tim. 6:1-2; Titus 2:9-10.) The situation of Onesimus presents Paul with a unique challenge. On the one hand he must do his legal duty to return a runaway slave to his master, Philemon, a friend and fellow member of the church. On the other hand he must teach a principle revolutionary to his own time, that "in Christ" there are no slaves and no freedmen but only brothers, and discreetly ask that Philemon forgive Onesimus and accept him back, not as a slave but as a fellow saint and brother in Christ.

At first glance this short letter may appear to be merely a personal note from Paul to one of his friends about a private and relatively trivial matter—the forgiveness of a runaway slave. Upon closer inspection, however, we see that the letter is addressed not to Philemon alone but to several other individuals, as well as the members of the church in Colossae, and that it eloquently teaches a very important gospel truth for Christians of all ages: the gospel has the power to transform human relationships. Therefore Paul's earnest personal plea to Philemon that he forgive Onesimus and accept him back—not as a slave but as "a brother beloved" (v. 16)—becomes a universal appeal for love, forgiveness, and fellowship. A careful study of this brief epistle reveals much about the warmth and concern of Paul for his fellow saints and his ability to gently but firmly persuade them to more fully accept the radical change of heart required by the gospel of Jesus Christ.[5]

Structure of the Epistle

The epistle to Philemon has the same basic structure as the rest of the Pauline epistles and contains four standard elements also found with some variations in other contemporary Near Eastern and Hellenistic letters.[6] These common elements are as follows: an introduction, including the name of the sender and the addressee, and a salutation, or greeting usually consisting of a formal blessing; a thanksgiving, expressing gratitude to God and often to the addressee; the body of the letter, which contains the purpose and message of the letter; and a conclusion with a final salutation and blessing. The structure of Philemon can be outlined as follows:

1-3	Introduction and Salutation
4-7	Thanksgiving and Petition
8-20	Body of the Letter: Intercession for Onesimus
21-25	Conclusion and Salutation

Introduction and Salutation

Paul introduces the letter with the information that he is a "prisoner of Jesus Christ" (v. 1). This same phrase occurs in the epistle to the Ephesians (3:1; 4:1) and in 2 Timothy (1:8), both of which were clearly written while Paul was in prison, and is generally considered to be a literal reference to Paul's imprisonment rather than as a symbolic reference to his ministry. This assumption raises the related problem of the date of the letter. The historical narrative in Acts refers to two specific periods of imprisonment: when Paul was imprisoned in Caesarea before he was sent to Rome (Acts 24:27), thought to be between the years A.D. 58 and 60, and the Roman imprisonment mentioned at the end of Acts, where we read that "Paul dwelt two whole years in his own hired house, and received all that came in unto him" (28:30), dated A.D. 61-63.[7] In addition, Paul alludes to many other imprisonments in the course of his ministry that have not been recorded in Acts. (2 Cor. 11:23.) While arguments have been made for various places and dates,[8] the imprisonment at Rome from A.D. 61 to 63 best fits the context for the letter to Philemon as well as the letters to the Colossians, Ephesians, and Philippians, which also come from the same period.[9]

The letter is primarily addressed to Philemon "our dearly beloved, and fellowlabourer" (v. 1). Because he had slaves and the church met in his house, we cannot help but suppose that Philemon was a wealthy citizen with some influence in the Christian community in Colossae. In addition, the letter is addressed to "our beloved Apphia," whom we might suppose to be Philemon's wife (and whose mutual consent as the lady of the house would be properly sought by Paul in the matter of a slave); to "Archippus our fellowsoldier"; and to the members of the church who met in the house of Philemon (v. 2). Archippus is mentioned in Paul's epistle to the Colossians as being responsible for the ministry at Colossae (Col. 4:17), and therefore we may conclude that Philemon is a fellow citizen of Colossae and perhaps that Archippus is his local church leader. The fact that the letter is initially addressed to the church at large strongly suggests that the principle Paul is trying to teach has significance beyond the specific case of Philemon and Onesimus.[10]

The final part of the introduction is a salutation in the form of a blessing: "Grace to you, and peace, from God our Father and the Lord Jesus Christ" (v. 3). This phrase is a common formula used by Paul in the introductions to some of his letters; here it is directed to all of the aforementioned individuals and the community as a whole (in the second person plural). Unfortunately, often the reader skims over this formulaic benediction and misses the profound doctrinal lesson it contains. Scholars have pointed out that the blessing of *peace* occasionally appears together with *mercy* in the greetings of Jewish letters, and that the Greek word *grace* (*cháris*) is strongly reminiscent of the usual epistolary Greek greeting (*chaírein*, "greeting").[11] However, the combination of *grace* and *peace* is unique to Paul. He has ingeniously combined two of the ordinary conventions of his time to create a blessing appropriate to the Christian message. It seems clear that the *peace* referred to is the "peace on earth" (see Luke 2:14) brought about by the *grace* of the atonement of Jesus Christ.[12] This grace and peace come from God our Father and the Lord Jesus Christ. Thus the words *greeting* and *peace,* which had nearly become secular clichés in their respective epistolary traditions, are transformed by Paul into a sacred blessing capturing the very essence of the gospel of Jesus Christ.

Thanksgiving and Petition

Verses 4 through 7 contain a statement of thanksgiving similar to those found in other Pauline epistles, especially 1 Thessalonians 1:2-5 and Colossians 1:3-8. Paul thanks God for the love and faith toward Jesus Christ and toward the saints that Philemon has demonstrated in the past (vv. 4-5.)[13] This statement is followed by the beginning of the petition Paul is making to Philemon.

The King James translation of verse 6 is rather awkward—"that the communication of thy faith may become effectual by the acknowledging of every good thing which is in you in Christ Jesus." As attested by the notes in the LDS edition of the King James Bible, the Greek words *communication* (*koinōnía*) and *effectual* (*energés*) may be profitably translated with other meanings that may better express the meaning of the phrase. Following the suggestions found in the LDS edition, we would have "I pray that the *participation* of thy faith may become *active* by the acknowledging of every good thing which is in you in Christ Jesus."[14] In this verse Paul is expressing the desire that the faith Philemon has demonstrated in the past, through his love and service toward the saints, may be active and produce good works in the future as well.

In verse 7 Paul again commends Philemon for his applied faith by good works in the past, saying, "We [Paul and Timothy] have great joy and consolation" in Philemon's love for his fellow saints "because the bowels [or hearts] of the saints are refreshed" on account of him. This verse provides a transition from the thanksgiving to the body of the letter, where Paul will continue his petition on behalf of Onesimus.

Body of the Letter: Intercession for Onesimus

Paul's purpose in writing the letter is carefully laid out in verses 8 through 20. His intercession on behalf of Onesimus is a model of careful rhetoric, alternately appealing to logic, emotion, and the common bond of fellowship as followers of Christ. In verse 8, he continues his petition set forth in verses 4 to 7 by subtly suggesting to Philemon that due to his position as an apostle, he could be "bold" in Christ to "enjoin" (Gr. *epitássein* = to command) him to do that which was "convenient" (Gr. *anêkon* = that which is required or fitting). In other words, he could order him to do his duty. But he would rather make his request "for love's sake" (v. 9). To this Paul adds an emotional appeal, reminding Philemon that he (Paul) is getting old and is imprisoned.

In verses 10 and 11, Paul makes a word play on Onesimus's name, which in Greek means useful, by juxtaposing it with two adjectives (*áchrēston* and *eúchrēston*) meaning useless/unprofitable and useful/profitable. He recognizes that in the past Onesimus had run away and had indeed been "unprofitable" to Philemon. But now, because he has become converted to Christianity through the teaching of Paul (v. 10), he has at last become "profitable" both to Paul and to Philemon (v. 11). Paul is sending him back to Philemon, although he would have liked to have kept him to assist in his missionary labors (vv. 12-13). Paul intimates in verse 14 that if Philemon were agreeable, perhaps Onesimus might indeed return to the ministry with Paul.

Finally Paul makes his long-awaited request: that Philemon forgive Onesimus and accept him back, "not now as a servant, but above a servant," as a fellow saint and a "brother beloved" (vv. 15-16). Paul is clearly asking that Philemon forgive Onesimus, and, while not explicit, the language strongly suggests that he is also asking Philemon to give Onesimus his freedom. Paul again makes an appeal to his own mutual relationship with Philemon and asks that he receive Onesimus back even as himself (v. 17). He promises that he will be personally responsible to Philemon for any financial debts owed or damages incurred by Onesimus. At the same time, he states he will not even mention that Philemon's debt to Paul was substantial and, probably referring to the fact that Paul was instrumental in his conversion, that it included his "own self."

Paul concludes his plea in verse 20 with a literary envelope referring back to verse 7, where he had mentioned the joy he had already experienced in Philemon's manifestation of love that had refreshed the hearts of the saints. Now he asks that his heart might again have joy of Philemon in Christ and that his heart, just as those of the saints, might also be refreshed (v. 20).

The epistle to Philemon is replete with language revealing the intimate human relationships brought about by Christianity and enjoyed by the members of the covenant community. For example, in verses 1 and 2 Paul refers to Timothy as "our brother" (Gr. *ho adelphós*); to Philemon as "our dearly beloved" and later on in verse 20 as "brother"; to Apphia as "our beloved" (Gr. *hē adelphḗ* = sister); and to Archippus as "our fellowsoldier." In verse 10 Paul fondly refers to Onesimus as his "son" by virtue of the fact that through Onesimus's conversion he became symbolically begotten by Paul. In the conclusion of the letter, Paul refers to his companion Epaphras as his "fellowprisoner in Christ Jesus" and to Marcus, Aristarchus, Demas, and Lucas as his "fellowlabourers" (vv. 23-24).

Hence the relationships shared by members of the church are expressed in the sacred and intimate terms of family relationships—of brother and sister, father and son—and with terms of fellowship in both the labors and the afflictions of the ministry. Based on the mutual acceptance of Jesus Christ and the commitment to service in his name, complete strangers—Jew and Gentile alike—are inseparably bound together by the love and brotherhood eloquently expressed by the simple terms of *brother* and *sister*.[15] Thus, through the Atonement we experience a transformation of relationships in that we become sons and daughters of Christ and brothers and sisters in Christ.

Paul's plea for Onesimus is based on this concept—that acceptance of the gospel of Jesus Christ creates a community of saints and that their common bond radically alters all existing socially imposed relationships. His argument is carefully constructed on the premise that Philemon has "love . . . toward the Lord Jesus" as well as toward "all saints" (v. 5), and that Philemon has demonstrated this love and the saints have benefited from it in the past (v. 7). Paul too has developed this same love for Jesus Christ and for his children and therefore has extended his love and concern to Onesimus (v. 10). Although Onesimus has "departed for a season" by running away from his legal responsibilities as Philemon's slave, he now returns as a member of the church, and therefore Philemon should "receive him for ever; not now as a servant, but above a servant" in the eternal relationship as a "brother beloved" in the gospel—"both in the flesh, and in the Lord" (vv. 15-16).

The simple logic of Paul's argument profoundly illustrates a principle that is revolutionary in both ancient and modern times: membership in the kingdom of God transcends the transitory modes of human relationships directed by race, gender, or social status. Although Christianity at the time of Paul was not able to abolish the institution of slavery, which was so deeply ingrained into society, Paul boldly teaches the doctrine that just as before God all are alike— "black and white, bond and free, male and female" (2 Ne. 26:33; Gal. 3:28)—so are we as his children brothers and sisters. Throughout the course of history this principle, imbedded in Christianity from the beginning, has slowly but surely resulted in the eradication of slavery.

Conclusion and Salutation

Paul concludes his request on behalf of Onesimus with a statement of his confidence that Philemon would be obedient to all he had written him and that he knew Philemon would even do more than he had been explicitly asked to do (v. 21). It is possible this is another veiled expression of hope that Philemon would grant Onesimus his freedom from slavery, a request that seems pervasive throughout the letter but is nowhere stated directly. Then Paul tells Philemon to prepare him a place to stay since he hopes he will be able to personally pay him a visit in the near future (v. 22). By adding this final touch to his personal appeal for Onesimus, Paul may be indirectly advising Philemon that he would indeed follow up on the situation, perhaps with a personal visit to Philemon's house, to see how the matter turned out. In the words of one commentator, referring to Paul's carefully constructed and sustained request, "How could anyone resist such an appeal?"[16]

To the conclusion are added further salutations from various individuals residing with Paul. Epaphras, one of the early founders of the Christian community in Colossae, who is now a "fellowprisoner in Christ Jesus" with Paul, sends his greetings along with Marcus, Aristarchus, Demas, and Lucas, Paul's "fellowlabourers" in the mission field. All of these men are also mentioned in the epistle to the Colossians

(Col. 4:9-17). The final blessing (v. 25), "the grace of our Lord Jesus Christ be with your spirit" (JST, "be with *you*"), forms another elegant literary envelope with the opening blessing (v. 3) and reminds the saints of the divine auspices under which the work of the kingdom must go forth.

Conclusion

The inescapable question that every reader asks is what was the outcome of this little drama. Although the scriptures are silent, we would like to assume that Philemon, if he was truly the Christian Paul believed him to be, accepted the request gracefully and, understanding the principle Paul was teaching, received Onesimus as a brother and granted him his freedom. And in the dubious case that Philemon's charity was not sufficient in and of itself, there was additional motivation to comply because the request was backed up by authority of the church vested in Paul and because of the community pressure from his fellow saints to whom the letter was also addressed.

A tantalizing hint as to what may have happened to Onesimus can be found in a letter written to the church in Ephesus by Ignatius, Bishop of Antioch, in the early second century. In this letter Ignatius says that the Ephesians are truly blessed with a noble bishop, a man full of love, and admonishes them to follow his example. Oddly enough this man had the name of a slave—Onesimus.[17] While positive identification of this Onesimus with the runaway slave of the epistle to Philemon remains tenuous, it is not impossible.[18] Whether this is our Onesimus or not we may never know for sure. But we can be sure that just like Onesimus, once a runaway and an "unprofitable" servant to his master, we too can indeed through the gospel become "profitable" in the service of the Lord Jesus Christ.

Notes

1. Richard Lloyd Anderson, *Understanding Paul* (Salt Lake City: Deseret Book, 1983), p. 239, discusses the possibility that Paul visited Colossae

or at least made contact with some of the individuals there when "all they which dwelt in Asia heard the word of the Lord" from Ephesus. (Acts 19:10.)

2. Onesimus is named as the letter carrier in both Colossians (4:7, 9) and Philemon (vv. 10-12). In addition, all the people mentioned in Philemon also are mentioned in Colossians 4:9-17. It seems almost certain that the two letters were written at the same time.

3. Anderson, pp. 240-42, gives a review of some of the documents from the period that illustrate ancient attitudes toward slavery. For a concise discussion of the practice of slavery in New Testament times, see W. G. Rollins, "Slavery in the New Testament," *Interpreter's Dictionary of the Bible,* 4 vols. and Supplement (New York and Nashville: Abingdon Press, 1962-76), Supplement, pp. 830-32.

4. The ancient evidence suggests that such names, while not used exclusively for slaves, generally point to servile status or background. For a more complete list and discussion, see Rollins, p. 831.

5. The most recent and comprehensive work on the Apostle Paul and his writings by a Latter-day Saint scholar is Richard Lloyd Anderson, *Understanding Paul.* The discussion of the epistle to Philemon can be found on pages 238-44. A useful non-LDS commentary is Eduard Lohse, *Colossians and Philemon* (Philadelphia: Fortress Press, 1971).

6. A short discussion of how some of these elements compare with the Near Eastern and Hellenistic letters can be found in Lohse, pp. 5-6, 12-14, where he discusses these elements in the epistle to the Colossians.

7. Anderson, pp. 393-98, provides a useful chronological reconstruction of Paul's life and ministry.

8. The subscript preserved at the bottom of the text in the KJV, "written from Rome to Philemon, by Onesimus, a servant," is an editorial addition probably added at a somewhat later date. In the Marcionite tradition this subscript reads that the epistle was written from Ephesus. Because of this and Paul's mention of great hardship in Ephesus (1 Cor. 15:32), some have postulated that one of the unspecified imprisonments referred to in 2 Corinthians 11:23 was at Ephesus. Proponents of this hypothetical imprisonment at Ephesus, which is in the same geographical vicinity as Colossae, claim that this would help to explain how Onesimus and Paul met, Paul's seeming reference in Philemon 1:22 to an imminent visit, and to the fact that Epaphras is a "fellowprisoner" with Paul—without having to suppose that Paul was much farther away in Rome. For a complete discussion, see Lohse, pp. 165-67. Sea transportation was readily available from Asia Minor to Rome, and therefore the argument that Rome was far from Colossae is not necessarily a compelling one.

9. The common historical context and the mutual relationship of the contents of these four epistles is accepted and demonstrated by Anderson throughout his discussion of each epistle, found in pp. 230-309.

10. While the letter is addressed in the plural to these three individuals and the other members of the church in the salutations at the beginning (1-3) and at the end of the letter (23-25), it should be noted that the body of the letter is in fact specifically directed to Philemon in the second person singular ("thee").

11. Lohse, p. 5, in his discussion of the similar phrase found in Colossians 1:2, cites a biblical example of the use of *peace* in the Near Eastern tradition from Daniel 4:1, where a letter opens: "Nebuchadnezzar the king, unto all peoples, nations, and languages, that dwell in all the *earth;* Peace be multiplied unto you." The common Greek greeting *chairein* is found in James 1:1, where it is translated "greeting," as well as in Acts 15:23, 29, and 23:26, 30. While ultimately going back to a common root, *cháris* and *chairein* are two different words with distinct meanings. The suggestion made here is that it may be significant that they sound the same and therefore their similar function creates an obvious word play.

12. Lohse, pp. 5-6, 10.

13. Lohse, p. 193, points out that verse 5 may be a nice chiasm a-b-b-a [a = love; b = faith; b = Jesus Christ; a = saints] "Hearing of thy *love* and *faith,* which thou hast toward the *Lord Jesus,* and toward all *saints* = "love toward all saints" and "faith toward the Lord Jesus."

14. The Revised Standard Version translates this verse "I pray that the sharing of your faith may promote the knowledge of all the good that is ours in Christ." Lohse discusses the difficulties of the passage (pp. 4-6) and renders "May your sharing in the faith become effective in the knowledge of all the good that is in us for the glory of Christ."

15. It is worthy of note that the Greek term for *sister* (as well as the Hebrew and Aramaic terms) does not derive from a different root than *brother* (as in English) but rather is simply the feminine form of the same word, emphasizing that *brother* and *sister* are two aspects of the same category rather than two different categories.

16. M. E. Lyman, "Letter to Philemon," in *Interpreter's Dictionary of the Bible* 3:783.

17. Ignatius, Letter to the Ephesians 1:3 (Apostolic Fathers, Loeb Classical Library).

18. Ignatius's letter was written in the first decade of the second cen-

tury, and therefore many argue that the Onesimus known from the New Testament would probably be dead by that time. If he was a young man at the time he returned to Colossae in A.D. 61 (Paul does call him his "son" or "child"), it is possible that he was an elderly man at the time of the letter to the Ephesians. Beyond this we can only speculate.

12

THE PASTORAL EPISTLES
(1, 2 Timothy; Titus)

BRUCE A. VAN ORDEN

Paul's last known epistles were addressed to his trusted associates Timothy and Titus. Often these three letters are designated as pastoral epistles since Timothy and Titus were priesthood leaders in Ephesus and Crete respectively, and the first two of these letters especially contain counsel on church organization, discipline, and methods. In addition, these letters are highly personal and reflect the apostle's faith and feelings toward the end of his eventful life. Thus these letters help us understand what happened to Paul after the near-biographical account of Luke ended abruptly in Acts 28.

The first epistle to Timothy and the epistle to Titus were written after Paul was released in A.D. 63 from his first imprisonment in Rome. Whether they were written before or after his probable visit to Spain is unclear. If before, they likely were composed in 63; if afterward, probably in 65. The second epistle to Timothy was written after Paul was imprisoned a second time in Rome and undoubtedly shortly before his death, which most scholars believe occurred in 67.

Timothy and Titus were among Paul's most loyal assistants in the ministry. Paul converted Timothy in the Galatian city of Lystra on his first missionary journey. Timothy was the son of a Greek father and Jewish mother, Eunice. (Acts 16:1-3; 2 Tim. 1:5.) His name, which

---

Bruce A. Van Orden is assistant professor of Church history and doctrine at Brigham Young University.

means "honoring God" or "honored by God," may have been given him by his pious mother and grandmother, who taught him from the holy scriptures from his youth up. Paul loved Timothy dearly and referred to him as his "beloved son, and faithful in the Lord." (1 Cor. 4:17.) He also called Timothy "my own son in the faith" (1 Tim. 1:2) and "my dearly beloved son" (2 Tim. 1:2).

When Paul revisited Lystra in A.D. 49 during his second missionary journey, he asked Timothy, who may have been no more than a teenager, to accompany him as his assistant. He ordained the youth to the ministry and circumcised him to avoid any possible difficulty in bringing the gospel to the clusters of Jews in the cities of the Roman Empire. Timothy became one of the most constant companions of the apostle. His history is virtually the history of Paul's missions. He was with Paul when the apostle wrote at least seven of his letters. "Paul had many powerful companions, but not one continued to be closer to him," writes Richard Lloyd Anderson.[1]

Titus was a Greek convert. His name is never mentioned in Acts, so all that is known of him is gathered from the references to him in the Pauline epistles. Not unlike Timothy, Titus is addressed by the apostle as his "own son after the common faith." (Titus 1:4.) Paul took Titus along to the Jerusalem Conference in A.D. 49 as an example of his Gentile converts and used him as a test case for the idea that a Gentile did not need to conform to Jewish ritual when he was converted to the Christian faith. The fact that Titus was not compelled to be circumcised confirmed Paul's position. (Gal. 2:1-5.) When Paul was in Ephesus during the third missionary journey, three times he sent Titus to Corinth to help bring about peace among the saints there. Successful in Corinth, Titus was later assigned to labor in Crete until he was called to meet with Paul. Thereafter he presided over the branches on that island. From 2 Timothy 4:10 we learn that Titus visited the imprisoned Paul in Rome and then went on missionary labors to Dalmatia, which is now part of Yugoslavia.

The occasion for writing 1 Timothy is evident from the epistle. Upon his return to Ephesus, Paul found the city to be the storm center of false teaching, even as he had prophesied years earlier. (Acts 20:29-30.) He dealt with the leaders of the trouble (1 Tim. 1:19-20), but left Timothy in charge of the situation when he went into Macedonia (1

Tim. 1:3). Feeling that Timothy would need encouragement and authorization to proceed with the difficult task entrusted to him, Paul wrote this noteworthy epistle.

When Paul left Titus in Crete, he fully expected to return. But when he found he could not, he wrote the epistle to Titus to provide definite instructions about the duties of those who minister in the church.

The second epistle to Timothy was written under the adverse circumstances of Paul's lonely second imprisonment. The Roman emperor Nero had placed the blame of the great fire of Rome upon the saints and launched a series of intense persecutions against the Christians in Rome. Friends could still visit Paul, but the apostle was restricted in his ability to preach the gospel. Apparently only Luke remained with him. In spite of this negative setting, Paul remained optimistic and buoyed up by his faith in Christ.

Instructions to Priesthood Leaders

Paul was critically concerned about the encroaching apostasy in the branches of the church. Hence he wrote to trusted overseers Timothy and Titus (who had roles perhaps similar to stake presidents today) and gave them instructions on how to cope with false teachers in their midst. He also gave them wise counsel on being leaders and handling affairs in their congregations, most all of which is useful for church leaders even today.

Preach Sound Doctrine

Immediately after giving his greetings of love to Timothy, Paul instructed his youthful aide to "charge some that they teach no other doctrine . . . from which some having swerved . . . unto vain jangling." (1 Tim. 1:3, 6.) Apparently Gnostic Judaists, men who aspired to be "teachers of the law" yet who wholly misunderstood the full nature of the law, were teaching "contrary to sound doctrine" and were making inroads in Ephesus. (1 Tim. 1:3-11.) Likewise Paul instructed Titus in Crete to "speak thou the things which become sound doctrine" to counter those who "profess that they know God; but in works they deny him." (Titus 2:1; 1:16.) Paul well knew that false teachers can quickly lead believers into forbidden paths, so he desired that both Timothy and Titus select priesthood leaders and teachers who would maintain doctrinal loyalty.

Timothy was charged to "keep that which is committed to thy trust" by not allowing "profane and vain babblings." (1 Tim. 6:20.) The King James translators used *science* when the word should have been rendered *knowledge*. Translated more understandably in our modern language, Paul instructed Timothy to "turn a deaf ear to . . . the contradictions of so-called 'knowledge', for many who lay claim to it have shot wide of the faith." (1 Tim. 6:20, New English Bible.) The ancient Gnostics received their name from the Greek term meaning *knowledge*. "Like many sects that have broken from the Church today," Dr. Anderson explains, "the Gnostics generally claimed secret doctrines to add to the Church's public message."[2]

Elder Bruce R. McConkie explained the application of Paul's instruction to today's setting: "Teachers in the Church represent the Lord in their teaching. The Church is the Lord's; the doctrine is the Lord's. Teachers speak at the invitation of the Lord and are appointed to say what he wants said, nothing more and nothing less. There is no freedom to teach or speculate contrary to the revealed will. Those who desire to express views contrary to gospel truth are at liberty to find other forums or to organize churches of their own. But in God's Church, the only approved doctrine is God's doctrine."[3]

Qualification for Leadership

In the early New Testament church as well as in the modern church, no prior formal training was required to serve in a leadership capacity. Timothy and Titus, as ordained priesthood leaders, had further responsibility to seek out and commission other leaders over the branches. Both well knew that "no man taketh this [priesthood] honour unto himself, but he that is called of God, as was Aaron." (Heb. 5:4.) They also realized that the ordinance of laying on of hands was necessary to bestow priesthood offices and power. (1 Tim. 4:14; 5:22.) Paul's instructions to Timothy and Titus about the selection of bishops and deacons were filled with caution to insure that only worthy and experienced men would receive these responsible positions. "Self-appointed and congregationally appointed leaders are ruled out in the procedure of the Early Church, which had a regular line of authority from Christ and his apostles," Dr. Anderson states.[4]

The title *bishop* evolved from the Greek *episcopos,* which means overseer. Bishops were to care for their flock, suggesting their image of pastors or shepherds. (Eph. 4:11.) The bishop leads the flock by looking out for its welfare.

Paul's descriptions of the qualifications for bishops are nearly identical in 1 Timothy 3:1-7 and Titus 1:5-8. The apostle emphasized that bishops should be "blameless," "vigilant," "not self-willed," "sober," "temperate," "patient," "given to hospitality," and "not greedy of filthy lucre." The bishop should have control over his own house; otherwise, asked Paul, "how shall he take care of the church of God?" Paul summarized that the bishop should not be a novice (1 Tim. 3:6), but experienced as a member and a leader.

Paul stated that the bishop must be "the husband of one wife." (1 Tim. 3:2; Titus 1:6.) Some commentators have seen in this instruction a prohibition against polygyny, including the Latter-day Saint system wherein most bishops in the nineteenth century were polygamous. Since having more than one wife was virtually unknown in Paul's day, particularly in the Church of Jesus Christ, a better interpretation of Paul's instruction is "sexual loyalty to the lawful spouse." For example, the New English Bible renders the verse "faithful to his one wife." And at the present time, when the practice of plural marriage has been suspended in the restored church, a bishop is to have only one wife and to be unswervingly faithful to her.

First Timothy 3:8-13 describes the qualifications for deacons. Paul listed deacons following bishops in Philippians 1:1, as he did here in his letter to Timothy. In the Greek, *diakonos* means helper or servant. Like bishops, deacons were expected to go through the two stages of proving worthiness and then being called. (1 Tim. 3:10.) Deacons were to be qualified as well: "grave, not doubletongued, not given to much wine, not greedy of filthy lucre." (1 Tim. 3:8.) But they would function under the direction of the bishop and not have presiding authority.

It was the judgment of Paul that the deacon should be a married man. (1 Tim. 3:11-12.) In that day a man was not considered qualified to take part in the ministry until he was thirty years of age. The restored church began with older deacons and lowered the age many years later only when there were numerous priesthood holders and when boys could receive regular supervision from experienced priesthood leaders. In ancient times it was also possible for a boy to be ordained to the priesthood. Noah was only ten years old when he was given the priesthood under the hands of Methuselah. (D&C 107:52.)

Welfare Instructions

In 1 Timothy 5, Paul instructed his co-laborer on the welfare principles of self-sufficiency, caring for the widows, and providing occasional temporal assistance to full-time laborers in the kingdom. Paul never emphasized the contemplative and devout life at the expense of appropriately caring for oneself. As Richard Lloyd Anderson states, "Behind 1 Timothy 5 is the commitment to productive labor, exemplified by Paul's regular tent-making, and requiring industry as a condition of full fellowship in 2 Thessalonians 3."[5]

Foremost in Paul's welfare instructions were his sober, oft-quoted admonitions to heads of households who have responsibility to provide for their families: "But if any provide not for his own, and specially for those of his own house, he hath denied the faith, and is worse than an infidel." (1 Tim. 5:8.) Church leaders in the last dispensation have taken Paul's lead and likewise instructed the members. For example, President Spencer W. Kimball declared: "No true Latter-day Saint, while physically or emotionally able will voluntarily shift the burden of his own or his family's well-being to someone else. So long as he can, under the inspiration of the Lord and with his own labors, he will supply himself and his family with the spiritual and temporal necessities of life."[6] A year after explaining the foregoing, President Kimball added, "I like to think of providing for our own as including providing them with affectional security as well as economic security. When the Lord told us in this dispensation that 'women have claim on their husbands for their maintenance' (D&C 83:2), I like to think of *maintenance* as including our obligation to maintain loving affection and to provide consideration and thoughtfulness as well as food."[7]

On the subject of widows, Paul counseled younger widows to

marry righteously again, bear children, and guide a household. (1 Tim. 5:14.) He decried idleness in widows and those who were "tattlers" and "busybodies." (1 Tim. 5:13.) Regarding elderly widows, Paul first encouraged family members to provide for their care: "If a Christian man or woman has widows in the family, he must support them himself; the congregation must be relieved of the burden, so that it may be free to support those who are widows in the full sense of the term." (1 Tim. 5:16, New English Bible.) This fully corresponds with the modern welfare principle of the family being asked to care for their own before turning to the church. As President Kimball explained, "The responsibility for each person's social, emotional, spiritual, physical, or economic well-being rests first upon himself, second upon his family, and third upon the Church if he is a faithful member thereof."[8] To qualify for church assistance in Paul's day, as in ours, widows were to demonstrate their worthiness for such assistance in a variety of ways. (See 1 Tim. 5:10.)

Also in Paul's day, as in ours, "there are times when elders spending their full time in the ministry, should receive temporal help from the Church, especially for their families," according to Elder McConkie.[9] (See 1 Tim. 5:17-18; D&C 75:24.)

In 1 Timothy 6, Paul provided pastoral instructions on the unrighteous acquiring of this world's wealth. He reminded Timothy, "For we brought nothing into this world, and it is certain we can carry nothing out." (1 Tim. 6:7.) Paul was concerned lest the "rich fall into temptation and a snare, . . . for the love of money is the root of all evil." (1 Tim. 6:9-10.) Paul's advice to Timothy on dealing with the wealthy included, "Instruct those who are rich in this world's goods not to be proud, and not to fix their hopes on so uncertain a thing as money, but upon God, who endows us richly with all things to enjoy." (1 Tim. 6:17, New English Version.) In like manner, Elder Spencer W. Kimball queried, "Why another farm, another herd of sheep, another bunch of cattle, another ranch? Why another hotel, another cafe, another store, another shop? Why another plant, another service, another business? Why another of anything if one has that already which provides the necessities and reasonable luxuries? . . . Certainly when one's temporal possessions become great, it is very difficult for one to give proper attention to the spiritual things."[10]

Strengthen Faith in Christ

Surely some of Paul's most significant pastoral instructions to Timothy are admonitions for the latter to strengthen his faith in Christ. These admonitions usually came in the form of aphorisms:

"For there is one God, and one mediator between God and men, the man Christ Jesus." (1 Tim. 2:5.)

"Hold fast the form of sound words, which thou hast heard of me, in faith and love which is in Christ Jesus." (2 Tim. 1:13.)

"Thou therefore, my son, be strong in the grace that is in Christ Jesus." (2 Tim. 2:1.)

"Thou therefore endure hardness, as a good soldier of Jesus Christ." (2 Tim. 2:3.)

"For God hath not given us the spirit of fear; but of power, and of love, and of a sound mind. Be not thou therefore ashamed of the testimony of our Lord, nor of me his prisoner: but be thou partaker of the afflictions of the gospel according to the power of God." (2 Tim. 1:7-8.)

The latter passage is a particular favorite of a powerful minister of Christ, President Gordon B. Hinckley. After citing these verses, President Hinckley has said: "Who among us can say that he or she has not felt fear? I know of no one who has been entirely spared. Some, of course, experience fear to a greater degree than do others. Some are able to rise above it quickly, but others are trapped and pulled down by it and even driven to defeat. We suffer from the fear of ridicule, the fear of failure, the fear of loneliness, the fear of ignorance. Some fear the present, some the future. Some carry the burden of sin and would give almost anything to unshackle themselves from those burdens, but fear to change their lives. Let us recognize that fear comes not of God, but rather that this gnawing, destructive element comes from the adversary of truth and righteousness. Fear is the antithesis of faith. It is corrosive in its effects, even deadly."[11]

Timothy was instructed, as a priesthood leader, to continue learning from "the holy scriptures, which are able to make thee wise unto salvation through faith which is in Christ Jesus." (2 Tim. 3:15.) Indeed, all scripture, Paul said, is valuable in the ministry of a leader "for doctrine, for reproof, for correction, for instruction in righteousness." (2 Tim. 3:16.)

A modern prophet, President Ezra Taft Benson, in an address reminiscent of the pastoral instructions of Paul to Timothy, admonished priesthood leaders to emphasize scripture study above all other things in their callings: "Immerse yourselves in the scriptures. Search them diligently. Feast upon the words of Christ. Learn the doctrine. Master the principles that are found therein. There are few other efforts that will bring greater dividends to your calling. There are few other ways to gain greater inspirations as you serve."[12]

General Instructions

Paul gave a number of general instructions to Timothy and Titus to aid them in their pastoral ministry. These instructions were shorter and did not fit into the larger categories already mentioned.

Paul encouraged the saints to pray "for all men; for kings, and for all that are in authority; that we may lead a quiet and peaceable life in all godliness and honesty." (1 Tim. 2:1-2; see also Titus 3:1-2.) As President Spencer W. Kimball explained, doing this "will help develop loyalty to country and to leaders. One can hardly be critical of Church leadership if honest prayers are offered for [government leaders]. Children will come to honor leaders for whom they pray."[13]

Paul's advice to Timothy included suggestions to women in the church. He encouraged them to "adorn themselves in modest apparel" and to avoid worldly styles and fashions. (1 Tim. 2:9.) Book of Mormon prophets concur, as Elder Bruce R. McConkie pointed out: "The Nephite prophets repeatedly identified the wearing of costly clothing with apostasy and failure to live by gospel standards. (Jac. 2:13; Alma 1:6, 32; 4:6; 5:53; 31:27-28; 4 Ne. 24; Morm. 8:36-37.)"[14] More controversial were Paul's instructions for the women to remain silent in the services. But, as Joseph Fielding Smith explained, "Times have changed from what they were in the days of Paul. The counsel that Paul gave in the branches of the Church in his day was in strict conformity to the law of the times in which he lived."[15] Paul's most important statement about women stands through all ages of time: "She shall be saved in childbearing." (1 Tim. 2:15.)

Twice Paul warned the saints not to give heed to "endless genealogies." (1 Tim. 1:4; Titus 3:9.) To modern Latter-day Saints who, in the spirit of Elijah, righteously seek out information about their kindred dead, this counsel may seem strange. The dictionary in the LDS edition of the Bible explains that this reference "is probably to exaggerated stories of the heroes and patriarchs of early Hebrew history, such stories being at that time very popular among the Jews. Paul's denunciation of 'endless genealogy' was not of the scriptural and spiritually rewarding study of one's ancestry, but was a criticism of the self-deceptive practice of assuming that one can be saved by virtue of one's lineage."[16]

Of great importance to Paul was that Timothy would continue to develop spiritual attributes and godliness. (1 Tim. 4:8.) "Let no man despise thy youth," he reminded Timothy, "but be thou an example of the believers, in word, in conversation, in charity, in spirit, in faith, in purity." (1 Tim. 4:12.) Furthermore, he encouraged Timothy to flee the seeking of worldly wealth and "follow after righteousness, godliness, faith, love, patience, meekness." (1 Tim. 6:11.) Paul explained to Titus that "unto the pure all things are pure, but unto them that are defiled and unbelieving is nothing pure." (Titus 1:15.) Finally Paul urged his priesthood leaders to refrain from arguing and strife: "And the servant of the Lord must not strive; but be gentle unto all men, apt to teach, patient, in meekness instructing those that oppose themselves." (2 Tim. 2:24-25.)

Apostasy

Most Latter-day Saint missionaries recall that Paul's letters to Timothy contain prophecies about an impending apostasy. Indeed, three of the most frequently quoted passages in the New Testament about apostasy are found in either 1 or 2 Timothy. A careful examination of these passages reveals that they deal with personal apostasy and a falling away from truth and righteousness in the latter days, even after the gospel and true church had been restored to the earth.

The first of these is in 1 Timothy 4:1-3, wherein Paul indicates that the Spirit expressly taught him that in the last days many would "depart from the faith," would give heed to "seducing spirits," would speak "lies in hypocrisy," and by so doing would forbid to marry and command to abstain from meats. Regarding these two prohibitions of the apostates, the word of the Lord is clear in this last dispensation: "Whoso forbiddeth to marry is not ordained of God, for marriage is ordained of God unto man.... And whoso forbiddeth to abstain from meats, that man should not eat the same, is not ordained of God." (D&C 49:15, 18.) An editorial in the *Church News* elucidates the problems of "forbidding to marry" in our day: "Since eternal life may only be achieved through celestial marriage, Satan does all within his power to forbid men and women to marry. Celibacy, living together out of wedlock, homosexuality, adultery, abortion, and birth control are but a few of the many methods employed to pervert men's minds and prevent the creation and continuance of this holy union. In the words of President Harold B. Lee, 'Satan's greatest threat today is to destroy the family, and to make mockery of the law of chastity and the sanctity of the marriage covenant.'"[17]

Perhaps the most frequently cited New Testament prophecy about apostasy is found in 2 Timothy 3:1-7. "This know also, that in the last days perilous times shall come," began Paul. Then he listed twenty-one separate evil attributes that would characterize individuals in the last days, such as "unthankful," "without natural affection" (homosexual), "incontinent" (intemperate), and being "disobedient to parents." President Spencer W. Kimball reaffirmed, "I feel sure that Paul was looking foward to these last days when he said ... they would swear unrighteously, would disavow God and all sacred things; they would be disobedient to parents. Certainly we have come to a day when the youth leave their parents, disregard their training, and with what they may feel is justified, abandon their parents, move away from them. This is disastrous."[18]

Paul's last prophecy on apostasy is found in 2 Timothy 4:3-4. "For the time will come when they will not endure sound doctrine," he began. "And they shall turn away their ears from the truth, and shall be turned unto fables." Elder Neal A. Maxwell, in an address to scholars and practitioners of behavioral sciences, declared, "The appetite of man for 'fables' and the turning away from truth is not confined to the behavioral sciences, but it is present there also." He indicated that "unchecked drives for sexual gratification and indulgence" are fables prophesied by Paul. He added, "The growing heresy, that disarming fable that there is a private morality, not only turns many away from the truth but also threatens to bury man in an avalanche of appetite."[19]

President Kimball, ever prepared to defend the standards of the

Church against immorality, declared the idea that homosexuality is accepted by God to be a fable prophesied by Paul: "'God made me that way,' some say, as they rationalize and excuse themselves for their perversions. 'I can't help it,' they add. This is blasphemy. Is man not made in the image of God, and does he think God to be 'that way'? Man is responsible for his own sins. It is possible that he may rationalize and excuse himself until the groove is so deep he cannot get out without great difficulty, but this he can do. Temptations come to all people. The difference between the reprobate and the worthy person is generally that one yielded and the other resisted."[20]

Personal Feelings and Farewell

Paul's last known epistle is 2 Timothy. Paul dearly loved Timothy, his son in the gospel, and desired that he labor to endure to the end, even as he, Paul, was striving to do. This epistle is widely appreciated for its demonstration of the love and tender feelings of the beloved apostle. Inadvertently Paul revealed much courage as he recounted his experiences and decisions. "Paul's final example of courage is as precious as are the words of his letter," writes Richard Lloyd Anderson.[21]

Paul exudes pathos about his last days in mortality in his last chapter to Timothy. He remarks that his previous disciple Demas had now forsaken the ministry, "having loved this present world." (2 Tim. 4:10.) He adds, "Only Luke is with me. Take Mark, and bring him with thee: for he is profitable to me for the ministry." (2 Tim. 4:11.) Paul then asks the simple favor of Timothy that he bring the cloak he had left in Troas, and, as an afterthought, also to bring the books and parchments. (2 Tim. 4:13.)

Most significant is Paul's declaration about his expected demise as he reflects upon the previous thirty years of his ministry: "For I am now ready to be offered, and the time of my departure is at hand. I have fought a good fight, I have finished my course, I have kept the faith. Henceforth there is laid up for me a crown of righteousness, which the Lord, the righteous judge, shall give me at that day: and not to me only, but unto all them also that love his appearing." (2 Tim. 4:6-8.)

From this statement, President Marion G. Romney concluded: "Surely Paul, in his soul, enjoyed perfect freedom. The Apostle's conclusion that the reward won by him is to be available to others suggests that there must be a pattern of living by which each of us may attain it, and I believe there is." President Romney then counseled, "Freedom thus obtained—that is, by obedience to the law of Christ—is freedom of the soul, the highest form of liberty. And the most glorious thing about it is that it is within the reach of every one of us, regardless of what people about us, or even nations, do. All we have to do is learn the law of Christ and obey it. To learn it and obey it is the primary purpose of every soul's mortal life."[22]

Surely Paul's letters to Timothy and Titus are of great worth to the saints of the latter days. To heed their teachings is to be on the path toward the sanctification of our own souls.

Notes

1. Richard Lloyd Anderson, *Understanding Paul* (Salt Lake City: Deseret Book, 1983), p. 315.

2. Ibid., pp. 318-19.

3. Bruce R. McConkie, *Doctrinal New Testament Commentary,* 3 vols. (Salt Lake City: Bookcraft, 1965-73), 3:70-71.

4. Anderson, *Understanding Paul,* p. 327.

5. Ibid., p. 335.

6. *Conference Report,* October 1977, p. 124.

7. *Conference Report,* October 1978, p. 63.

8. *Conference Report,* October 1977, p. 124.

9. McConkie, *Doctrinal New Testament Commentary* 3:91.

10. *Conference Report,* October 1953, p. 54.

11. "God Hath Not Given Us the Spirit of Fear," *Ensign* 14 (October 1984): 2.

12. "The Power of the Word," *Ensign* 16 (May 1986): 81.

13. *BYU Speeches of the Year,* October 1961, p. 3.

14. McConkie, *Doctrinal New Testament Commentary* 3:79.

15. Joseph Fielding Smith, *Answers to Gospel Questions,* 5 vols. (Salt Lake City: Deseret Book, 1957-65), 3:65-66.

16. Dictionary, LDS Edition of the King James Version of the Bible, p. 678.

17. *Church News,* August 19, 1972, p. 3.

18. *Brisbane Area Conference Report,* March 1976, p. 20.

19. "Some Thoughts on the Gospel and the Behavioral Sciences," *Ensign* 6 (July 1976): 73-74.

20. "President Kimball Speaks Out on Morality," *Ensign* 10 (November 1980): 97.

21. Anderson, *Understanding Paul,* p. 365.

22. "The Perfect Law of Liberty," *Ensign* 11 (November 1981): 45.

13

JESUS CHRIST, SYMBOLISM, AND SALVATION
(Hebrews)

JOSEPH F. MCCONKIE

Among New Testament books, Romans is the most abused, Revelation the most misunderstood, and Hebrews the most neglected. Admittedly, Hebrews is a difficult book. It is to the New Testament what Leviticus is to the Old: Leviticus announces the Mosaic system, while Hebrews explains it. In it, Paul shows how the gospel grew out of the soil of the Levitical order. By the light of the gospel restored in his day, he shows how the Levitical system was intended as a bridge by which those in the wilderness of carnality could cross over to the rest of the Lord.

None of the books in the New Testament, the Gospels included, are more Christ centered than Paul's epistle to the Hebrews. In it, Paul seeks to show Christ as the fulfillment of the Mosaic system. The imagery of the Mosaic system finds its reality in Jesus of Nazareth and his atoning sacrifice. A marvelously purposeful law has now seen the accomplishment of its purpose. The shadow of Christ has now become the reality of Christ.

Christ as the Personification of the Father

"God, who at sundry times and in diverse manners spake in time past unto the fathers by the prophets, hath in these last days spoken

---

Joseph F. McConkie is associate professor of ancient scripture at Brigham Young University.

unto us by his Son," Paul begins his epistle to the Hebrews. Let us paraphrase: God, who, on a great variety of occasions and in a host of ways, spoke to the prophets of old, has also spoken to us. Indeed, he has granted us the most sublime and instructive of revelations—his own Son! The Son, Paul tells us, is in the "brightness of his [Father's] glory, and the express image of his person." (Heb. 1:3.) Thus, the manifestation of the Son is the revelation of the Father. To know the Son is to know the Father. As the Son expressed it, in response to the request of one of his disciples that they be shown the Father, "He that hath seen me hath seen the Father." (John 14:9.)

Though the scriptures tell us little of the Father, in a comparative sense, they tell us much of the Son—and to know the Son is to know the Father. The example and doctrine of one is the example and doctrine of the other. Christ constituted a living, moving, breathing revelation of his Father. "The Son can do nothing of himself," Christ said, "but what he seeth the Father do: for what things soever he doeth, these also doeth the Son likewise." (John 5:19.) Again, "I do nothing of myself; but as my Father hath taught me, I speak these things." (John 8:28.) And yet again, "If ye had known me, ye should have known my Father also: and from henceforth ye know him, and have seen him." (John 14:7.)

As all prophets are types and shadows of Christ, so Christ is a type and shadow of his Father: it could not be otherwise. Christ could hardly come and say, "I am the antithesis of the Father; in no way are we the same. He does things his way and I do things mine. Now come follow me. I will be your example in all things." Nor could his prophets come, saying, "We agree with Christ in some things, but certainly not in everything. We must be true to ourselves. In some ways we seek to be like him and in others we do not."

The very concept of salvation is of oneness and unity. It is a concept in which the Godhead professes to be one, the apostles and prophets one, the congregation one, husband and wife one, and the family unit one. Christ stated the principle thus: "If ye are not one ye are not mine." (D&C 38:27.) Thus, types, shadows, similitudes, and likenesses, in all their forms, become the common denominator for teaching the gospel.

In addition to being in the brightness of his Father's glory and the express image of his person, Paul explains that Christ has been "appointed heir of all things" (1:2), and that following the atoning sacrifice, he took his place "on the right hand of the Majesty on high" (1:3). He received of his Father's fullness and became equal with him in power, might, and dominion (D&C 76:94-95), or, as John stated it, "He received all power, both in heaven and on earth, and the glory of the Father was with him, for he dwelt in him" (D&C 93:17). Thus, Christ was "crowned with glory and honour" (Heb. 2:9) and became the personification of the Father.

We Too Are of the Heavenly Family

Having described Christ's relationship with the Father, Paul now asserts that "both he that sanctifieth and they who are sanctified are all of one" (Heb. 2:11), meaning one family. That is, he who sanctifies and they who are sanctified are of one origin. Modern translations state it thus: "For the one who sanctifies, and the ones who are sanctified, are the same stock." (New Jerusalem Bible; compare New English Bible.) The "one" is not Adam (cf. Acts 17:26) or Abraham (cf. Heb. 2:16), but God, the Father of the spirits of all men. "The Spirit itself beareth witness with our spirit," Paul had observed in his epistle to the Romans, "that we are the children of God: and if children, then heirs; heirs of God, and joint-heirs with Christ; if so be that we suffer with him, that we may be also glorified together." (Rom. 8:16-17.)

Paul cited Old Testament texts to sustain his argument that we and Christ are children of the same Father. It was prophesied, Paul noted, that the Christ would not be ashamed to declare the name of God unto his "brethren" of the "church" (Heb. 2:12; Ps. 22:22), and that Christ would be called upon to "trust" as with all of God's "children" (Heb. 2:13; Ps. 18:2; Isa. 8:18). Though he is God's son, Christ did not take upon himself the "nature of angels." (Heb. 2:16.) It was for him to work out his salvation with fear and trembling like the rest of God's children, "in all things." Paul said, "it behoved him to be made like unto his brethren." (Heb. 2:17.) Were this not the case, Christ's life would be of little value to us as an example. We could not be expected to pattern our lives after someone whose nature was so very different from our own that following in his footsteps would be impossible.

It is our kinship with Christ, our descent from the same Father, that gives meaning to the divine plan for the salvation of men. We too are in the image and likeness of God (Gen. 1:26; Mosiah 7:27; D&C 20:18); we too are heirs, even joint-heirs with Christ; we too may receive of his fullness (D&C 93:19), sit upon thrones (D&C 132:19), and become equal with him "in power, and in might, and in dominion" (D&C 76:95). Thus, salvation comes to us as it did to Christ, by becoming one with the Father. The whole system of salvation centers in the doctrine of oneness and unity. As Christ is the revelation and manifestation of the Father, so we too are to be manifestations of the Father. As Christ was a living, moving, breathing revelation of his Father, so all who would be saved must be the same. This principle of similitude, or oneness, is the key that unlocks the book of Hebrews.

Priesthood Ordination as a Type for the Messiah

It is generally understood that both the priests of the Levitical order and the presiding high priest were types for the Messiah. As they functioned in their office, they constituted living prophecies of what Christ would do and be. What has gone virtually unobserved is that the call, preparation, and ordination to the priesthood are also a Messianic prophecy. Paul and Alma are our two most instructive teachers on this subject. Let us review some of the insights granted us by these two.

Alma explains, "The Lord God ordained priests, after his holy order, which was after the order of his Son, *to teach* these things unto the people." (Alma 13:1; italics added.) This announces the manner in which the call and ordination to the priesthood come as a teaching device. Priests, he tells us, were ordained "after the order of his Son, in a manner that thereby the people might know in what manner to look forward to his Son for redemption." (Alma 13:2.) Thus Alma sees ordination to the priesthood as a type by which those of Old Testament times were to identify the Messiah and by which they were to understand the nature of his atoning sacrifice.

To establish his point, or explain the manner in which priesthood ordination is a Messianic type, Alma reminds us that those who hold the priesthood are "called and prepared from the foundation of the world according to the foreknowledge of God, on account of their exceeding faith and good works; in the first place being left to choose good or evil; therefore they having chosen good, and exercising exceedingly great faith, are called with a holy calling, yea, with that holy calling which was prepared with, and according to, a preparatory redemption for such." (Alma 13:3.)

By Alma's description, we learn that key elements associated with ordination to the priesthood, or the authority to stand in the stead of God, include being called, prepared, proven in faith, and established in good works "from the foundation of the world." All who are so called typify Christ, who was called in the councils of heaven to his redemptive office on "account of his exceeding faith and good works." More explicitly, none hold the priesthood of God or any office within it save they have been chosen to do so by God. Authority, or office in the kingdom of God, is not by our choice but by his. False priests, prophets, and messiahs serve at their own bidding, not that of heaven. God chose those whom he has prepared, a preparation that commenced long before the spirit was housed in a mortal tabernacle. As to preparation, Alma spoke not of schools and degrees, but of the development of "exceedingly great faith" and of the doing of works of righteousness.

Teaching the same principle, Paul tells us that Christ "took not on him the nature of angels; but he took on him the seed of Abraham." (Heb. 2:16.) The Messiah was to be mortal and, as such, subject to all the frailties of the flesh that afflict his fellows. Further, he was to be the seed of Abraham, for such was the promise given to the Father of the Faithful. (See Gal. 3:16.) He was, as Moses had prophesied, to come forth from the midst of his brethren. (Deut. 18:15.) He was to be called of God, as Aaron had been called (Heb. 5:4); that is, Aaron's call to serve as Israel's high priest was but a type foreshadowing the call that would be given in some future day to a fellow Israelite, who would offer the crowning sacrifice in Israel's behalf. The Messiah, Paul taught us, was to be prepared, not in the disciplines of men but in the discipline of God. "Though he were a Son, yet learned he obedience by the things which he suffered; and being made perfect, he became the author of eternal salvation unto all them that obey him; called of God an high priest after the order of Melchisedec." (5:8-10.)[1]

How, then, were those of Jesus' day to identify the Messiah? How were they to recognize him who was to preside among them as their Great High Priest? First, they knew he would be of Abraham's seed, for all who held the priesthood must rightfully claim Abraham as their father. (Abr. 2:8-11.) Second, they knew that, as the seed of Abraham, Christ would come forth from their midst; he would be one of their brethren. Such he had been in the pre-earth life and such he would be in mortality. Third, they knew he would take no honor unto himself and that he would await the call of God. Fourth, he would be ordained to the priesthood, by the laying on of hands, as had been Aaron and all true priesthood holders in ages past. Fifth, he would be fully obedient to all the laws and statutes of God. Sixth, he would abound in good works. Seventh, he would have exceedingly great faith and, as such, have great power with God. Finally, a matter obvious to those of past ages but lost upon many of our modern day, Christ would be a man— for only men functioned as priests and priesthood holders. Such was the prophetic profile of the Great High Priest, and such is the profile of all who would claim priesthood, be they ancient or modern.

The Priest and High Priest as Messianic Types

Having established the call to the priesthood as a prophetic type for the Christ, we now turn our attention, more specifically, to the offices of priest and high priest in the Aaronic order as they officiated in the church anciently. Paul will be our tutor and the book of Hebrews our text, as we see how these ancient offices functioned so as to teach and testify of the Messiah and of his atoning sacrifice.

In this epistle to the Hebrews, Paul refers to Christ as "an high priest" (4:15; 5:1, 6, 10; 6:20; 7:26; 8:1; 9:11; 10:21), "a great high priest" (4:14), "a merciful and faithful high priest" (2:17), "the Apostle and High Priest of our profession" (3:1), and "an high priest after the order of Melchisedec" (5:10). Unfortunately, the etymology of the word *priest* is uncertain.[2] Of a certainty, however, is the fact that the priest (*cohen*) in Old Testament times functioned as a mediator between God and man. Strong suggests that the primary root means "to mediate."[3] It has also been suggested that *cohen* is derived from a verb meaning "to minister," or in the noun form, "a minister."[4] Its Greek root is a derivative of *sacerdos,* signifying that which is sacred or holy.[5] Such definitions seem wholly appropriate, by way of describing the nature of the office of a priest as found in the Old Testament, and consistent with Paul's description of Christ as the "great high priest."

All priests were types for Christ. To understand their office and calling was to understand the nature of the Messiah's ministry. Their duties, as summarized in Deuteronomy, were to watch over and guard the covenant, to teach the law of God, and to make the ritual offerings required by the law. (Deut. 33:9-10.) The performance of their ministry placed the priests in a dual mediational role. In their ritual performance, they functioned as a mediator between the people and God. In teaching the law, they represented God to the people. As the priest was mediator between God and man, so Israel was called to be the vehicle of the knowledge and salvation of God to the nations of the earth. As the priest was to be holy, so the nation was to be holy. Indeed, it had been the desire of the Lord initially that Israel be a "kingdom of priests, and an holy nation." (Ex. 19:6.) It was Israel's refusal to live such a standard that led to the priesthood being confined to the tribe of Levi.

Sundry duties were associated with the office of high priest, including: (1) entrance into the most holy place (Lev. 16:3); (2) mediating with God for the people (Ex. 28:29); (3) bearing the sins of his people (Ex. 28:38); (4) offering incense—a symbolic act representing the ascension of Israel's prayers (Lev. 16:12-13); (5) making atonement (Lev. 16:32); (6) judging of uncleanness, in establishing worthiness to enter the presence of the Lord (Lev. 13:2); and (7) blessing the people (Num. 6:23). In two matters, the office of high priest was particularly distinguished from that of the ordinary priest. The first was his responsibility to communicate the mind and will of God to the people. To do so, he had been granted the use of the Urim and Thummim. Second, each year, on the Day of Atonement, he entered the Holy of Holies, where he would sprinkle the blood of a sin offering on the mercy seat. This was done to seek forgiveness for the sins of his people in a manner foreshadowing the atonement yet to be made by Christ. (See Lev. 16.)

The priesthood, which occupied a mediational position between God and Israel, testified to the holiness that God demands for access to him. No principle was better understood among the ancients than the doctrine that no unclean thing could enter his presence. The ritual system, with its sacrifices, shows the seriousness of sin and testifies that a life must be given before forgiveness can be obtained. The very existence of the priesthood establishes the need for a mediator. No common man could make the sacrifice that provided access to God. Only one clothed with priesthood and the robes of righteousness, one called and chosen of God, could serve at the altar and enter the holy place or the Holy of Holies.

In Jesus Christ, Israel was to see their faithful and spotless Mediator and high priest. In him every mediational role in the Old Testament finds its fulfillment: (1) Christ rent the veil and entered the true holy place—heaven, the abode of God (Heb. 9:24); (2) in heaven, Christ labors as a mediator in our behalf (Heb. 9:24); (3) Christ bore the sins of the elect (2 Cor. 5:21); (4) Christ's ascension and intercession appear to be the spiritual fulfillment of the ascending smoke of incense; (5) Christ offered himself as an atonement for our sins; (6) through the atonement, Christ becomes the judge of all and will yet come on that great and dreadful day to reward all according to their works; and (7) through Christ and the atonement, all the blessings of the gospel become a reality to those seeking after them.

Entering the Rest of the Lord

The entrance of the high priest into the Holy of Holies and his passing through the sacred veil of the temple was a type for that future day when the Son of God would rend the veil to enter the heavenly temple and stand in the presence of God. Having satisfied the demands of justice through his atoning sacrifice, Christ could now commence his great work of mercy and mediation in behalf of all whose labors attested that they had accepted him. By virtue of his mercy and grace, the faithful of all ages could now also enter into the holiest place. "So now, my friends," Paul explained, "the blood of Jesus makes us free to enter boldly into the sanctuary by the new, living way which he has opened for us through the curtain, the way of his flesh. We have, moreover, a great priest set over the household of God; so let us make our approach in sincerity of heart and full assurance of faith, our guilty hearts sprinkled clean, our bodies washed with pure water." (Heb. 10:19-22, New English Bible.)

The purpose of the atonement was to remove the effects of the Fall whereby men were cast out of the presence of God. Through his sacrifice, Christ opened the door through which we might return to the divine presence. To return to the presence of the Lord is, in the language of the scriptures, to obtain the "rest of the Lord." Paul reminded the Hebrew saints of Moses' efforts to bring the children of Israel into that rest while they were yet in the flesh. He was unable to do so because of their unbelief and the hardness of their hearts. (See Ps. 95:7-11; Heb. 3:8-11.) Blessings that are obtained on the same grounds in the meridian day were lost on the same grounds. Paul warned that if the meridian saints hardened their hearts in unbelief, they too would forfeit the privilege of entering into God's rest. "Let us labour therefore to enter into that rest, lest any man fall after the same example of unbelief." (4:11.)

The appropriateness of Paul's warning, with an expanded explanation of its implications, is given to our day through the Prophet Joseph Smith. This revelation traces Moses' priesthood back to Adam and identifies it as the authority by which the gospel is administered. It tells us that this priesthood, the very priesthood restored in our day, holds the keys of the mysteries of the kingdom and the key of the knowledge of God. Further, it tells us that this priesthood is given to prepare those of the house of faith to be brought into the presence or rest of the Lord. Moses, having the same priesthood, sought the same end. We are told that he "sought diligently to sanctify his people that they might behold the face of God; but they hardened their hearts and could not endure his presence; therefore, the Lord in his wrath, for his anger was kindled against them, swore that they should not enter into his rest while in the wilderness, which rest is the fulness of his glory. Therefore, he took Moses out of their midst, and the Holy Priesthood also," giving them in its stead the lesser or Aaronic Priesthood. (D&C 84:19-25.)

Thus, those of our day have been clearly warned that failure to use the priesthood for the purpose for which it has been given—namely, to sanctify us so that we might enter into the divine presence—will result in that priesthood and the fullness of gospel blessings being taken from us. The principle can apply no differently to us than it did to the children of Israel as they wandered in the wilderness or as they joined with the church of Christ in the meridian of time.

Melchizedek as a Type for Christ

It stands to reason that if the priesthood is a type for Christ, Melchizedek, whose life personifies what a priesthood holder ought to be, is also a type for the Savior. Paul so identifies him to the Hebrews. By interpretation, he tells us that the name Melchizedek means "King of righteousness." (Heb. 7:2.) *Melech* (Melek) is the Hebrew word for king, while *Sedek* (Zedek) means just or righteousness. No more appropriate name could have been used as a substitute for the name of deity in referring to the priesthood. The priesthood is the authority of our king, an authority that can be used only in righteousness. Paul also notes that Melchizedek was the King of Salem, which he interprets as "King of peace." (7:2.) *Salem* is a form of the Jewish greeting *shalom*, meaning "peace to you." Thus, Gideon named the place where the Lord gave him the promise of peace, "Jehovah-shalom." (Judg. 6:23-24.)

In the Bible text, we read that Melchizedek is "without father, without mother, without descent, having neither beginning of days, nor end of life; but made like unto the Son of God; [abiding] a priest continually." (Heb. 7:3.) This statement, an obvious Bible error, has been the source of much mischief and nonsense among uninspired writers. From the revelation on the priesthood previously cited, we learn that it is the priesthood and not Melchizedek to which reference is being made in the verse. (See JST, Heb. 7:3; also D&C 84:17.) In identifying the Melchizedek Priesthood as being "without father, without mother, without descent," Paul is simply emphasizing that the

Greater Priesthood, unlike the Lesser Priesthood, is not the exclusive province of the tribe of Levi. With the restoration of a higher order of things, it was righteousness that qualified one for the priesthood, not descent from Levi. Further, our corrected text reads, "And all those who are ordained unto this priesthood are made like unto the Son of God, abiding a priest continually." (JST, Heb. 7:3.)

Alma also describes Melchizedek as a classic type for Christ. "Now this Melchizedek was a king over the land of Salem; and his people had waxed strong in iniquity and abomination; yea, they had all gone astray; they were full of all manner of wickedness; but Melchizedek having exercised mighty faith, and received the office of the high priesthood according to the holy order of God, did preach repentance unto his people. And behold, they did repent; and Melchizedek did establish peace in the land in his days; therefore he was called the prince of peace, for he was the king of Salem; and he did reign under his father." (Alma 13:17-18.) Alma's profile of Melchizedek is of a great preacher of righteousness, a teacher of repentance, whose message, once it was accepted by his people, established perfect peace among them. This prince of peace then ruled Salem as prophet, priest, and king, which he did "under his father." The likeness to Christ is made even more perfect by adding the description from the Joseph Smith Translation, from which we learn that Melchizedek "was called the king of heaven by his people, or, in other words, the King of peace," and that his people "wrought righteousness, and obtained heaven." (JST, Gen. 14:34-36.)

Mosaic Ordinances Prefigured Christ's Ministry

This was not an epistle to Gentiles, but to Hebrews, those schooled in the law of Moses. It was one thing to know the law and entirely another to know the reason for the law. Similarly, in our day it is one thing to know what the Bible says and entirely another to know what the Bible means. Israel had her tabernacle—within the temple; the altar, ark, veil, Holy of Holies, and so forth—in which sacrifices and cleansing ordinances were performed, which Paul, by the spirit of revelation, now identifies as similitudes of the coming of the Son of God. Through these ordinances, the faithful among the ancients obtained a forgiveness of sins and learned what was required of them to obtain the rest of the Lord.

Let us briefly identify the symbolism associated with those parts of Israel's ancient temple worship referred to by Paul in Hebrews 9:

Tabernacle: The tabernacle was a portable temple of the Lord, the place of the divine presence, and thus represents the kingdoms of heaven. The outer court represents the telestial order, the holy place the terrestrial order, and the Holy of Holies, the celestial world, the place where the throne of God is found.

Candlestick: The seven-branched candelabrum of the tabernacle was part of the furniture of the holy place. It was not lighted by candles, but by pure olive oil in cup-shaped containers resting on the head of each of its branches. (Ex. 25:31-40.) Its light represents the light of the Holy Spirit. The seven branches or stems represent the fullness and perfection of the revelations of God and could be taken as affirmation that they would burn brightly in seven great gospel dispensations.

Table: Paul's reference is to the table of shewbread that stood on the north or right side as one entered the holy place. It faced the candlestick and upon it were to be placed twelve loaves of bread made of fine (unleavened) flour. Paul does not identify its symbolism. Its equivalent in our day could be the sacrament table.

Shewbread: Literally translated, the name *shewbread* means "the bread of faces," or "the bread of the presence," signifying that this bread was placed before the face of the Lord or in his presence. That there is a common symbolism between the Sabbath ritual in which the priests were to eat the shewbread and the ordinance of the sacrament, as introduced by Christ, seems apparent.

Sanctuary: The sanctuary, in this text, refers to the holy place.

Veil: Paul's reference is to the thick curtain separating the Holy of Holies from the holy place in the temple. The rending of the veil symbolizes the removal of the barrier between man and God, for man is thus enabled "to enter into the holiest by the blood of Jesus." (Heb. 10:19.) Thus, the faithful and obedient can, in the fullest and most complete sense, enter into the rest of the Lord.

Holiest of All: By holiest of all, Paul is referring to the Holy of

Holies. This, the most sacred place in the temple, is the symbolic representation of the heavenly temple where the throne of Gód sits.

Golden Censer: The vessel used for the burning of incense in the holy place was known as the golden censer. (Paul seems to indicate that this was housed in the Holy of Holies. There is nothing in the Old Testament that corroborates this.) The smoke rising from the vessel is a symbol of the prayers of Israel rising to God. (Ps. 141:2.)

Ark of the Covenant: Housed within the Holy of Holies, the ark of the covenant signifies the divine presence and as such is the most sacred symbol in ancient Israel.

Manna: Among the sacred relics found within the temple was a golden pot containing some of the manna sent down from heaven as food for Israel during their wilderness wanderings. This bread from heaven typifies the spiritual salvation that could be had only through Christ, who is the Bread of Life.

Aaron's Rod: To affirm his call to Aaron and his tribe to labor in the priesthood in preference to the other tribes, the Lord instructed Moses to have each of the tribes bring a rod or branch with the name of their prince on it. These twelve rods were then placed before the Lord in the Holy of Holies. The following morning when Moses went to the sacred place, he found the rod of Aaron covered with buds, blossoms, and even mature almonds. The other rods remained as barren as before. (Num. 17.) As I have written elsewhere, "The symbolism associated with this test was most deliberate: A rod, or branch, had been chosen to represent each of the twelve tribes or families of Israel; each had its name carefully placed upon it. By tradition, the rod, as a staff or sceptre, represented one's position and authority. Together, all were presented before the Lord. By making Aaron's rod bud, blossom, and put forth fruit, the Lord demonstrated once again that it was for him to choose those who will stand in his stead, be filled with his power, and bring forth his fruits."[6]

Tables of the Covenant: The tables of the covenant refers to the tablets upon which the Ten Commandments were written.

Cherubim: The images of two cherubim were placed over the mercy seat of the ark in the Holy of Holies. Cherubim are angels, set to guard the way before the presence of the Lord. They are to see that no unclean thing enters the divine presence.

Mercy Seat: The mercy seat is the golden lid to the ark of the covenant: This lid, which covers the ark, is a symbolic representation of the manner in which the Atonement overarches or covers all that is sacred. The name comes from the Hebrew *kapporeth,* which, in turn, comes from the root *kaphar,* meaning to cover or expiate. It implies the making of an atonement, a cleansing or forgiving.

Though Paul did not detail the meaning of each of these items associated with the temple, his purpose was to emphasize that each was intended as a witness of Jesus as the Christ.

Conclusion

Hebrews was not written to Gentiles, but to Jews. It was written to those schooled in the law of Moses. Yet it took Paul, a living prophet, to unfold its symbolism and explain the meaning of Mosaic rituals to the Jewish saints of his day. Through his eyes they came to see that all things associated with the Mosaic law centered in and testified of Christ. Similarly, in this epistle Paul seeks to bring the Hebrew Saints to the understanding that everything in the gospel centers in Christ. Salvation is not the result of ritual performance nor is it the result of a verbal declaration. Rather, salvation consists of our becoming one with Christ.

Christ was in the express image of his Father's person and the brightness of his glory. As such, he personifies what a saved being is. Thus, he shows the way for all who desire salvation. Salvation comes by taking upon ourselves his name, by saying and doing what he would say and do. For us to obtain salvation means we will obtain that same brightness and glory. Such brightness and glory can be obtained only by taking upon ourselves his name and learning to do as he would do. Christ was a living prophecy of his Father. We must become living prophecies of Christ. Paul declared it thus: "Now the God of peace, that brought again from the dead our Lord Jesus, that great shepherd of the sheep, through the blood of the everlasting covenant, make you perfect in every good work to do his will, working in you that which is wellpleasing in his sight, through Jesus Christ; to whom be glory for ever and ever. Amen." (13:20-21.)

Notes

1. On the original manuscripts of the Joseph Smith Translation of the Bible, the following note is found (N. T. manuscript no. 2, folio 4, p. 139): "The 7th and 8th verses allude to Melchizedek, and not to Christ." (See Robert J. Matthews, *"A Plainer Translation": Joseph Smith's Translation of the Bible* [Provo: Brigham Young University Press, 1975], pp. 383-84.) Since Melchizedek—in name (his name literally means "my king is righteousness" or simply "king of righteousness") and in deed—was a remarkable type of Christ, it would appear that Hebrews 5:7-8 would have reference to both Melchizedek and Christ. (See Bruce R. McConkie, *Doctrinal New Testament Commentary,* 3 vols. [Salt Lake City: Bookcraft, 1965-73], 3:157; *The Promised Messiah: The First Coming of Christ* [Salt Lake City: Deseret Book, 1978], p. 450.)

2. Brown, Driver, and Briggs, in their work *A Hebrew and English Lexicon of the Old Testament* (Oxford: Clarendon Press, 1978), make no attempt at definition.

3. James Strong, *Strong's Exhaustive Concordance* (Nashville: Regal Publishers, Inc.), "Dictionary of the Hebrew Bible," p. 54.

4. William Gouge, *Commentary on Hebrews* (Grand Rapids, Michigan: Kregel Publications), p. 182.

5. Strong, *Strong's Exhaustive Concordance,* "Dictionary of the Greek Testament," p. 37. See also Gouge, *Commentary on the Hebrews,* p. 182.

6. Joseph Fielding McConkie, *Gospel Symbolism* (Salt Lake City: Bookcraft, 1985), p. 73.

14

A STRING OF GOSPEL PEARLS
(James)

LARRY E. DAHL

As one contemplates the book of James, several questions come to mind: Who wrote the book of James? To whom did he write? When? Why? What messages for them and for us are to be found in the book?

Background

There are several persons mentioned in the New Testament who have the name James. Although there is no conclusive agreement among Bible scholars, it is generally agreed that the author of this epistle is James, the Lord's brother, also referred to as James the Just. He occupied an important position in the church at Jerusalem: he was one of the three "pillars" of the church at Jerusalem (along with Peter and John) who extended the hand of fellowship to Paul after his remarkable conversion (Gal. 1:19; 2:9); he played a key role in the council at Jerusalem dealing with the question of whether Gentile converts were expected to be circumcised and abide by other requirements of the Jewish law (Acts 15); and he received Paul's report of his missionary labors among the Gentiles and counseled him concerning his associations with Jewish Christians (Acts 21). Is it possible that he was a member of the presidency of the church, replacing the other James,

---

Larry E. Dahl is associate professor of Church history and doctrine and director of Doctrine and Covenants research in the Religious Studies Center at Brigham Young University.

who was killed by Herod? (Acts 12:2.) If so, that would explain his prominent role at the Jerusalem Council, and the fact that Paul, an apostle, repeatedly reported to him when he was in Jerusalem.[1]

In the opening verse of the epistle, the writer identifies himself simply as "James, a servant of God and of the Lord Jesus Christ." That he did not explain himself more specifically suggests that he was well known to those he was addressing—"the twelve tribes which are scattered abroad." (James 1:1.) Did he mean literally the twelve tribes of Israel, or was he perhaps using the term to refer to covenant Israel— believers in Jesus Christ, members of the church—whether blood Israel or adopted "heirs according to the promise" (Gal. 3:29)? Because most of literal Israel had been taken captive, scattered, and "lost," and were therefore not apt to receive his epistle, it seems appropriate to believe that he was addressing covenant Israel, somewhat scattered, but known and available.

When did he write? If the author is indeed James, the Lord's brother, the epistle was written before A.D. 62. There is substantial evidence that James, the brother of the Lord, was killed about A.D. 62 by Jewish leaders who took the law into their own hands at a time when there was no Roman procurator in Judea (between the death of Festus and the arrival of Albinus, procurators).[2] Richard Lloyd Anderson comments: "Eusebius quotes Josephus on the death of the brother of the Lord and adds: 'Such is the story of James, whose is said to be the first of the so-called general epistles.' ... James' lack of warnings of apostasy verifies this early date—all the known later letters speak sharply of false teachers."[3]

If James was not writing to denounce or warn against apostate teachers who evidently entered the scene later, why did he write? No reason is given in the epistle itself. The purpose does not seem to be to convince readers of the divinity of Christ or of the authority of the church or its leaders. These things seem to be assumed. The epistle is not a well-organized treatise on a major theme, or even two or three themes, but is more like a sermon, highlighting many gospel truths and exhorting readers to apply the principles they profess to believe. This is similar to some of the general conference addresses of President Spencer W. Kimball in the middle and late 1970s. Perhaps as a leader of the church in his day, James saw signs of spiritual sickness among the saints—lack of faith and certitude, buckling under the weight of trials and temptation, hypocrisy, selfishness, loose tongues, a strong attraction to the world with its standards of behavior and judgment, love of riches, violation of conscience—and felt pressed to counsel, correct, encourage and strengthen his fellow church members. Do you notice how hauntingly modern the problems sound? Undoubtedly, the epistle of James is as needed in our day as it was in his.

Seen in this light, rather than being an "epistle full of straw, because it contains nothing of the gospel,"[4] the book of James is an epistle that contains the very essence of the gospel—"pure religion" (1:27), the "royal law" (2:8), a guide to overcoming a "multitude of sins" (5:20)—and is timelessly current.

This brings us to an examination of the messages contained in the epistle. James speaks of several gospel truths. Among them, we may each find some that strike responsive chords in our hearts.

A Pattern for Finding Answers
(James 1:5)

Perhaps the most familiar and most often quoted verse in the book of James as far as Latter-day Saints are concerned is James 1:5: "If any of you lack wisdom, let him ask of God, that giveth to all men liberally, and upbraideth not, and it shall be given him." Of this verse Joseph Smith said, "Never did any passage of scripture come with more power to the heart of man than this did at this time to mine. It seemed to enter with great force into every feeling of my heart. I reflected on it again and again." (JS–H 1:12.) The verse had such a profound effect on Joseph at that time because of his great need. Observing the "war of words, and tumult of opinions" concerning which church was right, he was troubled and yearned to know how he could find answers for himself. As he was reading the scriptures, the Spirit of the Lord penetrated his mind and heart when he came to the particular passage that would direct him toward resolving his difficulty. He was humble enough to follow the message of the scripture, and the result was a new dispensation of the gospel on the earth, a restitution of all things, a restoration of truth, power, and priesthood with inestimable eternal significance for all mankind.

Is there a pattern for truth seekers here? An honest, troubled heart yearning for resolutions, scriptures, the Spirit, humility and courage to receive and obey the message. Surely we too can be directed toward answers to our questions, as Joseph Smith was. Our answers may not be found in this particular verse, because our needs may not be the same as his (on the other hand, they may be very much the same); and the results of our endeavors may not stretch as far and deep as did Joseph's. But there can come to each of us a kind of personal dispensation of truth and power (even a "restoration" if we have become casual or have strayed) that for us is glorious, with eternal significance. But we must follow the pattern: we must search the scriptures with real intent, humility, and courage, setting the stage for the Spirit to focus our minds and our hearts upon those truths which are of particular importance to us now.

Trials and Afflictions
(James 1:2-4, 12-19; 5:7-11)

"My brethren, count it all joy when ye fall into divers temptations." (James 1:2.) The Joseph Smith Translation changes "divers temptations" to "many afflictions." To many persons, this seems to be strange doctrine. Why "count it all joy" when we are afflicted in one way or another? Why do faithful people, who are earnestly striving to do all they know they should do, suffer hardship and heartbreak, sometimes for long periods, or repeatedly? Does it have to be this way? Couldn't an omnipotent God pave the road of life, at least for those who would obediently and happily walk thereon? Further, why did the Savior, who was fully obedient and totally innocent, have to endure incomprehensible suffering? That suffering and trials are essential in the plan of salvation is unmistakably clear, though not always easy to accept. It has to do with "law, irrevocably decreed in heaven before the foundation of this world." (D&C 130:20.) It has to do with the "justice of God" in executing that law with exactness (Alma 7:20; 42:14; Jacob 4:10), making it possible for us to have unwavering faith in Him.[5] It has to do with agency and its misuse by us and by others. (Alma 14:11; 60:13; D&C 103:3-4.) And, painfully, it has to do with our being tested and tried, proven "to see if [we] will do all things whatsoever the Lord [our] God shall command [us]." (Abr. 3:25.)

Father Lehi taught, "For it must needs be, that there is an opposition in all things," stressing that without opposition, neither righteousness nor happiness nor the eternal purposes of God (and therefore, our own purposes) could be brought about. (2 Ne. 2:11-13.) The Lord has reminded us repeatedly in this dispensation that he will have a tried people:

> My people must be tried in all things, that they may be prepared to receive the glory that I have for them, even the glory of Zion; and he that will not bear chastisement is not worthy of my kingdom. (D&C 136:31.)
>
> For he will give unto the faithful line upon line, precept upon precept; and I will try you and prove you herewith . . . for I have decreed in my heart, saith the Lord, that I will prove you in all things, whether you will abide in my covenant, even unto death, that you may be found worthy. (D&C 98:12-14.)
>
> Therefore, they must needs be chastened and tried, even as Abraham, who was commanded to offer up his only son. For all those who will not endure chastening, but deny me, cannot be sanctified. (D&C 101:4-5.)

As we experience and observe trials and afflictions, we often see what appear to be inequities. People are tested and afflicted in different ways, in different degrees. As Elder Boyd K. Packer explains, "Some are tested by poor health, some by a body that is deformed or homely. Others are tested by handsome and healthy bodies; some by the passion of youth; others by the erosions of old age. Some suffer disappointment in marriage, family problems; others live in poverty and obscurity. Some (perhaps this is the hardest test) find ease and luxury. All are part of the test, *and there is more equality in this testing than sometimes we suspect.*"[6]

Understanding this principle, James could truly encourage his readers to "count it all joy" and remind them that "trying of [their] faith worketh patience . . . that [they] may be perfect and entire, wanting nothing." (James 1:3-4.) Perhaps also because he understands that such trials are difficult, James admonishes that we "stablish [our] hearts," or be resolute, firm, and anchored, and look to the prophets "for an example of suffering affliction, and of patience." (James 5:7-11.)

James reminds us that we must not blame God for every trouble. Much of what we suffer is because of our own doing, "being drawn away of [our] own lust, and enticed." (James 1:14.) He assures us that in God there is "no variableness, neither shadow of turning" (James 1:17; see also Alma 7:20), and that God's gifts to us are good and perfect (James 1:17). "Wherefore, my beloved brethren," he says, "let every man be swift to hear, slow to speak, slow to wrath. . . . Lay apart all filthiness . . . and receive with meekness the engrafted word, which is able to save your souls." (James 1:19-21.)

Faith and Works
(James 1:22-27; 2:14-15; JST⁷)

"Be ye *doers* of the word." (James 1:22; emphasis added.) Anything less than this is self-deception. James points out the incongruency of claiming to have faith in God without doing the works of God. That is as foolish as the position of the devils who "believe and tremble," who acknowledge God and his power, but who do not obey the laws that bring the blessings. In the final analysis, our works (our thoughts, feelings, and actions) identify the object or objects of our faith. Correctly understood, faith and works are not the same thing, but they are inseparable companions. To have faith is to have confidence and trust in something sufficient to motivate us to action. If there is no action, there is no faith. We can exercise faith in a myriad of things, but faith in anything but the God of Israel is powerless to save us.

James also teaches us that faith and works serve to build one another—faith leads to works, and by works, faith is made perfect. (James 2:22.) If we can generate enough faith in the promises of God to obey, he is bound to bless us. (D&C 82:10.) Experiencing those blessings will in turn build our confidence that his promises are sure, leading to further obedience. How do we start the cycle? "Faith cometh by hearing" (Rom. 10:17), through studying the scriptures (Hel. 15:7-8), as a gift of the Spirit to those who ask in humility and with real intent (1 Cor. 12:9; Alma 22:15-18), and if we will simply "awake and arouse [our] faculties, even to an experiment upon [God's] words" (Alma 32:27).

With these things in mind, the seemingly endless debate over whether we are saved by faith or by works is almost meaningless. The truth is, we are saved by grace—the grace of God and of Jesus Christ as expressed in the reality of the plan of salvation made possible through the Infinite Atonement. Our resurrection ("salvation" from the grave) is assured totally by grace, without regard to faith or works. (1 Cor. 15:22.) However, our "salvation" from hell and the devil, and the level or degree of that salvation, depend a great deal upon our faith and works. There are eternal rewards commensurate with every level of faith and works, from perdition to exaltation. But grace is essential here too, to make faith and works efficacious. Hence, Nephi's testimony that "it is by grace that we are saved, after all we can do" (2 Ne. 25:23) and James's exhortation to be "doers of the word" make sense. Indeed, "pure religion and undefiled before God and the Father" is not contained in vain and unbridled *claims* of belief (James 1:26); rather it is exemplified in *works:* "to visit the fatherless and widows in their affliction, and to keep [oneself] unspotted from the vices of the world." (JST, James 1:26-27.)[8]

Loose Tongues (1:26; 3:3-18; 4:11-12)

"If any man among you seem to be religious, and bridleth not his tongue, . . . this man's religion is vain" (James 1:26); "And the tongue is a fire, a world of iniquity" (3:6); "The tongue . . . is an unruly evil, full of deadly poison" (3:8). James points out that mankind has learned to control or tame almost everything—ships, horses, beasts, birds, serpents, and things in the sea—except the tongue. (3:3-7.) He decries the fact that with the same mouths we bless God and curse men, producing both sweet and bitter fruit, a condition that is against the natural order of things, and "ought not so to be." (James 3:9-12.) Rather than stirring up "bitter envying," "strife," and "confusion" with falsehoods, James reminds us that the "wisdom that is from above is first pure, then peaceable, gentle, and easy to be intreated, full of mercy and good fruits, without partiality, and without hypocrisy." (James 3:13-17.)

An unruly tongue can fan the flames of rumor, spread gossip, betray confidences, destroy trust, and cause embarrassment and pain, even if what is talked about is true. President Spencer W. Kimball said, "Lies and gossip which harm reputations are scattered about by the four winds like the seeds of a ripe dandelion held aloft by a child. The degree and extent of the harm done by the gossip is inestimable."[9] Whenever we are tempted to speak ill of another, perhaps we should remember the Savior's teachings about what has become known as the golden rule (Matt. 7:12), and about motes and beams (Matt. 7:1-5). Also we should note James's explanation that when we speak evil of another, we are in a sense judging that person and putting ourselves in God's place. After declaring that there is but one lawgiver, he asks, "Who art thou that judgest another?" (James 4:11-12.)

Another dimension of loose talk is profanity and vulgarity. Elder Dallin H. Oaks, a modern apostle, addressed that issue in general conference in April 1986. Some excerpts from his discussion follow:

> For many in our day, the profane has become commonplace and the vulgar has become acceptable. Surely this is one fulfillment of the Book of Mormon prophecy that in the last days "there shall be great pollutions upon the face of the earth." (Morm. 8:31.) The people of God have always been commanded to abstain from language that is profane or vulgar....
>
> Satan seeks to discredit the sacred names of God the Father and his Son, Jesus Christ, the names through which their work is done. He succeeds in a measure whenever he is able to influence any man or woman, boy or girl, to make holy names common and to associate them with coarse thoughts and evil acts. Those who use sacred names in vain are, by that act, promoters of Satan's purposes.
>
> Profanity is profoundly offensive to those who worship the God whose name is desecrated. We all remember how a prophet reacted from a hospital bed when an operating room attendant stumbled and cursed in his presence. Even half-conscious, Elder [Spencer W.] Kimball "recoiled and implored: 'Please! Please! That is my Lord whose name you revile'" (*Improvement Era*, May 1953, p. 320.)...

Profanity also takes its toll on the one who uses it. . . . The Spirit of the Lord . . . is offended and withdraws. . . .

Vulgar and crude expressions are also offensive to the Spirit of the Lord. . . .

A speaker who mouths profanity or vulgarity to punctuate or emphasize speech confesses inadequacy in his or her own language skills. Properly used, modern languages require no such artificial boosters. A speaker who employs profanity or vulgarity to catch someone's attention with shock effect engages in a babyish device that is inexcusable as juvenile or adult behavior. Such language is morally bankrupt. It is also progressively self-defeating, since shock diminishes with familiarity and the user can only maintain its effect by escalating its excess.[10]

There is yet another aspect to controlling the tongue that is worthy of serious consideration. Our ability and willingness to control our tongues is directly related to how much revelation the Lord is willing to give us. "Remember that that which cometh from above is sacred, and must be spoken with care, and by constraint of the Spirit." (D&C 63:64.) Promising that marvelous signs and healings would follow true believers in the early church, the Lord cautioned: "But a commandment I give unto them, that they shall not boast themselves of these things, neither speak them before the world; for these things are given unto you for your profit and for salvation." (D&C 84:73.) Later he declared: "Talk not of judgments, neither boast of faith nor of mighty works." (D&C 105:24.) The Prophet Joseph Smith taught that "the reason we do not have the secrets of the Lord revealed unto us, is because we do not keep them but reveal them; we do not keep our own secrets, but reveal our difficulties to the world, even to our enemies, then how would we keep the secrets of the Lord?"[11] President Brigham Young counseled as follows:

Should you receive a vision or revelation from the Almighty, one that the Lord gave you concerning yourselves, or this people, but which you are not to reveal on account of your not being the proper person, or because it ought not to be known by the people at present, you should shut it up and seal it as close, and lock it as tight as heaven is to you, and make it as secret as the grave. The Lord has no confidence in those who reveal secrets, for He cannot safely reveal Himself to such persons.[12]

That man who cannot know things without telling any other living being upon the earth, who cannot keep his secrets and those that God reveals to him, never can receive the voice of his Lord to dictate him and the people on this earth.[13]

President David O. McKay called special spiritual experiences "heart petals."[14] Surely it would take some special inspiration to share them with others. The spirit of the occasion would have to be right, and the motive would have to be to build another or to build the kingdom, not self-aggrandizement.

Whether the tongue is undisciplined in the area of gossip, profanity and vulgarity, or the unwise telling of sacred things, it needs to be controlled. Great blessings can flow from schooled tongues; great harm can come from loose tongues.

Double-mindedness
(James 1:6; 3:10; 4:1-12)

Double-mindedness means being torn between two enticements, being tossed to and fro by divided loyalties, attempting to give attention to both simultaneously, or devoting oneself to one and then the other, alternately. Either approach is fruitless, leaving the person fragmented and ineffective in both camps. Such an approach pleases the devil but not the Lord. The Lord's way is to "have no other gods" before him (Ex. 20:3), to "seek . . . first the kingdom of God, and his righteousness" (Matt. 6:33), to "serve him with all [our] heart, might, mind and strength" (D&C 4:2), to yield "to the enticings of the Holy Spirit" (Mosiah 3:19), to prove that we are "determined to serve Him at all hazards."[15] We must put on the whole armor of God (D&C 27:15-18; Eph. 6:10-18), experience a change of heart that will make us "firm and steadfast" (Hel. 15:7-8), "sure and steadfast" (Ether 12:4), anchored and immovable in proclaiming and defending the truth of heaven. In a pluralistic world, some may see this posture as narrow, even bigoted and arrogant, wooden, uncaring, self-righteous. But the Savior was none of these, and none was more unbending and resolute in the cause of right doctrine and right behavior than he. By his own words, we are to follow his example. (Matt. 4:19; 5:48; 3 Ne. 27:27.) But how can we judge *and* be tolerant, preach justice *and* mercy, be uncompromising *and* cooperative, advocate faith *and* reason, be heaven-bent *and* world-concerned, have our heads in the clouds *and* our feet on the ground, as it were, all at the same time, and not be double-minded? This can be done only with a gospel view of things— a view that admits to a God in heaven, a purposeful creation, a plan of salvation, a Savior, continuous revelation to prophets and to individuals, and the wisdom and ultimate necessity of everyone's yielding to that system.

Temporarily, the world may reject God and the gospel view. James tells us that "whosoever therefore will be a friend of the world is the enemy of God." In fact, he indicates that those who give their allegiance to the world rather than to God are "adulterers and adulteresses." (James 4:4.) Although he may be referring literally to sexual immorality, it is more probable that he is speaking figuratively of adultery—that is, the bride (the Lord's covenant people) has been unfaithful to the bridegroom (Christ), has given her heart or part of it to another suitor (the world). (See Isa. 54:5-6; Jer. 3:14, 20; 31:32; Ezek. 16; Hosea 2.) Such double-mindedness is not acceptable to the Bridegroom; he desires and expects complete loyalty—single-mindedness. Single-mindedness toward God does not preclude concern for and efforts to improve the world, but it does require an uncompromising commitment to doing things the Lord's way. And that way is offensive to some. One simply cannot fully serve God without offending the devil—and one cannot be double-minded without offending God.

James points out several cases of double-mindedness: faith versus lack of faith in prayers (1:5-6); blessings versus cursings from the same tongue (3:10); allegiance to God versus allegiance to the world (4:1-4); being subject to the one lawgiver versus judging the law and others (4:11-12); and submitting to God versus yielding to the influence of the devil (4:6-7). He challenges those affected to overcome their double-mindedness by submitting themselves to God—to be humble, draw near to him, and purify their hearts—promising that in response, God will draw near to them and lift them up (4:6-10). James also admonishes the appropriate reaction to the devil and his temptations: "Resist the devil, and he will flee from you" (4:7).

Keeping the Whole Law
(James 2:10)

"For whosoever shall keep the whole law, and yet offend in one point, he is guilty of all." (James 2:10.[16]) Does that mean that those who are not perfect are considered guilty concerning even the laws they have not broken? How are we to interpret this passage? James uses this statement to emphasize the fact that the "royal law" requires that we love our neighbors as ourselves; and regardless of whatever else we may do toward our neighbor that is decent and right (even if we keep every other aspect of the law as it pertains to our neighbor), if we "have respect of persons" because of riches, we have broken that royal law and thereby deny ourselves the blessings that keeping it would bring. (James 2:1-9.)

Another scriptural example of someone's keeping all the law but one point, and thereby missing *all* that he could have had, is the sad story of the rich young man who came to Jesus asking what he had to do to gain eternal life. (Matt. 19:16-26.) Jesus reminded him of the critical commandments. The young man responded: "All these things have I kept from my youth up: what lack I yet?" When told that to be perfect he must give up his wealth, the young man "went away sorrowful: for he had great possessions." Several issues and lessons could be extracted from that exchange, but the point to be made here is that failing in any requirement of the law can rob us of eternal life. Joseph Smith said: "Any person who is exalted to the highest mansion has to abide a celestial law, and the whole law too," and "I spoke to the people, showing them that to get salvation we must not only do some things, but everything which God has commanded."[17]

Those who attain exaltation must be "cleansed from *all* their sins." (D&C 76:52; emphasis added.) Certainly there are eternal kingdoms and rewards to correspond with every level of obedience. However, it only takes one area of deficiency to keep us from "all that [our] Father hath." (D&C 84:38.) That seems to be the point James is making. Thankfully, we have been given a probationary time to learn total obedience. It is not required by Monday morning, as it were—at least not *next* Monday. But we should not use the Lord's willingness to be patient with us as an excuse to be casual or lazy about self-improvement. King Benjamin taught the proper balance: "See that all these things are done in wisdom and order; for it is not requisite that a man should run faster than he has strength. And again, it is expedient that he should be diligent, that thereby he might win the prize; therefore, all things must be done in order." (Mosiah 4:27.)

Riches
(James 1:9-11; 2:1-13; 5:1-6)

At three different points in his epistle James discusses riches, twice to warn about how transitory they are (1:9-11; 5:1-6), and once to decry using them as the reason for giving respect or honored social position (2:1-13). Immediately a defensive chorus (usually made up of those who are rich and those who intend to become so) swells in unison: "There is nothing wrong with having money. It takes money to help build the kingdom. Many of the leaders of the church are wealthy." No contest! The Lord does not condemn riches. In fact, he promises them to the obedient and is pleased when he can bestow them. (D&C 59:16-20.) However, he has repeatedly warned—and history has proven—that worldly wealth brings with it the potential, and more often than not the reality, of the very evils James identifies in his epistle: social distinctions based on wealth and oppression of the poor (2:1-9), foolish reliance upon and unwarranted stockpiling of wealth (5:1-3), selfish withholding of honest wages by fraud (5:4), and wanton hedonism, enjoyed at the expense of others (5:5-6).

The Lord promised the early saints of this dispensation "the riches of the earth," but warned them to "beware of pride, lest [they] become as the Nephites of old." (D&C 38:39.) What did riches do to the Nephites? "There began to be some disputings among the people; and some were lifted up unto pride and boastings because of their exceedingly great riches, yea, even unto great persecutions. . . . And the people began to be distinguished by ranks, according to their riches and their chances for learning; yea, some were ignorant because of their poverty, and others did receive great learning because of their riches. . . . And thus there became a great inequality in all the land, insomuch that the church began to be broken up." (3 Ne. 6:10-14.)

Such a condition prevailed among the Nephites just prior to the coming of the Savior to them and the destruction of the more wicked part of the society. For about two hundred years after the Savior's visit, the Nephites lived prosperously, both spiritually and temporally: "They had become exceedingly rich, because of their prosperity in Christ." But "in this two hundred and first year there began to be among them those who were lifted up in pride, such as the wearing of costly apparel, and all manner of fine pearls, and of the fine things of the world. And from that time forth they did have their goods and their substance no more common among them. And they began to be divided into classes; and they began to build up churches unto themselves to get gain, and began to deny the true church of Christ." (4 Ne. 1:23-26.)

Evidently riches were causing problems for the early Christians at the time James wrote. Are there any worrisome signs today? In the church there are both rich and poor. Perhaps some are selfishly rich, but many freely share their good fortune to further the Lord's work and help those in need. It takes a constant vigil, however, to see that worldly riches do not rob us of the riches of eternity. The prophet Jacob gave us a key that can unlock the door to the simultaneous enjoyment of both temporal and spiritual prosperity. (Jacob 2:17-18.)

Position and Knowledge Bring Responsibility
(James 3:1; 4:17)

James cautions against seeking to be "masters" because of the greater condemnation that could attend. (James 3:1.) Later he adds, "To him that knoweth to do good, and doeth it not, to him it is sin." (James 4:17.) That position and knowledge bring responsibility is taught repeatedly in the scriptures. "For of him unto whom much is given much is required; and he who sins against the greater light shall receive the greater condemnation." (D&C 82:3.) "Therefore repent ye, repent ye, lest by knowing these things and not doing them ye shall suffer yourselves to come under condemnation." (Hel. 14:19.) "For the atonement satisfieth the demands of his justice upon all those who have not the law given to them.... But wo unto him that has the law given, yea, that has all the commandments of God, like unto us, and that transgresseth them, and that wasteth the days of his probation, for awful is his state!" (2 Ne. 9:26-27.)

Two notable examples are Corianton and Joseph Smith. Corianton was a missionary who left his labors to go after the harlot Isabel. In reproving his wayward son for this conduct, Alma said, "Yea, she did steal away the hearts of many; but this was no excuse for thee, my son. Thou shouldst have tended to the ministry wherewith thou wast entrusted." (Alma 39:3-4.) Joseph Smith succumbed to the pressures of Martin Harris's pleadings about taking the 116 pages of the Book of Mormon to show others. Though the Lord finally permitted the request, he sharply censured Joseph in these words: "For, behold, you should not have feared man more than God. Although men [that is, men without your calling and knowledge] set at naught the counsels of God, and despise his words—yet you should have been faithful." After inviting Joseph to repent, the Lord added, "Except thou do this, thou shalt be delivered up and become as other men, and have no more gift." (D&C 3:7-8, 11.)

Sometimes young Latter-day Saints question why their friends can do wrong things and seem to live quite contentedly, while the Latter-day Saint who joins them in these activities suffers much guilt and unhappiness. The truth of the matter is that the Latter-day Saint knows better and has been called out of the world and blessed with knowledge and the gift of the Holy Ghost. Joseph Smith taught that "God judges men according to the use they make of the light which He gives them."[18] We are not judged by the light God gives others, and others are not judged by the light he gives us. To violate true conscience is sin, regardless of what others know or do. We know and God knows the measure of light we have been given, and our spiritual health depends upon our giving heed to it.

Forgiveness of Sins
(James 5:14-20)

In the last few verses of the epistle, James talks about a relationship between healings and forgiveness and between saving souls and forgiveness. Concerning the forgiveness of sins that can accompany a healing, Joseph Fielding Smith said: "If by the power of faith and through the administration by the elders the man is healed, it is evidence that his sins have been forgiven. It is hardly reasonable to think that the Lord will forgive the sins of a man who is healed if he has not repented. Naturally he would repent of his sins if he seeks for the blessing by the elders."[19] James's instructions support the idea that a spirit of faith and repentance is present with such forgiveness—the sick person is to "call for the elders" (5:14), the prayer is to be a "prayer of faith" (5:15), and contrition is suggested by the "confess your faults" passage (5:16). Forgiveness is predicated upon law as are all other blessings (see D&C 130:20-21) and must be assumed in this instance. But what a great comfort it is to those who are repentant to know that when hearts are right, anointings are given, and healings are granted, not only the body but also the soul is made well.

How does saving souls relate to forgiveness? James says that "he which converteth the sinner from the error of his way shall save a soul from death, and shall hide a multitude of sins." (James 5:20.) Whose sins? The converted sinner's sins, or the sins of the one who helped to turn him around? The answer is yes. Sins of both parties are taken care of in the process. The converted sinner changes his life as past sins are forgiven and not repeated in the future. And the one who helped the sinner is undoubtedly affected by the experience—commended, uplifted, encouraged by the Spirit, and inspired to new levels of righteousness. After quoting James 5:19-20, Spencer W. Kimball wrote:

> Every person who is beginning the long journey of emancipating himself from the thralldom of sin and evil will find comfort in the thought expressed by James. We could expand it somewhat and remind the transgressor that every testimony he bears, every prayer he offers, every sermon he preaches, every scripture he reads, every help he gives to stimulate and raise others—all these strengthen him and raise him to higher levels.
>
> The proper motivation for missionary work of any kind, as for all Church service, is of course love for fellowmen, but always such work has its by-product effect on one's own life. Thus as we become instruments in God's hands in changing the lives of others our own lives cannot help but be lifted. One can hardly help another to the top of the hill without climbing there himself.[20]

Truly a multitude of sins is hidden—not winked at or covered over, but dealt with, repented of, and forgiven, not to be mentioned again. (See Ezek. 18:21-23).

Conclusion

The epistle of James has much substance, and James has a way of saying things that impresses them upon the mind. Some of these impressive statements include:

"If any of you lack wisdom, let him ask of God" (1:5).

"A double minded man is unstable in all his ways" (1:8).

"Be swift to hear, slow to speak, slow to wrath" (1:19).

"Pure religion and undefiled before God ... is this, To visit the fatherless and the widows in their affliction, and to keep himself unspotted from the world" (1:27).

"If ye fulfil the royal law according to the scripture, Thou shalt love thy neighbour as thyself" (2:8).

"Faith, if it hath not works, is dead" (2:17).

"By works was faith made perfect" (2:22).

"The tongue is a fire, a world of iniquity" (3:6).

"Ye have not, because ye ask not. Ye ask, and receive not, because ye ask amiss" (4:2-3).

"The friendship of the world is enmity with God" (4:4).

"Resist the devil, and he will flee from you" (4:7).

"Who art thou that judgest another?" (4:12).

"To him that knoweth to do good, and doeth it not, to him it is sin" (4:17).

"The effectual fervent prayer of a righteous man availeth much" (5:16).

Perhaps the summary of the epistle is captured in James's exhortation: *"Be ye doers of the word, and not hearers only"* (1:23).

Notes

1. For additional information, see the Bible Dictionary in the LDS edition of the King James Version, under the heading "James."

2. Josephus, *Antiquities of the Jews* 20.9.1, and *Ecclesiastical History* 2.23.9-18.

3. Richard Lloyd Anderson, "James and His Letter," *Guide to Acts and the Apostles' Letters,* Religion 212 Syllabus (Provo, Utah: Brigham Young University, 1983).

4. This is Martin Luther's assessment in comparing James to some of the writings of Peter, John, and Paul. See New Testament Preface, cit. John Dillenberger, *Martin Luther* (1961), p. 19, as quoted in Anderson, *Guide to Acts and the Apostles' Letters.* Perhaps Luther's appraisal is due to the fact that James seems to assume, rather than argue for, belief in the divinity and absolute necessity of Christ and the validity of the gospel. Also, it may be due to Luther's attachment to the idea of salvation by grace, not works. The unrelenting focus in the book of James is upon works.

5. Joseph Smith, *Lectures on Faith* (Salt Lake City: Deseret Book, 1985), lecture 4.

6. Boyd K. Packer, "The Choice," *Ensign* 10 (November 1980): 21; emphasis added.

7. There are sixteen verses in James where the wording is changed in the Joseph Smith Translation: 1:2, 12, 21, and 27; 2:2, 4, 10,14, 15, 16, 19, 22, and 25; 3:1. Note that seven, or nearly one-half, of those changes are in 2:14-25, concerning the issue of faith and works. And it is in these verses (especially verses 19, 20, and 22), that the changes add to our knowledge, not just state more clearly the ideas already understandable in the King James Version.

8. See Joseph Fielding Smith, *Doctrines of Salvation,* comp. Bruce R. McConkie, 2 (Salt Lake City: Bookcraft, 1954): 306-11.

9. Spencer W. Kimball, *The Miracle of Forgiveness* (Salt Lake City: Bookcraft, 1969), p. 54.

10. *Conference Report,* April 1986, pp. 66-69.

11. *Teachings of the Prophet Joseph Smith,* comp. Joseph Fielding Smith (Salt Lake City: Deseret Book, 1976), p. 195.

12. *Journal of Discourses,* 26 vols. (Liverpool: F. D. Richards and Sons, 1851-86), 4:288.

13. Ibid., p. 287.

14. *Millennial Star,* January 1963, p. 13.

15. *Teachings of the Prophet Joseph Smith,* p. 150.

16. The Joseph Smith Translation renders this verse "For whosoever shall, save in one point, keep the whole law, he is guilty of all," which is technically a more accurate statement of the principle.

17. *Teachings of the Prophet Joseph Smith,* pp. 331-32.

18. Ibid., p. 303.

19. *Doctrines of Salvation* 3:177-78.

20. *The Miracle of Forgiveness,* p. 205.

15

THE SUBLIME EPISTLES OF PETER
(1, 2 Peter)

MONTE S. NYMAN

The writings of Peter are often neglected in a study of the New Testament. This is not by intent but by circumstance. Because these writings are located near the end of the New Testament and because Paul's letters are so intriguing and challenging, many just never get to Peter's. Some people also have not realized the significance of Peter's writings and thus have not given them proper priority. To neglect Peter's writings in a study of the New Testament epistles is similar to eating a roast beef dinner without a serving of roast beef. There are lots of potatoes, vegetables, rolls, butter, and salad, but the meat is missing. An analysis of Peter and his writings illustrates why this is true.

Peter's writings concern the three main missions of the church, as outlined by the First Presidency:

> To proclaim the gospel of the Lord Jesus Christ to every nation, kindred, tongue, and people;
> To perfect the Saints by preparing them to receive the ordinances of the gospel and by instruction and discipline to gain exaltation;
> To redeem the dead by performing vicarious ordinances of the gospel for those who have lived on the earth.[1]

Monte S. Nyman is professor of ancient scripture, associate dean of Religious Education, and director of Book of Mormon research in the Religious Studies Center at Brigham Young University.

Peter deals with these purposes in a succinct and specific manner.

Peter was the most important figure in the meridian of time after the death of the Savior. He was the president of the Church of Jesus Christ and held the "keys of the kingdom" in that dispensation. (Matt. 16:18-19; 17:1-9; 18:17-18; D&C 7:7; 27:12; and Preface to D&C 13.) The words of the president of the church are to be received as if from the Lord's own mouth. (D&C 21:5.)

Further justification for giving Peter's writings a prominent place is found in the words of the Prophet Joseph Smith: "Peter penned the most sublime language of any of the apostles."[2] *Sublime* means elevated in thought, noble, majestic, inspiring. This fits not only the language of Peter but also the doctrine he teaches. The Prophet Joseph said many other things about Peter's writings that will be quoted later.

Another reason for giving Peter's writings a high priority is that many other presidents of The Church of Jesus Christ of Latter-day Saints have singled out Peter's writings. President Joseph F. Smith was pondering over the scriptures when his mind reverted to the writings of the apostle Peter. To those who believe that revelation consists of "sudden strokes of ideas" coming into one's mind,[3] it is not difficult to believe that President Smith's attention to Peter's testimony was inspired by the Lord. When he opened the Bible and read the third and fourth chapters of the first epistle of Peter, he was greatly impressed with 1 Peter 3:18-21 and 4:6, more so than he had ever been before. As he pondered these things, one of the great revelations of this dispensation concerning the work for those in the spirit world and one of the major missions of the latter-day church was revealed. (D&C 138:1-11.)

Other presidents have also been inspired by Peter's writings. President David O. McKay said: "I have a great admiration in my heart for Simon Peter, president of the Twelve Apostles,"[4] a response that came as he also reflected upon Peter's writings. These reflections will be treated below in the context of Peter's writings. President Spencer W. Kimball, speaking to the Brigham Young University student body in 1971, gave one of his many classic addresses entitled "Peter, My Brother."[5] This talk, given in response to a negative statement on a church marquee, is a must for those who want to appreciate the man Peter and his writings.

The First Epistle of Peter

Peter's first epistle was written to members of the church scattered throughout parts of Asia. In his salutation, he calls them strangers because he had never met them; yet he acknowledges that they are the elect according to the foreknowledge of God. In other words, the elect are those who have been chosen or foreordained to receive salvation through their faith. The theme of this epistle is that through the sanctification of the spirit and faith in the grace of the atonement of Jesus Christ, members can endure their trials and temptations and attain salvation (1:2-9). This is another way of bringing about the perfection of the saints. In the rest of the epistle, Peter gives counsel and reminds the people of doctrines and blessings that can enable them to attain this most precious gift of salvation. The beauty and the power of these admonitions remind us that we, as members of Christ's church today, can also attain our salvation if we heed the same counsel. It becomes more realistic to us if we equate this epistle with the opening addresses of our modern-day prophets, seers, and revelators at general conference.

After he reminds the saints that all of the prophets have taught, testified, and prophesied of salvation through the coming of Christ (1:10-12), Peter's *first admonition* is that they be holy in all their conversations as was Christ (1:13-16). He warns against reverting to their former habits, which they had practiced in ignorance, and emphasizes this by quoting from Leviticus 11:44.

Peter's *second admonition* is that the saints are to love one another fervently and with pure hearts (1:22). He bases this counsel upon the love the Father shows to his children "without respect of persons" (1:17), the love of Christ who was chosen or foreordained to redeem them. This love, which they have experienced in accepting the truth taught to them, has led to their rebirth. The love between a convert and a missionary can be understood only by those who experience it, just as God's love and Christ's love for us is only truly appreciated when experienced. Peter substantiates this statement with a scripture, citing Isaiah 40:6-8 as evidence that the word of God, which they had obeyed to bring about their newly born condition, is eternal. Having known these experiences, "the object of [their] faith, even the salvation of [their] souls (JST, 1 Pet. 1:9) was based upon their ability to lay aside malice, guile, and hypocrisy and to love one another according to the sincere "milk" or basic teachings of the word of God (2:1-3).

Before giving his third admonition, Peter lays a foundation upon which to build his other admonitions (2:4-9). He compares the listeners to stones out of which "a spiritual house, an holy priesthood" is built to offer sacrifices unto God through Jesus Christ (2:4-5). The chief cornerstone of this house is Jesus Christ, as the scriptures had foretold (2:6; Ps. 118:22). As a part of this spiritual house, the cornerstone will prevent them from being confounded, while, to the disobedient, that same cornerstone will become a stumbling block and an offense (2:7-8). Peter reminds them that they are a chosen generation, the foreordained house of Israel to whom this blessing was promised. (See Deut. 32:7-8.) Further, the priesthood, or authority to offer sacrifices in this house, is a royal priesthood, the priesthood of the king, or what the Book of Mormon and the Doctrine and Covenants call the priesthood of the Son of God. (Alma 13:7-9; D&C 107:1-4.) He also declares them to be a holy nation, a people who have been forgiven of their sins and are collectively accepted as a righteous people of God. He tells them they are a peculiar people, meaning that their ways are different from the ways of the rest of the world (2:9). Such things as following a health code (the Word of Wisdom) or wearing a temple garment are examples of this, as is acceptance of such doctrines as the premortal life and a personal God. It should be noted that a similar description of people was revealed to Moses on Mount Sinai. His people were to be a "peculiar treasure" unto God on condition that they accept the opportunities revealed to them. (Ex. 19:5-6.) Paul also speaks of the time when Jesus Christ will appear again and purify unto himself a peculiar people zealous of good works. (Titus 2:13-14.) God's people are always considered peculiar in the eyes of the world. Peter reminds his readers that in times past they, a foreordained people (the house of Israel), were rejected as God's people because of their failure to follow His counsel, but now they have again been extended the arm of mercy. With this foundation laid, Peter delivers his *third admonition:* to abstain from the lusts of the flesh, which war against the soul, and thus be good examples among the Gentiles (2:11-12).

Peter's *fourth admonition* is for the saints to submit to the ordinances of man or, as the following verses disclose, to the laws of the land—the will of God, that which will silence the ignorance of foolish men (2:13-16).

The next series of admonitions were addressed to specific groups. The *fifth admonition* is to those who were servants. Since, under the laws of the land, servitude was legal, Peter's advice was for them to submit themselves to their masters and endure whatever suffering this may bring. To comfort them, he refers to the suffering Christ endured, as was prophesied by Isaiah. (2:18-25; Isa. 53:4-11).

The *sixth admonition* is to wives, encouraging them to be good examples in a spiritual sense rather than through worldly or physical enticements (JST, 3:1-4). This example will win to the Lord others who might tend to go astray. Peter cites Sarah's obedience to righteous Abraham as an example for the women (3:5-6).

In the *seventh admonition,* Peter turns his attention to husbands, reminding them that they are to honor their wives, for they are heirs together of the grace of life (3:7). This is undoubtedly a reference to the eternal nature of the marriage covenant in the Lord.

Peter's *eighth and final admonition* to the members is an affirmation of the Savior's golden rule: "Therefore all things whatsoever ye would that men should do to you, do ye even so to them." (Matt. 7:12.) In Peter's words, "be ye all of one mind" and look to the blessings of God that will follow the righteous even if it requires that they suffer for their righteousness. He admonishes the saints to shun evil and do good, for the Lord is with the righteous. Their good conduct will lead to missionary work (JST, 3:8-17). To give them support in the face of suffering, he cites the suffering to which Christ subjected himself in order to bring us to God. Then, in an apparent attempt to show how good things will come from the enduring of suffering, he gives a treatise on Christ's going into the spirit world while his body was in the tomb, in order that all people might have the opportunity to receive the gospel. (3:18-22.) This great section of writing was what led President Joseph F. Smith to receive his revelation about Christ's mission in the spirit world. (See D&C 138.) The Prophet Joseph Smith's inspired translation of the Bible also clarifies Christ's mission (see JST, 3:20; 4:1, 6): it stresses that the Savior ministered to only *some* of those in the spirit world—namely, the righteous. (Cf. D&C 138:20-22, 29-30.) In Peter's final counsel to be "all of one mind," he urges them to have charity, which will prevent a multitude of sins, and to use their individual gifts of the Spirit to help each other (JST, 4:7-10). He further counsels them to speak or minister as the oracles of God, having authority as his servants, according to the ability with which God has blessed them (4:11).

After pronouncing a probable hearty "Amen" (4:11), Peter adds a postscript: They will face trials, as worthy candidates for the celestial kingdom; but they should rejoice rather than despair because they are suffering for Christ. He warns against suffering for the wrong reasons but tells them that it is good to suffer as Christians. In other words, we do not seek for suffering or persecution, but if it comes to us because we are living as Christians, we need not be ashamed. Peter reminds us that judgment must begin at the house of God and the righteous will scarcely be saved (4:12-19; compare 1 Ne. 22:16-19; D&C 112:23-26).

In another apparent postscript, Peter addresses the elders,[6] those in leadership positions, and tells them to feed the flock of God, not by constraint nor for filthy lucre, but as shepherds, until the chief Shepherd shall appear (5:1-4). Several other admonitions are given to the elders, including the comment that the younger (perhaps in service rather than age) are to submit to the elder. This system of hierarchy is also followed in the church today.

The first epistle of Peter is full of timely admonitions that will bring us salvation if we will exercise our faith and follow them. This theme of the epistle is just as significant to us today as it was to the members in Asia in Peter's day.

The Second Epistle of Peter

Peter's second epistle is addressed to a more select audience than the first: to members of the church who had attained the same faith in God and Jesus Christ as had Peter and the apostles. The main theme of the letter is that through the grace of God and of Jesus their Lord, many great and precious promises had been extended to these members, and by attaining these promises, they could be "partakers of the divine nature" and escape the corruption of the world. This theme was also a theme of President David O. McKay. In general conference in October 1960, after quoting 2 Peter 1:4, President McKay said: "I have a deep admiration in my heart for Simon Peter, President of the Twelve Apostles, . . . who was only two and a half years—a little more—in the personal presence of his Lord. Before that he did not care much for the Church, but before this writing he had a testimony of the divinity of the Sonship of Jesus Christ. More than that, he had experienced that communion of the spirit with his Resurrected Lord, and speaks here of being a partaker of the divine nature."[7] On another occasion, President McKay declared: "Peter was quite a doubtful man as he grew to manhood before he knew Christ, but long afterwards he was praying and said that we have been made partakers of the divine nature. He knew it, and you will know it some day if you will do the will, be true to self."[8] To be a partaker of the divine nature is to know the power of God and to experience the Holy Ghost in one's life. (D&C 76:31, 35.)

In the rest of chapter 1, Peter gives instructions on what a member of the church should do after having been a partaker of the divine nature. He explains that, having escaped the corruption of the world, the saints should give all diligence to "add to [their] faith virtue; and to virtue knowledge; and to knowledge temperance; and to temperance patience; and to patience godliness; and to godliness brotherly kindness; and to brotherly kindness charity." (2 Pet. 1:5-7.)

In commenting on these verses, Joseph Smith said: "It is not wisdom that we should have all knowledge at once presented before us; but that we should have a little at a time; then we can comprehend it. . . . The principle of knowledge is the principle of salvation. This principle can be comprehended by the faithful and diligent; and every one that does not obtain knowledge sufficient to be saved will be condemned. The principle of salvation is given us through the knowledge of Jesus Christ."[9]

The Prophet acknowledged the depth and complexity of this chapter of Peter's epistle, declaring: "There are three grand secrets lying in this chapter which no man can dig out, unless by the light of revelation, and which unlocks the whole chapter as the things that are written are only hints of things which existed in the prophet's mind, which are not written concerning eternal glory. I am going to take up this subject by virtue of the knowledge of God in me, which I have received from heaven. The opinions of men, so far as I am concerned, are to me as the crackling of thorns under the pot, or the whistling of the wind."[10]

He then summarized the grand secrets or keys to unlocking Peter's writings. The first, "knowledge is the power of salvation," is the essence of the statement just quoted. The second key is based on 2 Peter 1:10, making one's calling and election sure. The Prophet explained this principle:

> Notwithstanding the apostle exhorts [the saints] to add to their faith, virtue, knowledge, temperance, etc., yet he exhorts them to make their calling and election sure. And though they had heard an audible voice from heaven bearing testimony that Jesus was the Son of God, yet he says we have a more sure word of prophecy, whereunto ye do well that ye take heed as unto a light shining in a dark place. Now, wherein could they have a more sure word of prophecy than to hear the voice of God saying, This is my beloved Son.
>
> Now for the secret and grand key. Though they might hear the voice of God and know that Jesus was the Son of God, this would be no evidence that their election and calling was made sure, that they had part with Christ, and were joint heirs with Him. They then would want that more sure word of prophecy, that they were sealed in the heavens and had the promise of eternal life in the kingdom of God. Then, having this promise sealed unto them, it was an anchor to the soul, sure and steadfast. Though the thunders might roll and lightnings flash, and earthquakes bellow, and war gather thick around, yet this hope and knowledge would support the soul in every hour of trial, trouble and tribulation. Then knowledge through our Lord and Savior Jesus Christ is the grand key that unlocks the glories and mysteries of the kingdom of heaven.[11]

The experience of hearing an audible voice, to which Peter refers (as does Joseph Smith), is undoubtedly that of the Savior taking Peter, James, and John up on the mountain where he was transfigured before

232

them. (Matt. 17:1-9.) From the Prophet's explanation, it seems that the three apostles did not have their calling and election made sure on that occasion. If not, this experience pointed their souls to that third key of Peter's writings given by the Prophet: "It is one thing to be on the mount and hear the excellent voice, etc., and another to hear the voice declare to you, You have a part and lot in that kingdom."[12] The Joseph Smith Translation does not settle the issue but does give a further consideration: "We have *therefore* a more sure *knowledge of the word* of prophecy, *to which word of prophecy* ye do well that ye take heed, as unto a light that shineth in a dark place until the day dawn, and the day star arise in your hearts: Knowing this first, that no prophecy of the *scriptures* is *given* of any private *will of man.*" (JST, 2 Pet. 1:19-20; italics indicate changes in JST.) The disciples' more sure knowledge was the voice declaring their assured part and portion of the kingdom. The record does not say when this happened, but Peter reminds his readers that this does not come through the private or personal desires of man, but through the revelation of the Holy Ghost (v. 21), or the Holy Spirit of Promise, which is the Holy Ghost's stamp of approval upon an ordinance or experience (D&C 132:26; Eph. 1:13-14).[13]

Though the Prophet did not comment on the other chapters of 2 Peter, the same keys seem to apply.

In his epistle, Peter warns against assuming that eternal life can be attained automatically or easily. As the Lord explained in the latter days, mankind "may fall from grace," therefore, "even let those who are sanctified take heed." (D&C 20:32, 34.) Peter points out the dangers of following false prophets and some of the ways in which they may attack. Using examples from the Old Testament, such as Noah and the citizens of Sodom and Gomorrah, he talks about those who, "with feigned words," would "make merchandise" of the saints. (2 Pet. 2:3.) He assures the saints that the Lord will deliver those who are godly out of such temptations and speaks of the punishment that will come upon the ungodly (2:9), particularly those who "walk after the flesh in the lust of uncleanness," and "despise governments" and speak evil of dignitaries (2:10). In support of the idea that these are warnings to those who are sanctified or whose calling and election is made sure, Peter declares that if such individuals are overcome by temptations after gaining the knowledge of the Lord, their "end is worse with them than the beginning," and "it had been better for them not to have known the way of righteousness." (2 Pet. 2:20-21.)

Having delivered his timely warning, Peter now turns to the preventive measures for not being overcome. The saints are to be mindful of the words spoken by the holy prophets and of the commandments of the apostles of the Lord Jesus Christ. (2 Pet. 3:2.) This is, of course, another example of many admonitions in the standard works to search the scriptures. He warns of those scoffers in the last days who will question the second coming of the Lord Jesus Christ (3:3), and gives three guidelines or reminders of his first coming: first, "that one day with the Lord [is] as a thousand years" for man; second, that the delay of his coming is such that all will have an opportunity to repent; and third, that Christ "will come as a thief in the night" to the wicked, when the people of the world are not looking for him or least expect him (3:8-10; cf. D&C 106:4).

As a conclusion to his comments, Peter admonishes the people to be "holy" in their conversation and godly in their actions as they look for and work for the coming of the Lord. Those who are diligent will be "found of him [the Lord] in peace, without spot, and blameless." (2 Pet. 3:11-14.) Peter points to Paul as a second witness to his testimony, while acknowledging that some who are unlearned and unstable wrest with Paul's writings and other scriptural writings as well.

The second epistle of Peter is full of timely instructions that are quite different from those of the first epistle, and contains important and perhaps deep doctrine that the Prophet Joseph Smith has unlocked through revelation. This doctrine of making one's calling and election sure, said the Prophet, "ought (in its proper place) to be taught, for God hath not revealed anything to Joseph, but what He will make known unto the Twelve, and even the least Saint may know all things as fast as he is able to bear them."[14]

Such are the epistles of Peter. He was the president of the Twelve Apostles, president of the Church of Jesus Christ, and he penned the most sublime language of any of the apostles. May we each study his writings and learn how we may be elevated in thought and become more noble and majestic subjects in the kingdom of God.

Notes

1. Spencer W. Kimball, *Conference Report,* April 1981, p. 3.

2. *Teachings of the Prophet Joseph Smith,* comp. Joseph Fielding Smith (Salt Lake City: Deseret Book, 1976), p. 301.

3. Ibid., p. 151.

4. *Conference Report,* October 1960, p. 115.

5. Spencer W. Kimball, "Peter, My Brother," *Speeches of the Year* (Provo: BYU Press, 1971).

6. Some scholars question Peter's authorship of this epistle because he calls himself an elder. However, as shown in D&C 20:38, an apostle is an elder and is addressed as such in the Church today.

7. *Conference Report,* October 1960, pp. 115-16.

8. *Conference Report,* April 1963, p. 95.

9. *Teachings of the Prophet Joseph Smith,* p. 297.

10. Ibid., p. 304.

11. Ibid., p. 298.

12. Ibid., p. 306.

13. Ibid., p. 149.

14. Ibid. For a detailed treatment of this subject, see Bruce R. McConkie, *Doctrinal New Testament Commentary,* 3 vols. (Salt Lake City: Bookcraft, 1965-73), 3:325-55.

16

THE EPISTLES OF JOHN
(1, 2, 3 John)

Thomas W. Mackay

Three of the letters known as the General Epistles (that is, James, 1 and 2 Peter, 1, 2, and 3 John, and Jude) were apparently written by the apostle John. While the second and third epistles are very brief, the first is much more extensive in its development of doctrinal themes. The major messages in 1 John are fellowship, obedience, light and darkness, love, anti-Christ, being like God, and the intercession of Christ. Before discussing these points, we appropriately examine in a cursory fashion questions of textual reliability, authenticity, and authorship, including date and setting for the three epistles. Our body of evidence includes biblical manuscripts, patristic citations, and some historical notes by Eusebius. Although a few commentaries were composed on individual General Epistles, such as Augustine on 1 John, nothing systematic and comprehensive was produced before the Venerable Bede of Jarrow, who wrote in Anglo-Saxon England during the first two decades of the eighth century.[1]

Authorship and Authenticity

The Johannine authorship of the three Epistles of John is strongly attested. Polycarp and other sources of the second century quote from the first epistle. By the fourth century, the epistles were among

---

Thomas W. Mackay is professor of Greek and Latin at Brigham Young University.

the *homologoumena* or generally accepted books, while 2 Peter, Jude, and the book of Revelation were still not universally received. Since the unnamed author is an eyewitness (1 John 1:1-4; 4:14), since the style and language are similar to that of John's Gospel, and since the references in the second century name the author as John, this has been practically unanimously accepted through the centuries.

While the language itself is similar, however, the arrangement of thoughts and ideas does differ. The first epistle does not have the same unified grouping of ideas and motifs that we immediately detect in the Gospel of John. Consequently, in discussing the epistle, we will reach out to draw together different passages somewhat removed from each other.

According to Irenaeus, a late second-century writer, John spent the latter part of his life in and near Ephesus. We also note that the letters to the seven churches in Revelation 2 and 3 were addressed to Ephesus and six important cities in surrounding Asia Minor: Smyrna, Pergamum, Thyatira, Sardis, Philadelphia, and Laodicea. Although the precise destination of 1 John is not given, we may safely presume that it was to people in those areas. Further, the content of 1 John presupposes an acquaintance with the Gospel, and it also refers to doctrinal problems from apostates. Thus, the date may be between about A.D. 70 and 90, probably closer to the latter date. But the problems of anti-Christ were already being signaled by Paul in the fifteen years before A.D. 62, when he was taken to Rome. Second Peter prophetically and Jude historically both point to the incipient apostasy of the "Great Gap" of A.D. 70 to 100; 1 John is to be dated to that period. According to Hegesippus, who compiled an early history of the Christian church and whose writings were quoted and used by Eusebius in the beginning of the fourth century, this is the time when the Gnostics began to flourish and to teach openly what they had secretly been espousing:

> Until then the church remained a pure and uncorrupted virgin, for those who attempted to corrupt the healthful rule of the Savior's preaching, if they existed at all, lurked in obscure darkness. But when the sacred band of the Apostles and the generation of those to whom it had been vouchsafed to hear with their own ears the divine wisdom had reached the several ends of their lives, then the federation of godless error took its

beginning through the deceit of false teachers who, seeing that none of the Apostles still remained, barefacedly tried against the preaching of the truth the counter-proclamation of "knowledge falsely so-called."[2]

The author of 2 John is an *elder* (Greek *presbyteros*), a term used in the late first and early second century for *apostle,* even as it is used today by the Latter-day Saints. (See D&C 20:38.) In writing to the "elect lady and her children" John warns against deceiving teachers and false doctrines. In the *Didache* (an authentic Christian text of the late first century, first discovered and published about a century ago), the anonymous author warns members of the church to shun anyone who taught for pay.[3] Again, the circumstances of 2 John fit best about A.D. 90, and 3 John, addressed to a local leader named Gaius, was probably composed about the same time.

Textual Reliability: The "Johannine Comma"

The text of the epistles is fairly well attested in the early manuscripts of the fourth to sixth centuries, and there are no early papyri such as we find particularly for the Gospels and the Pauline corpus. There are just a few words in the "Received Text," used by translators for the King James Version, that have quite probably been added to what John originally wrote, but for the most part they make no appreciable difference to most readers. However, one significant passage in 1 John 5:7-8 has clearly been added, the so-called Johannine Comma. Translated, the text for those two verses should read as follows, using the words of the Authorized Version: "For there are three that bear record, the spirit and the water and the blood, and these three agree in one."[4] As the textual problem of the passage has been adequately treated elsewhere, we restrict our observations to noting that (1) there are only four late Greek manuscripts in which the passage is found, and three of the four have had it added by someone writing centuries later than the original scribe of the manuscript; (2) patristic evidence for the passage is scanty at best, for it is not in the Greek Fathers, and the Latin Fathers use it only in the later period; (3) the earliest attestation of the passage is in a late fourth century Latin treatise composed by the Spanish heretic Priscillian or one of his followers; (4) it is found in none of the manuscripts of the ancient translations of the Bible except progressively in Latin manuscripts emanating from North Africa and Italy, but not in the manuscripts that preserve Jerome's Latin Vulgate translation, namely the Fuldensis (ca. 541-47), the Amiatinus (ca. 690 and before 716), or the Vercelli (early ninth century).[5] So the more expanded passage in the Authorized Version does not accurately represent what John wrote.

Doctrinal Themes

Fellowship. The primary purpose of 1 John is to state the terms and effects of our fellowship with God or our failure to develop such a relationship. In Greek, the word for *fellowship* is *koinonia*, a noun from the adjective meaning common or shared. The corresponding verb, *koinoneo*, means to share, to have a share, to participate, and so the agent or person who does such an action is a companion, partner, or sharer (*koinonos*). Therefore, the abstract noun translated *fellowship* also means association, communion, close relationship, participation, or sharing and was appropriately used regarding the marital relationship.

Inherent in the notion of Christian fellowship is the idea of sharing property and livelihood such as characterized the Saints, as recorded by Luke in Acts 2:44-45: "And all that believed were together, and had all things common [*koina*]; and sold their possessions and goods, and parted them to all men, as every man had need." Ignatius, writing in the first decade of the second century, reaffirms this Christian association. Such an ideal was also practiced in some of the early Greek philosophical brotherhoods, and Plato's famous saying is that "friends have things in common" (*koina ta ton philon*) or "the possessions of friends are shared."

For John, there are natural consequences of having a fellowship with God: we do not walk in the darkness but rather in the light of God (1 John 1:5-7), and so the atoning blood of Christ cleanses us if we acknowledge and confess that we as mortals have sinned (1 John 1:7-9). Otherwise we deceive ourselves and the truth is not in us. We love; we do not hate. We foster light and truth; we shun deception and darkness.

The sinner who confesses his faults has Jesus for an advocate or intercessor, a mediator who is called to intervene and help (Greek *parakletos*, Latin *advocatus*). This is the term used in John's Gospel for the Spirit (John 14:16, 26; 15:26; 16:7), and at John 14:16, his calling the Holy Spirit "another comforter" (*parakletos*) implies that Christ, too, is a comforter or mediator, just as he is so identified at 1 John 2:1.

Since fellowship includes the notion of personal acquaintance or knowledge, John states that we who know him will have our manner of life in accordance with God's commandments (1 John 2:3-5); we "walk in the light" (1 John 1:7).

Again, the whole idea of knowing God and associating with him after mortal death is one that can only be in truth, light, and obedience. We cannot fake our way into the kingdom. Therefore, perhaps the single most transcendent statement in the epistle is in 1 John 3:2-3: "Beloved, now are we the sons of God, and it doth not yet appear what we shall be: but we know that, when he shall appear, we shall be like him; for we shall see him as he is. And every man that hath this hope in him purifieth himself, even as he is pure." The natural consequence of coming to know God is to desire to emulate him, to have our closest friendship with him. And to be like God is to know him. Thus we more fully understand Jesus' prayer in John 17:3 where he defines eternal life as knowing God and Christ: "And this is life eternal, that they might know thee the only true God, and Jesus Christ, whom thou hast sent." In this verse the form of the Greek verb for *know* emphasizes the continuing personal acquaintance and friendship between God and man, a fellowship that commences in this life. Eternal life, therefore, becomes the natural continuation of a close association enjoyed in this life into the eternities. By John's definition, we ought definitely not to think of eternal life as something thrust upon a person unprepared or unacquainted with God and his ways. So at 1 John 3:2, "we shall be like him" points to the integrity of life by obedience to God's commandments, changing our nature to resemble God more closely. We cannot deceive God, who knows all things. (1 John 3:20.)

Hope. Another of John's doctrinal words is *hope.* In Greek there is a much stronger sense of expectation and anticipation than our word *hope* conveys. A preferable translation is "firm or confident expectation." In 1 John 3:3 we learn that those of us who expect to become like God and resemble Christ when we see him are motivated to purify ourselves, that is, to emulate God all the more. Our hope is founded on a literal sense of Christ's intercession: we come to know him and desire to follow his ways, and in turn, he plants deep in our hearts the confident expectation that "we shall be like him."

Love. Of all the characteristics of God, love is supreme. Christ's disciples are to love one another. (1 John 3:11; cf. John 13:34; 5:12, 17; 2 John 1:5.) By contrast, the works of darkness are hatred, anger, and jealousy, and such were the influences on Cain that motivated him to slay his brother. True love manifests itself by deeds of kindness and mercy, exhibiting compassion in very fact and not just in word. By manifesting toward our fellow mortals a sense of love, not hatred, we demonstrate that we have fellowship with God and emulate and mirror his love for us. (Cf. 1 John 4:16-21.)

Perfection. Elsewhere in the epistle, John (1 John 4:18)[6] uses a Greek word meaning perfect, complete, whole, adult, married, or one who had received his initiation ordinances (Greek verb *teleioo* from the adjective *teleios*; the baseword noun is *telos* from which the word telestial seems to have been formed).[7] The same verb is also found in John 4:34, where it means to fulfill or make complete. As an adjective, this word was a strong part of the Christian vocabulary, for Matthew uses it in Matthew 5:48: "Be ye therefore [*or,* ye shall then (accordingly) be(come)] perfect, even as your Father which is in heaven is perfect."

Anti-Christ. In 1 John we encounter the word *anti-Christ* (e.g., 1 John 2:18-23; 4:1-3). While we ordinarily associate the prefix *anti* with opposition and antagonism, the base meaning in Greek is "instead of" or "in place of." In John's words, it is as though Satan were setting himself up as a mirror image imitation of Christ, and that the falseness of the imitation intensifies the opposition that motivates Satan while also being a manifestation of the conflict of light and darkness. Since we must have the true intercessor and be filled with his true light and love, the counterfeit is the more reprehensible, for it provides a false security as it repulses God's own emissary.

And how are we to detect this anti-Christ? John's simple statement of confessing that Jesus has come in the flesh is disarming but precise.

Already during the last decades of the first century there was a growing heresy of Docetism (from the Greek word meaning to seem or to appear)—the notion that Jesus only *seemed* to be mortal. Clearly, John does not mean that someone must merely mouth the words that Jesus came in the flesh. The intent is that in such a confession, an entire range of doctrines is accepted, including the divine fatherhood of God, the literal atonement and resurrection of Christ, and the concomitant promise of resurrection and glory for mankind redeemed by the great expiatory sacrifice. And beyond words and doctrines, implicit in John's statement is the notion that the hearers will be able to discern the commitment and spirit underlying the confession— whether it is motivated by and reflects the love and spirit of God. Otherwise, it is another manifestation of the apostasy that was creeping into the church, for, as Paul's words to the Ephesian saints in Acts 20:29-30 indicate, the apostasy (a Greek word meaning an overthrow of political power, a deliberate defection of loyalty or a *coup d'état*) resulted from a revolution within the church, not external persecution: "For I know this, that after my departing shall grievous wolves enter in among you, not sparing the flock. Also of your own selves shall men arise, speaking perverse things, to draw away disciples after them."

This prophecy finds answer in the historical reflection by Hegesippus quoted earlier in this article. Thus, John indicates that "many false prophets" have already "gone out into the world" (1 John 4:1). He therefore encourages his readers to overcome the world (1 John 5:4-5) and to possess for and in themselves the witness or testimony of God. We are to be bearers of light, full of love, growing to become like God, so that he may receive us as his own, for "when he shall appear, we shall be like him."

Notes

1. David Hurst, editor, *Corpus Christianorum* 121A (Turnhout, Belgium: Brepols, 1984).

2. Eusebius *Hist. Eccl.* 3.33.7; see 1 Tim. 6:20.

242

3. *Didache* 11.6: "And when an Apostle goes forth let him accept nothing but bread till he reach his night's lodging; but if he ask for money, he is a false prophet."

4. More literally the verses read: "Because those who witness [*or*, the witnesses] are three, the spirit and the water and the blood, and the three are for the one [*that is*, are for one purpose or goal]."

5. Bruce M. Metzger, *The Text of the New Testament,* 2nd ed. (New York and Oxford: Oxford University Press, 1968); Bruce M. Metzger, *A Textual Commentary on the Greek New Testament* (London and New York: United Bible Societies, 1971); Raymond E. Brown, *The Epistles of John,* Anchor Bible, vol. 30 (Garden City, New York: Doubleday, 1982): 775-87.

6. "Fear does not exist in true love, but rather whole or complete love casts out fear because fear has [=brings] punishment [or, eternal retribution], and he who fears has not been made perfect (*teteleiotai*) in (God's) love."

7. Telestial in this sense probably means the last or final kingdom (of glory). In the New Testament, Paul uses the word *katachthonion* (Philip. 2:10) for telestial, in contrast to *epigeion* (terrestrial) and *epouranion* (celestial). Other contemporary documents may use the adjective *hypogeion* in the same sense.

17

REFUGE IN GOD'S LOVE
(Jude)

CATHERINE THOMAS

Jude's little letter evokes several intriguing questions for gospel students: Who was Jude and what was his authority to write to the saints? Why do several passages in Jude's letter bear strong resemblance to verses in 2 Peter? Why would Jude use apocryphal sources for his message? These are the main issues of Jude's letter, as well as his insight into the close of the early Christian dispensation, which revelation speaks also to us as we near the end of ours.

Who Was He?

"Jude, the servant of Jesus Christ, and brother of James." (Jude 1:1.)

He was modest. Instead of writing that he was the brother of the Lord, which he was (Matt. 13:55), he wrote that he was servant to the Lord and brother of James the apostle, who was also a brother of the Lord (Gal. 1:19). Was Jude an apostle? The Prophet Joseph Smith adds to this verse, "Jude, the servant of *God, called of* Jesus Christ, and brother of James." The Greek of Luke 6:16 and Acts 1:13 lists one of the apostles as "Judas of James," which is translated "Jude ... brother of James" (JST, Jude 1:1). The Greek name "Judas" is rendered "Jude" in English to distinguish him from the traitor and from the patriarch

---

Catherine Thomas is an instructor in ancient scripture and a doctoral candidate in ancient history at Brigham Young University.

Judah of the tribe of Israel. He was married and apparently traveled with his wife in his apostolic duties. (1 Cor. 9:5.) The fourth century historian Eusebius records (quoting Hegesippus) that the Roman emperor Domitian (A.D. 81-96) searched out any survivors of the family of the Lord to ascertain whether there was any threat to his reign among them. He found grandsons of Jude, simple farmers, whom he dismissed as harmless.[1]

Because of many similar passages in Jude and 2 Peter, scholars contend over which came first. Stylistic and other evidence suggests that Peter wrote first; somewhat later, Jude wrote his letter, using some of the senior apostle's ideas. A comparison of the two letters reveals that Jude added his own insights, that he was not merely derivative, but made a significant contribution of his own to the canon. Where Peter's letter points to the future when serious apostasy will infest the church, Jude's letter conveys the urgency, the crisis, of the actual present infection. If Jude indeed quoted Peter's letter, he must then have written some time after about A.D. 67, for 2 Peter is dated toward the end of Nero's reign (A.D. 54-68). Since Jude was apparently dead when Domitian went searching for members of the Lord's family, and the Apostasy had progressed, Jude's letter may be dated roughly at A.D. 80.[2]

The Love of God

"To them that are loved by God the Father, and preserved in Jesus Christ, and called: mercy unto you, and peace, and love, be multiplied." (Jude 1:1-2.)

The King James Version reads *sanctified* instead of *loved.* The two words in Greek, respectively, *(h)agiasménois* and *agapeménois,* are so similar that a scribe could easily mistake the one for the other. Manuscript evidence supports the word *loved* here. Further support for this correction comes from the end of Jude's letter where he says, "Keep yourselves in the love of God" (1:21), making the theme of God's love serve as a frame for his message. Another possible translation for this passage could be "to those who are loved in God the Father," or united in God the Father's love.

Jude comes right to his point: the crisis of apostasy is upon the saints. They live on a battlefield, though many saints then, as now, may not have realized the intensity of the conflict, so subtle, so sense-numbing are the adversary's weapons. Prophecies written earlier, for example, in 2 Peter or in Matthew 24:24 (or in 1 Enoch, which we will consider further on) declared that false teachers would seek to deceive and dismantle the church. The leaders also knew that they would succeed, but the fight was for individuals, not for the organization itself, and the messages written may have been at least as much for our day as for theirs. Satan and his colleagues had earnestly joined battle, turning God's love into lasciviousness and denying the Savior, the very personification of God's love. The saints too must be aware of the gravity of the contest. Paul declared, "For we wrestle not against flesh and blood, but against principalities, against powers, against the rulers of darkness of this world, against spiritual wickedness in high places. Wherefore take unto you the whole armour of God, that ye may be able to withstand in the evil day, and having done all, to stand." (Eph. 6:12-13.) Jude's letter teems with words about preservation, salvation, protection, guarding in God's love. Here he identifies a potent weapon against apostasy: the power of the love of God.

Jude and Apocryphal Works

"And the angels which kept not their first estate, but left their own habitation, he hath reserved in everlasting chains under darkness unto the judgment of the great day." (Jude 1:6.)

Jude cites examples of those delivered out of Egypt who later lost faith, of angels in the premortal world who left their high position and rebelled against God, of Israelites who perished in Sodom and Gomorrah, of the devil himself, and of Cain, Balaam, and Core. (Jude 1:5-11.) What do all these have in common? Once they all had knowledge of salvation, but they rebelled against it. Anarchy, then, is Jude's counter-theme.

It seems likely that Jude had before him, whether in mind or on desk, at least two apocryphal works. His reference to the angels who fell is quite similar to passages in the Jewish apocryphal book 1 Enoch. Compare Jude 1:6 with 1 Enoch 12:4: "Enoch, scribe of righteousness, go and make known to the Watchers of heaven who have abandoned [same Greek word as in Jude 1:6, *apolipóntes*] the high heaven, the holy eternal place.... There shall not be peace unto them even forever." And 1 Enoch 10:11-14: "And to Michael God said ... 'Bind [the Watchers] ... underneath the rocks of the ground until the day of their judgment and of their consummation, until the eternal judgment is concluded. In those days they will lead them into the bottom of the fire—and in torment—in the prison (where) they will be locked up forever.'"[3]

The Watchers is Enoch's name for the fallen angels. We shall find additional references to 1 Enoch in Jude. As Elder Bruce R. McConkie observes, the apocryphal 1 Enoch "contains many remarkable and inspired teachings and also considerable trashy nonsense."[4] Many apocryphal works were available to the early Christians. Several of these works (some of which the Lord warned Joseph Smith about in D&C 91) retain vestiges of truth that were only alluded to in the canon or were absent altogether. The doctrine of the premortal existence and the fall of Satan's followers was one of these truths. Called of God, Jude knew how to sift the truth. The Apostle Paul quoted from Greek poets, obviously not endorsing their works as scripture, but rather quoting from them what was true.[5]

"Likewise also these (filthy) dreamers defile the flesh, despise dominion, and speak evil of dignities.... In those things they corrupt themselves." (Jude 1:8, 10.)

These apostates defile the flesh ("filthy" does not occur in the Greek text) on the one hand and reject authority on the other. The two go together. Where one has forsaken internal discipline, he also rejects the external. Anarchists, these apostates reject all restraint on their desires. The Greek word *arché* in the passage, "the angels which kept not their first estate (*arché*)" has several meanings: beginning, origin, ruler, authority, rule, or office. Thus an anarchist is one who rejects authority. In a context similar to Jude's, Peter elaborated on anarchists: "[The Lord knows how to deal with] them that walk after the flesh in the lust of uncleanness, and despise government. Presumptuous are they, selfwilled, they are not afraid to speak evil of dignities." (2 Pet. 2:10.)

"Yet Michael the archangel, when contending with the devil... about the body of Moses, durst not bring against him a railing accusation, but said, The Lord rebuke thee." (Jude 1:9.)

Here Jude clarifies a text in 2 Peter. Peter refers obliquely to the event of Michael's and Satan's dispute in his letter: "Whereas angels, which are greater in power and might, bring not railing accusation against them before the Lord." (2 Pet. 2:11.) Jude's reference is more specific, and again it is from an apocryphal book, the Assumption of Moses. This book survives only in fragments, and this reference to the dispute between the devil and Michael is not preserved, but ancient writers give it as coming from the Assumption of Moses. Apparently in this apocryphal text Michael was commissioned to bury Moses. Satan opposed the burial on the ground that, as he was the lord of matter, the body should be given to him. He also slandered Moses by calling him a murderer (of the Egyptian).[6] But even where the devil acted in his usual anarchic role, Michael determined to leave the rebuke to God. Jude's allusion provides a helpful warning for zealous saints. Alma gives similar advice: "I would exhort you to have patience, and that ye bear with all manner of afflictions; that ye do not revile against those who do cast you out . . . *lest ye become sinners like unto them.*" (Alma 34:40; emphasis added.) And Alma again: "Now, as ye have begun to teach the word, . . . I would that ye would be diligent and temperate in all things. . . . Use boldness, but not overbearance; and also see that ye bridle all your passions, that ye may be filled with love." (Alma 38:10, 12.) This battle for souls then is not to be waged with rebukes and confrontations, but on a different front: in the heart of the saint.

"These are spots in your feasts of charity, when they feast with you, feeding [Gk. shepherding] themselves without fear." (Jude 1:12.)

Just what the *agápe* feasts or love feasts (see also 2 Pet. 2:13-14) of the earliest Christians were is not entirely clear. The saints have always been commanded to gather together in fellowship, to provide for needy saints, and to take the sacrament. Among the Jews, meals for fellowship and brotherhood were common; the Gentiles also had such gatherings.[7] As both groups became Christian, it was natural for them to continue this practice in what may have been sacrament-type meetings with the addition of fellowship suppers. Jude warns of licentious persons who enter into these member gatherings, outwardly saintly but inwardly rapacious.

This warning speaks to us in more than one way. We may not entertain many rapacious people in our gatherings, but we surely face the problems of licentiousness among us, some in our number being seduced in more subtle ways. Because spiritual experience taps our deepest feelings, and because intimacy arises in shared spiritual experience, the distinctions between God's love and human desire may blur. Satan, the great counterfeiter, deceives many through desire. The Greek word translated *lust* (*epithumía*) in the King James Version (see, for example, Jude 1:16) does not mean unlawful sexual desire, but may refer to any strong desire. Therefore, "lusts of the flesh" can refer to a craving for anything that pertains to the mind or the body. Under the adversary's influence, these cravings can become deeply compelling and begin to feel like real needs. His victims are tossed and driven and chained by desire, and they cannot remember their former spiritual knowledge. Deluded, some may try to give what they call love in order to get love. Jude makes the distinction between carnal and spiritual clear: those who prey on others to satisfy their own emotional or physical desires, even using love to get love, lack godly love and will feel forever hungry. God himself died to break these chains of hell and redeem us from the delusion and the grasp of the "awful monster." (2 Ne. 9:10.)

"Clouds they are without water, carried about of winds; trees whose fruit withereth, without fruit, twice dead, plucked up by the roots; raging waves of the sea, foaming out their own shame; wandering stars, to whom is reserved the blackness of darkness for ever." (Jude 1:12-13.)

Second Peter 2:17 calls the apostates "wells without water, clouds that are carried with a tempest." Jude seems to recall Peter's letter from memory, for he has mixed some of Peter's images, or perhaps he has deliberately modified them for his own purposes. Again Jude apparently alludes to 1 Enoch, where water and clouds and trees and the motions of stars and seas obey God according to divine law and harmony, but blasphemers and harsh speakers of the Lord (cf. Jude 1:15) are out of harmony with eternal law and must perish (1 Enoch 2:1-10; 18:14-16). Jude's apostates are like nature that operates outside God's law, representing spiritual barrenness and anarchy.

There is really only one law: the law of God. It governs the development to Godhood, preserving and sanctifying all who obey it. Many seek to become a law to themselves, and their private laws do not have power to protect them. "That which is governed by law is also preserved by law . . . [and] that which breaketh a law, and abideth not by law, but seeketh to become a law unto itself . . . cannot be sanctified by law." (D&C 88:34-35.) Jude urges the saints to find refuge in God's law and in his love. Lehi exclaims, "But behold, the Lord hath redeemed my soul from hell; I have beheld his glory, and I am encircled about eternally in the arms of his love." (2 Ne. 1:15.) Within that circle we have abundant inner life—richness of life. Jesus came to make entrance into the circle possible: to connect us with the Father and with his love. Outside the circle, the life we have is described as "nothing" by Nephi: "Wherefore, the Lord God hath given a commandment that all men should have charity, which charity is love. And except they should have charity they were nothing." (2 Ne. 26:30.) The Savior declared, "I am come that they might have life, and that they might have it more abundantly." (John 10:10.)

"And Enoch also, the seventh from Adam, prophesied of these, saying, Behold, the Lord cometh with ten thousands of his saints." (Jude 1:14.)

As we have seen, several of Jude's themes and figures occur in more than one apocryphal book. For example, both the book of Enoch and the Assumption of Moses treat the coming of the Lord in glory, the judgment of the wicked, and similar nature motifs alluding to the wicked. Jude may have had access to both books, but in what forms it is impossible to say. The most that can be safely said is that he shows familiarity with material traditional in his culture.[8] Of course, direct revelation is another significant source. Joseph Smith said that Enoch himself appeared to Jude and thus Jude was able to bear record of the vision of Enoch.[9] Compare Jude's Enoch prophecy (1:14-16) with Enoch's vision of the coming of the Lord as contained in the book of Moses:

> And the Lord said unto Enoch: As I live, even so will I come in the last days, in the days of wickedness and vengeance, to fulfil the oath which I have made unto you. . . . Then shalt thou and all thy city meet them there, and we will receive them into

our bosom, and they shall see us; and we will fall upon their necks, and they shall fall upon our necks, and we will kiss each other. . . . And it came to pass that Enoch saw the day of the coming of the Son of Man, in the last days, to dwell on the earth in righteousness for the space of a thousand years; but before that day he saw great tribulations among the wicked; and he also saw the sea, that it was troubled, and men's hearts failing them, looking forth with fear for the judgments of the Almighty God, which should come upon the wicked. (Moses 7:60, 63, 65-66.)

The similarities between the apocryphal book of Enoch and the inspired vision of Enoch are remarkable, as Hugh Nibley has observed.[10]

"To execute judgment upon all, and to convince all that are ungodly among them of all their ungodly deeds which they have ungodly committed, and of all their hard speeches which ungodly sinners have spoken against him. These are murmurers, complainers, walking after their own lusts; and their mouth speaketh great swelling words, having men's persons in admiration because of advantage [Greek for profit or gain]." (Jude 1:15-16.)

This verse also recalls a passage in the Assumption of Moses (the parentheses indicate places where the editor has tried to restore missing text): "But really they consume the goods of the (poor) saying their acts are according to justice, (while in fact they are simply) exterminators, deceitfully seeking to conceal themselves so that they will not be known as completely godless because of their criminal deeds (committed) all the day long, saying, 'We shall have feasts, even luxurious winings and dinings. Indeed, we shall behave ourselves as princes.' They, with hand and mind, will touch impure things, yet their mouths will speak enormous things, and they will even say, 'Do not touch me, lest you pollute me in the position I occupy.'"[11]

The very presence of these apostates signals the arrival of the "last time." (Jude 1:18.) This may refer to two periods in history: the termination and apostasy of the early Christian era, and the latter part of our own dispensation prior to the Second Coming. Compare here 2 Peter 2:13 and 18, which treat the same subject in similar vocabulary. Peter also seems to allude to this apocryphal work.

The Power of the Love of God

"But ye, beloved, building up yourselves on your most holy faith, praying in the Holy Ghost, keep yourselves in the love of God, looking for the mercy of our Lord Jesus Christ unto eternal life." (Jude 1:20-21.)

The earlier verses in Jude have been primarily a warning against and a description of hard-core apostates. No rebuke, no confrontation with them will avail any good thing. But Jude indicates now that to build oneself up in the faith, praying in the Holy Ghost, and keeping oneself in the love of God, especially extending refuge to others, are the most potent armaments in the battle against apostasy.

"And of some have compassion, making a difference: and others save with fear, pulling them out of the fire; hating even the garment spotted by the flesh." (Jude 1:22-24.)

This passage is difficult in the Greek and may have preserved a scribal error. A more likely translation may be, "Be helpful to the doubting (or hesitating) souls; save some by snatching them from the flames; on others have mercy in fear (be cautious), hating even the garment spotted from the flesh." Jude calls us to exercise discernment in offering love. We must love like God in order to be preserved and developed by his law. "Except ye have charity ye can in nowise be saved." (Moro. 10:21.) Through our personal gift of the Holy Ghost, we receive that divine element known as God's love. The use of this love prevents as well as covers a multitude of sins because of the power and insight God's love imparts. (JST, 1 Pet. 4:8.) God's love is not based on feeling, but transcends human emotion and is extended by true saints to all. It is based on godly perception and the intent to nurture spiritual growth; it embraces reverence for human agency.

What then is the nature of the battle? It is to cut through the delusions of our own power and submit to God's power and will. We may learn what love is not. It is a delusion to think that we can fix up or save another. If we try to change another, seeking to shape too specifically what we feel that person ought to be, say, give, or do, our help may really be interference. The more anxious, the more militant we are, the more we may turn away those who need our love. We want to *attract* others to the gospel. Those who practice kindness and tolerance draw others to the Lord. Through them, godly love flows as a spiritual gift. Such persons, revering agency, avoid feeling responsible for, or too anxious about, others' choices or behavior, no matter how closely related they may be. We learn to leave to God's tender care those whom we cannot influence. The prophet Jacob feared that his overanxiety for his charges would shake his firmness in the Spirit. (Jacob 4:18; cf. Alma 29:3-4, 7-8.) We can do God's work effectively only by doing it his way.

The Lord instructs those who would embark on soul-saving: "Faith, hope, charity and love, with an eye single to the glory of God, *qualify* him for the work. Remember faith, virtue, knowledge, temperance, patience, brotherly kindness, godliness, charity, humility, diligence." Then the Lord, acknowledging that we might feel deficient in a number of these qualities, adds, "Ask, and ye shall receive; knock, and it shall be opened unto you." (D&C 4:5-7; emphasis added.)

George F. Richards, president of the Council of the Twelve, related a unique experience with the love of God:

> More than 40 years ago I had a dream which I am sure was from the Lord. In this dream I was in the presence of my Savior as he stood mid-air. He spoke no word to me, but my love for him was such that I have not words to explain. I know no mortal man can love the Lord as I experienced that love for the Savior unless God reveals it to him. I would have remained in his presence, but there was a power drawing me away from him.
>
> As a result of that dream, I had this feeling that no matter what might be required at my hands, what the gospel might entail unto me, I would do what I should be asked to do even to the laying down of my life....
>
> If only I can be with my Savior and have that same sense of love that I had in that dream, it will be the goal of my existence, the desire of my life.[12]

"Now unto him that is able to keep you from falling, and to present you faultless before the presence of his glory with exceeding joy, to the only wise God our Saviour, be glory and majesty, dominion and power, both now and ever. Amen." (Jude 1:24-25.)
Observe the parallels in the foregoing verse with this verse from

Enoch's vision: "I am Messiah, the King of Zion, the Rock of Heaven, which is broad as eternity; whoso cometh in at the gate and climbeth up by me shall never fall; wherefore, blessed are they of whom I have spoken, for they shall come forth with songs of everlasting joy." (Moses 7:53.) Jude and Enoch have foreseen that a day when the soul devoted to the study and dissemination of God's love will be crowned with that final perfection which so eludes us in this life. (See Moro. 10:32-33.)

Jude's instruction to the early church and also to us is essentially this: (1) Let each saint beware, for in the battle for souls, even the very elect can fall; (2) let each seek refuge in the Spirit and love of God, ever refining himself; (3) let each get involved in providing loving refuge for others. Jude reminds us of our agency as well as our power to wield God's love. In this dispensation it is our great opportunity to assist in the preparations for the Second Coming of our Savior. As world conditions worsen and more refugees flee from the lusts of the flesh, the saints must provide the refuge.

Notes

1. Eusebius, *Ecclesiastical History* 3:20.

2. Richard Lloyd Anderson, "Jude and His Letter," *Guide to Acts and the Apostles' Letters* (Provo: BYU Press, 1983), p. 115.

3. James H. Charlesworth, *The Old Testament Pseudepigrapha*, vol. 1 (Garden City, New York: Doubleday, 1983).

4. Bruce R. McConkie, *Doctrinal New Testament Commentary*, 3 vols. (Salt Lake City: Bookcraft, 1965-73), 3:423.

5. H. C. Thiessen, *Introduction to the New Testament* (Grand Rapids, Michigan: Eerdmans, 1971), p. 294.

6. R. H. Charles, *Apocrypha and Pseudepigrapha of the Old Testament*, vol. 2 (London: Oxford University Press, 1913), p. 408.

7. J. D. Douglas, ed., *The New Bible Dictionary* (Grand Rapids, Michigan: Eerdmans, 1965), p. 712.

8. Charlesworth, *The Old Testament Pseudepigrapha*, p. 924.

9. *Teachings of the Prophet Joseph Smith,* comp. Joseph Fielding Smith (Salt Lake City: Deseret Book, 1976), p. 170.

10. Hugh Nibley, *Enoch the Prophet* (Salt Lake City: Deseret Book, 1986).

11. Charlesworth, "Testament of Moses," 7:1-10, vol. 1, p. 930.

12. As related by President Spencer W. Kimball, in *Ensign,* May 1974, p. 119.

18
"THINGS WHICH MUST SHORTLY COME TO PASS"
(Revelation)

GERALD N. LUND

"One of the Plainest Books . . . Ever Written"

The original Greek title for the book known to us in English as the book of Revelation is *Apocalypsis*. The word is formed from the preposition *apo*, which has the basic meaning of separation, and the verb *kalypto*, which means "to cover, cover up" or "to hide, veil, i.e. to hinder the knowledge of a thing."[1] Thus, *apocalypsis* means "to remove or take away the covering, to unveil so as to make seen," and this definition explains the book's English title, which is based on the verb *reveal*. Scholars and students of the New Testament have noted the seeming irony of that title. Many find this unique work of scripture anything but a revealing of that which is hidden or an uncovering of the unknown. Indeed, they say it is one of the most veiled and difficult of all the scriptural books. It is a book that can be simultaneously fascinating and frustrating, intriguing and irritating, exciting and exasperating. Someone even explained its difficulty by suggesting that the book was written in code so that John could safely smuggle it past his Roman guards on the prison island of Patmos. Some Latter-day Saints have concluded that Nephi's prophecy that certain "plain and precious things" of the Bible would be lost (1 Ne. 13:28-29) is especially

---

Gerald N. Lund is zone administrator for the Church Educational System.

true in the case of the book of Revelation. They think *all* the plain and precious things have been removed.

Though such explanations may make one feel good about his own inability to understand John's writings, they do not agree with the conclusion of the Prophet Joseph Smith, who said, "The book of Revelation is one of the plainest books God ever caused to be written."[2] Elder Bruce R. McConkie said, "Most of the book—and it is no problem to count the verses so included—is clear and plain and should be understood by the Lord's people." Further, he said that the Lord "has not withheld the book of Revelation, because it is not beyond our capacity to comprehend."[3]

Even the most complex and baffling thing is simple to those who fully understand it. This is true also of the book of Revelation, and it explains why the Prophet found it to be one of the plainest books God ever caused to be written. He understood the doctrine and the things that John saw and therefore found it to be a plain and easily understood book. While many things would probably add to our understanding of Revelation, three keys are: (1) pay the price required, (2) learn the divine esoteric language, and (3) learn the organizational structure of the book.

The Apocalypse was written primarily for saints of latter days. It reveals or uncovers the events of our own day and the near future. Therefore, it is of great value for us to put forth the effort necessary to make it a book of revealing, a book of revelation.

Paying the Price Required

It is obvious to even the beginning student of the scriptures that some portions of the scriptures are easier to understand than others. For example, the story of the sons of Mosiah and their mission to the Lamanites is exciting, fast moving, and easily understood. Isaiah, Revelation, and other portions of the scriptures are just the opposite, and most people have difficulty understanding them. Recognizing the greater difficulty of the book of Revelation, Elder Bruce R. McConkie said: "The language and imagery is so chosen as to appeal to the *maturing gospel scholar,* to those who already love the Lord and have some knowledge of his goodness and grace."[4] Clearly, we could not expect to sit down and read Revelation through once or twice and fully comprehend it. We must pay a price in diligent study, careful pondering, and spiritual development if the Apocalypse is to be a plain book. It was meant to be understood, but the Lord has apparently couched it in such a way that this understanding can be won only through personal effort. Three specific kinds of effort prove to be especially helpful in the case of the book of Revelation.

1. *We must develop a sensitivity to spiritual promptings as they relate to the study of the Revelation of John.*

When all is said and done, the book of Revelation can be understood only by revelation. "In this connection, however," Elder McConkie explained, "we must always remember that prophecy, visions, and revelations come by the power of the Holy Ghost and can only be understood in their fullness and perfection by the power of that same Spirit."[5] Often, as we study in the book, we find that the Spirit will gently confirm a particular interpretation of a passage or perhaps convey a quiet sense of uneasiness that suggests the interpretation is not correct. Following those subtle but very important promptings is one of the most important keys to understanding Revelation. And, of course, this sensitivity comes only when a price is paid in personal worthiness and by gaining experience in listening to the promptings of the Holy Ghost.

2. *We must have a broad knowledge of the gospel and the standard works.*

On a recent flight from Salt Lake City, as the plane came over the San Bernardino mountains and descended for its final approach into Los Angeles, we could see a grand vista spread out below us. Desert winds had polished away the smog, and the visibility was remarkable. The vast metropolis of Southern California lay sprawled out below in crystal clarity. A young couple excitedly commented on the panorama before their eyes. "Oh, look!" one would cry, "that must be an airport." And then a moment later, "Look at that big stadium coming up there," or "That must be a freeway interchange down there. Look at all those cars." A man in the seat in front of the couple looked down at exactly the same scene, but he saw much more. As the couple spoke, the man thought, "Yes, that's Norton Air Force Base, and the big stadium is the Rose Bowl. The interchange is where the Santa Monica, San Bernardino, Hollywood, Pomona, and Santa Ana freeways meet."

He could not only identify particular freeways, parks, schools, and other landmarks, he could even look down and say to himself, "There is Jim Jones's home, and Karl Fisher's, and there's the 7-Eleven store that opened up last month."

What made the difference in what these three people saw? Not what was there or even the clarity of the scene. It was their knowledge or lack of knowledge of the area. The man had lived in Los Angeles for several years. He had driven the streets, visited the houses, passed the parks, shopped in the stores. The young couple were visiting Los Angeles for the first time.

This analogy illustrates the importance of having a broad gospel knowledge if we are to understand Revelation. The Lord had John write the book for knowledgeable, spiritually aware Saints. Often, key concepts are not explained because John assumes his readers have a knowledge of the subject covered. He does not take time to say, as it were, "The big stadium is the Rose Bowl where some very important football games are played," and so on. He assumes that his readers are native to the area and that he need only mention the landmarks for them to know exactly what he refers to.

The area that John covers is the gospel and the scriptures, and the assumption is that his readers are natives of that area. The Lord has seen fit to reveal knowledge in a special way—as he himself says, "Here a little, and there a little." (D&C 128:21.) One concept is planted here and another there, and thus the scriptures form a great latticework of interwoven, interdependent concepts. The more familiar we are with that latticework and those concepts, the more quickly we will understand and recognize them when John uses them. And though John had only former-day scriptures, the power of inspiration is such that he uses many concepts and ideas that are found only in latter-day scripture. That is one reason why only the Latter-day Saints can understand Revelation. Many keys to the knowledge John assumes his readers have are not found in the Bible.

Note, however, that we are not saying that Latter-day Saints *will* understand Revelation, only that they *can*, if they will gain a broad knowledge of the gospel and the language of the four standard works. Only then will they recognize the concepts, images, and doctrines revealed to John.

*3. We must diligently study the book of Revelation itself, prob-
ing, pondering, and searching for understanding.*

The third price that must be paid in order to gain an understanding of Revelation is in the book itself. Our society is churning out so
much information so fast that it is a valuable asset to be able to read,
and read quickly. When this habit is carried over to the scriptures,
however, it becomes detrimental. The primary purpose of reading
scriptures is not to see how fast we can *cover* them but to see how
much we can *absorb* of what is in them. This is true of all scripture,
but it is especially true of Revelation. We must firmly grab ourselves
by the mental collar again and again and pull ourselves back, asking
the questions, "Why does the Lord say that? What is the Lord trying to
teach me with that image? Why does the Lord use that symbol? What
does this convey? Why is that important? How am I to interpret this?"

In many cases the very act of stopping, pondering, and probing for
meaning will bring additional insights and important understanding.
But often a further price of study must be paid through searching
other scriptures for knowledge and insight (in other words, increasing our general knowledge of the gospel). More will be said later
about how the scriptures can increase our understanding of Revelation, so let it suffice here to say only that time and time again the answer to the why or what or how of a specific verse can be clearly and
easily answered from the scriptures themselves. Sometimes, however,
the interpretation of a symbol or the explanation of a certain phrase is
found not in the scriptures but in an understanding of the history and
culture of John's time. We must realize that John wrote in a particular
setting and that his readers were part of that same setting. He did not
intend his writings to be obscure or incomprehensible to his readers.
He wrote in their language, he was part of the same cultural background and heritage as they were, and they were familiar with special
idioms or events that he used. Every language and culture develops
idioms—special phrases and ways of expression that are unique and
yet easily understood within the culture. For example, one night a
television talk-show guest referred to "the peanut farmer from
Georgia." There were probably very few of the thousands watching
who didn't know exactly what was meant by that phrase. But let's suppose that a thousand years from now, some enterprising archae-

ologist, excavating in the ruins of New York City, discovers a video-tape of this show and replays it. Will he not, upon hearing the phrase "peanut farmer from Georgia," be puzzled and miss the significance of the phrase?

That is the situation we face in the case of the Apocalypse. Many of the phrases were clearly understood by the saints of John's day, but we are far removed from those times, those situations, and that language. We must, through a study of nonscriptural sources, bridge that cultural gap and seek for the original, intended meaning. For example, in Revelation 13:16 John says: "And he [the beast] causeth all, both small and great, rich and poor, free and bond, to receive a mark in their right hand, or in their foreheads." Numerous interpretations of that passage have been given by various commentators, ranging all the way from saying it is a specific mark placed on the body of a person to wildly spiritualistic interpretations; however, knowledge of an ancient custom and a secondary practice derived from this custom sheds light on what John may have been trying to convey.

In the Roman empire there were vast numbers of slaves. Often a slave would run away from his master, go to a large city such as Rome, and try to disappear into the population. Since nothing about a human being marks him naturally as either a slave or freedman, such runaways could pass as free persons as long as no one could personally identify them. To protect against that practice, slave owners would often brand their slaves with marks to identify them, just as modern stockmen permanently mark their animals for identification. To make this brand impossible to hide under clothing, most slaves were marked either on the palm of the right hand or on the forehead directly above the eyes. Therefore, it would have been common in John's time to see a person walking down the street with a mark on his right hand or on his forehead and to instantly identify him as a slave.

Out of that practice grew a secondary custom. Worshipers of various gods in the Roman pantheon, to symbolize the fact that they were totally dedicated to their god—in other words, that they were slaves or servants of their god—would also mark themselves on the right hand or the forehead. In this case they would mark themselves with a symbol of their god. Thus, a person might be seen walking down the street with a thunderbolt on his forehead, which symbolized that he was totally devoted to—that is, a slave to—Jupiter. A person marked with a trident said symbolically, "I am a servant of Poseidon, the god of the sea," and so on. John's readers, familiar with that concept and its significance, would not have puzzled over what he meant. To say that a person had the mark of the beast suggested that he was a slave of, or totally subservient to, the beast. Note that John uses the same imagery in a positive sense, indicating that there are those who are sealed in their foreheads with the mark of God. (See Rev. 7:3.) This use clearly signifies that these are people who belong to God; they are God's servants. Thus, while it is true that only Latter-day Saints have the additional keys necessary to correctly interpret Revelation, a careful study of non-LDS sources can bring many valuable cultural, linguistic, and historical insights that can greatly enhance our understanding of John's vision.

An understanding of Revelation can be won by those willing to pay the price and put forth the required efforts in terms of study, pondering, and personal preparation. But if we expect to master the book at any lesser cost, we will likely be disappointed.

Learn the Divine Esoteric Language

Esoteric language is words and phrases that have special meaning or significance only to an initiated in-group. The story is told that during the Six-Day War of 1967, the Syrian government broadcast a warning to the Druze, an Arabic people living in northern Galilee, that Israeli troops were slaughtering this people. When thousands of the Druze began to flee to Syria, the Israeli army went on the radio and announced that the reports were false. Almost as one, the Druze returned to their homes. When asked by a reporter how they knew that the Israelis were telling the truth and that this was not just some propaganda trick, the people replied that Druze never lie. They said that when the Israelis put a Druze on the radio and he denied the Syrian reports, they knew it was true. "But," the reporter persisted, "how could you be sure it was really a Druze on the radio? It could have been an Israeli trick." One Druze shook his head. "The Druze religion is secret, known only to our own people. When the man on the radio used words and phrases that have special meaning only to a Druze, we knew he was Druze." This is a dramatic instance of the use of esoteric language.

The Lord told his disciples that he taught in parables so that those who are spiritually sensitive might receive the message of his teachings, but the message would be missed by those who "seeing see not; and hearing they hear not." (Matt. 13:13.) Elder McConkie said of the Lord's use of parables: "His purpose . . . was *not* to present the truths of his gospel in plainness so that all his hearers would understand. Rather it was so to phrase and hide the doctrine involved that only the spiritually literate would understand."[6] In other words the Lord used a form of spiritual esoteric language to simultaneously *reveal* and *conceal* the meaning, depending on his listeners' gospel readiness.

This is a concept that has tremendous implications for a study of Revelation, for this book is a book filled with esoteric language. Virtually every verse has words, phrases, symbols, numbers, and other verbal devices *that were designed to be understood* but *only by spiritually mature and sensitive Saints.*

As mentioned earlier, some Latter-day Saints have suggested that an explanation for the obscure nature of the book is that it was mutilated by apostate religionists who took out the "plain and precious things," as Nephi foresaw. But I am firmly convinced that just the opposite is true. Because these persons had no spiritual discernment, they missed the true significance of the divine esoteric language and left it relatively intact.

While it is risky to draw a conclusion from the Joseph Smith Translation changes, since it is unknown how that work would differ if the Prophet had had time to finish it, it is interesting to note the number of changes made in Revelation as compared to other books. For example, two books that have little symbolism or esoteric language underwent far more changes than did Revelation. In Genesis the Prophet changed 771 of 1,532 verses, besides adding 225 completely new verses. Thus, he altered well over 50 percent of the book and expanded it by another 15 percent. In Matthew he corrected 682 of 1,071 verses, or 64 percent of the total. By comparison, in Revelation he changed only 81 out of 393 verses, or 21 percent of the total. His statement that the book of Revelation is one of the plainest books God ever caused to be written seems to indicate that those changes satisfied him.

This, of course, provides the modern reader with the challenges of learning the significance behind the spiritually loaded terminology and imagery. Three things seem to be especially helpful in interpreting the esoteric language of Revelation: the scriptures, the writings of the modern prophets, and the nature of the symbols themselves.

1. *Do the scriptures themselves give the key to the esoteric language?*

Joseph Smith said, "I make this broad declaration, that whenever God gives a vision of an image, or beast, or a figure of any kind, He always holds Himself responsible to give a revelation or interpretation of the meaning thereof, otherwise we are not responsible or accountable for our belief in it. Don't be afraid of being damned for not knowing the meaning of a vision or figure, if God has not given a revelation or interpretation of the subject."[7] In hundreds of cases, we have no excuse for not understanding the divine imagery revealed to John, for the Lord has clearly specified how the symbols are to be interpreted. Sometimes the key is given in the same context as the symbol itself; other times he explains its significance later on in the vision; or in many cases, the key is given somewhere else in the standard works.

Examples of passages whose interpretation is given in context:

The "seven golden candlesticks" (Rev. 1:12) are "the seven churches" (Rev. 1:20).

The "golden vials full of odours [incense]" (Rev. 5:8) are "prayers of saints" (Rev. 5:8).

The "dragon" (Rev. 12:3) is "that old serpent, called the Devil, and Satan" (Rev. 12:9).

The "fine linen, clean and white" (Rev. 19:8) is "the righteousness of saints" (Rev. 19:8).

Examples of passages whose interpretation is given elsewhere in Revelation:

The "morning star" (Rev. 2:28) is Jesus Christ (see Rev. 22:16).

The "seven heads [of the beast]" (Rev. 13:1) are "seven mountains, on which the woman sitteth" (Rev. 17:9).

The "many waters" upon which the whore sits (Rev. 17:1) are "peoples, and multitudes, and nations, and tongues" (Rev. 17:15).

Examples of passages whose interpretation is given elsewhere in scripture:

The "rod of iron" by which the nations are broken into pieces (Rev. 2:27) is "the word of God," or the gospel (1 Ne. 11:25).

"Michael" (Rev. 12:7) is "Adam" (D&C 107:54).

"Babylon" (Rev. 14:8; 16:19; etc.) is a symbol of the world and spiritual "wickedness" (D&C 133:14).

The "white stone . . . [with] a new name" (Rev. 2:17) is a "Urim and Thummim" given to those who go to the celestial kingdom (D&C 130:10-11).

2. Do the prophets give the key to the esoteric language?

We believe that what is written or spoken by the prophets under the inspiration of the Holy Ghost constitutes scripture. (See D&C 68:2-5.) In some cases prophets of the last dispensation have given us further clues for interpreting the divine esoteric language of Revelation. Though technically it could be classed as canonized scripture and placed in the first category, one of the most important prophetic writings is the Joseph Smith Translation of the Bible. His corrections and additions to Revelation become important sources of interpretation. In addition he gave other clues in his sermons and writings, some of which dealt directly with John's visions. Other prophets and apostles have also provided us with significant interpretations that help us better translate the esoteric imagery.

The following are examples of interpretations given in the Joseph Smith Translation or other writings of Joseph Smith:

The seven "angels of the seven churches" (Rev. 1:20) become the "servants," or leaders, of the seven churches (JST, Rev. 1:20).

The "Lamb . . . having seven horns and seven eyes" (Rev. 5:6) becomes the "Lamb . . . having twelve horns and twelve eyes," perfecting the symbolism to identify Jesus and the twelve Apostles (JST, Rev. 5:6).

The "woman" and the "man child" (Rev. 12:1-5) are clearly identified as the "church of God" and "the kingdom of our God and his Christ" (JST, Rev. 12:7).

The "beast(s)" seen by prophets (Rev. 13:1-5) are representations of "the degenerate kingdoms of the wicked world."[8]

Examples of interpretations given by other apostles and prophets:

The "angel [flying] in the midst of heaven" (Rev. 14:6) represents the angels of the Restoration, including Moroni, Peter, James, and John.[9]

The time when "every island fled away" (Rev. 16:20) refers to the time when the continents will be rejoined into one land.[10]

The binding of Satan (Rev. 20:2-3) will be accomplished through the righteousness of the Saints.[11]

3. *Does the nature of the symbol give insights into its significance?*

The peoples of the ancient Middle East loved imagery and figurative language and used them constantly. They saw spiritual parallels in the natural characteristics of things that were around them every day. Animals, objects, events, and actions were observed and then used to express or teach figurative truths. In other words, the choice of symbols was not arbitrary or capricious; it was the nature of the item used that led to its use as a symbol. Therefore, if we take time to examine the symbols and ponder why the ancients chose them to represent symbolic truths, we often find important insights into their meaning. For example, trumpets were used anciently to sound an alarm, signal for battle, or announce the arrival of royalty. The sounding of trumpets therefore symbolized heralding or announcing something highly significant. This knowledge helps explain why the seven angels sound trumpets as each new judgment of the seventh seal is shown forth. (See Rev. 8 and 9.)

The candlestick is not a *source* of light but a *holder* of the light. Since the Church of Jesus Christ is not the actual source of truth but merely holds up Jesus Christ—the true light of the world—for all to see, the candlestick provides a beautiful representation of the church. (Rev. 1:12-13, 20; cf. 3 Ne. 18:24.)

Another example is the imagery of keys. (See Rev. 9:1; 20:1.) Anciently, locks were handcarved out of wood or hand-forged out of metal and were large, bulky, and very expensive. They were used only to protect valuable treasures or stores and were rarely owned by the common people. The keys for such locks were also necessarily large and were typically worn around the neck on a chain. Because of what they guarded, the keys were given only to highly trusted or respected individuals. Therefore, anciently, if one saw a man on the street wearing a key or keys, one could rightly assume that he was a man of power and authority. In this manner keys came to be a symbol not only of control over something but also of invested power and authority.

Again and again we find that taking time to ponder the natural characteristics of the item chosen as a symbol becomes an important key for understanding the imagery. We should constantly ask, What is it about this thing that would have caused it to be used symbolically? Often we can answer this question from our own experience, but sometimes further research is necessary to see what the item was or how it was used anciently. Here again we see how non-LDS sources may be of value to us; and, more important, we see that a price must be paid in personal thought, study, and effort. There are, perhaps, other ways for interpreting the divine esoteric language of Revelation, but these three—the scriptures, the prophets, and an examination of the symbol itself—are very helpful in understanding what was signified when John received the revelation. In some places in Revelation, none of these three sources provide the keys to understanding the language, and we must pass them over for now. But those passages are relatively few in number. For the most part, the Lord has made it possible to learn the key to what he says. It is an understanding of this esoteric language that then makes the book "one of the plainest books God ever caused to be written."[12]

Learn the Organizational Structure of the Book

One important question to be answered before we can understand any work of scripture has to do with its basic structure: how it was organized and the purposes for which it was written. The Book of Mormon follows a basically historical structure with pauses in the narrative to emphasize selected sermons; however, the chronological flow of the narrative is broken in several places. For example, Words of Mormon, written about A.D. 385, is inserted between writings completed more than five hundred years earlier. And Moroni, who wrote around A.D. 400, inserted into the record the Book of Ether, which begins at the time of the Tower of Babel, about 2200 B.C. There are also numerous digressions and flashbacks in the basic historical story line. But if we understand that Mormon was writing an abridgment of many records and that his purpose was to bear witness of Jesus Christ for those living in the latter days, these seeming anachronisms become perfectly logical and do not violate the basically chronological development of the book.

The New Testament, on the other hand, has a completely different organizational structure. There is no grand unifying chronological development. It is a series of short works and letters collected into one book, and it would be foolish to look for a narrative flow such as we find in the Book of Mormon.

Thus, knowing the organizational structure of a work becomes very important if we wish to better understand its contents. This is especially true of Revelation. Understanding how it is laid out becomes critical not only to understanding the book as a whole but also for interpreting specific imagery and symbolic language. Three concepts related to the organizational structure are particularly helpful to remember as we examine how Revelation is organized: (1) John's vision revealed the history and destiny of the earth in chronological order; (2) the major emphasis of the vision is on only a small portion of that chronological line; (3) the chronological narrative is interrupted periodically with "teaching interludes." Before examining each of these concepts, let us first note that we will be talking only about the actual vision given to John. The introductory material (chapter 1), the letters to the seven churches of Asia (chapters 2 and 3), and the concluding summary (chapter 22, verses 8 through 21) will not be discussed here. We will examine only what John saw when he saw that "a door was opened in heaven" and he was told to "come up hither." (Rev. 4:1.) This vision comprises the majority of the book (chapters 4 through 22) and is the heart of the Apocalypse.

1. *The vision given to John revealed the history and destiny of the earth in chronological order.*

Throughout the centuries one of the most hotly debated questions about Revelation has had to do with the question of where it fits into history, that is, was what John saw related to his own time (which for us makes it history), or did it depict only future events (which are now becoming current or near future for us), or was it a combination of both? Some scholars even suggest that the vision was to be interpreted spiritually and has no correspondence to actual events in

either history or prophecy. Impressive evidence and persuasive arguments are marshaled for each point of view. But as we have already
noted, the only way to understand Revelation is through revelation,
and again we see why only the Latter-day Saints have the key for understanding this work.

In March 1832 Joseph Smith received a revelation (D&C 77) in
which fifteen questions about the book of Revelation were asked and
answered. Though some people would like to have seen more than fifteen questions asked, upon careful study we find that these fifteen do
provide the key to understanding Revelation.

The word *key* is a good one. The Apocalypse is like a huge house
whose doors are locked and whose windows are shuttered. We can
peek in through a crack here and there and glimpse what is inside, but
most of it remains hidden from our view. Section 77, however, gives
us the key to the house. It does not tell us everything we would like to
know about John's vision, but it provides a means whereby we can
open the door, go inside the house, and begin to explore what is there.

The single most important clue for interpreting Revelation was
given in this revelation received by the Prophet. The first thing John
saw in heaven was a glorious being on a throne (Rev. 4:2-3) surrounded by various beings, all giving praise to him. The figure on the
throne represented Elohim because he reigns supreme in heaven. In
his right hand was a book (probably a scroll, since that was the common form of books of the day) that was sealed with seven seals. (Rev.
5:1.) An angel asked who was worthy to open the book, but no person
in heaven or on earth or under the earth was worthy. Sensing the significance of this, John began to weep. (Rev. 5:2-4.) Then he was shown
that there was no cause to weep because there was one person who
could open the book—the Lamb of God (Jehovah, or Jesus Christ).
When the Lamb took the book and prepared to open the seals, all
heaven burst forth in a great hymn of praise. (See Rev. 5:5-14.)

Understanding what is symbolized by the book in the right hand of
God becomes critical to understanding the book of Revelation, because the remainder of the vision is what John sees as the Lamb opens
the seals one at a time. Section 77 explains what the book symbolizes.
We are told that it symbolizes the history of the earth, which was to
last for seven thousand years (D&C 77:6), and that each seal repre-

sents one of the thousand-year periods (D&C 77:7). The book is shown in God's hand because it is under his control and management. Only the Lamb of God is worthy to open it because only through the atonement of Jesus Christ does the history and destiny of the world unfold.

If each seal represents one thousand years of the earth's history, then we can assume, since the seals are opened in order, one at a time, that Revelation is a chronological outline of the history of the earth.

Because John describes in figurative and highly symbolic language what he sees as each seal is opened, it is difficult for us to instantly recognize this chronology. But knowing what the structure is—that it is basically a chronological unfolding of the history of the earth—helps us tremendously in interpreting the symbols and understanding the book. Without this key to the organizational structure given in D&C 77, we can stray far afield in interpreting the book. For example, one Christian commentator was misled by not knowing how the book is structured. Speaking of the locusts seen as part of the opening of the seventh seal, John wrote, "And it was commanded them that they should not hurt the grass of the earth, neither any green thing, neither any tree; but only those men which have not the seal of God in their foreheads." (Rev. 9:4.) This commentator gives the following fascinating explanation of John's imagery. Speaking of the time when the armies of Mohammed swept out of Arabia and across most of the known world, he says:

> I have a copy of the military command given to this great cavalry army by Abu-bekr, their commander, in A.D. 632, when they were on the verge of entering upon their invasions of Syria. He dispatched a circular letter to the Arabian tribes which reads as follows: "When you fight the battles of the Lord, acquit yourselves like men, without turning your backs; but let not your victory be stained with blood of the women or children. *Destroy no palm trees, nor burn any fields of corn. Cut down no fruit-trees,* nor do any mischief to cattle, only such as you kill to eat." . . .
>
> The prophecy [of John] did not say that the more humane injunctions here would be scrupulously obeyed, but the prophecy did say that it was so commanded them. What a wonderful fulfillment of prophecy this is—a command given to the

advancing hosts, recorded in Scripture nearly 600 years before it was given by the military commander![13]

This is a brilliant and plausible explanation except for one serious problem. Revelation 9 takes place in the seventh seal or last thousand years (D&C 77:13), while the Moslem invasions described took place in the fifth thousand years!

Most Bible scholars assume that the person on a white horse seen when the first seal was opened (Rev. 6:2) symbolized Jesus Christ— again a reasonable and appealing explanation if we do not understand the chronology revealed in the vision. Knowing that the first seal represents the first thousand years (approximately 4000 to 3000 B.C.) and using John's imagery, we come to a different conclusion.

White. This symbol indicates righteousness, purity, sanctification.

Horse. In the ancient Middle East the horse was not used as a domesticated work animal, but was seen only at times of warfare and conquering armies. Therefore, throughout the Bible the horse is a symbol of war, conquest, and military power.[14]

Bow. In ancient warfare a man with a bow and arrow had one of the most effective weapons; it extended his power to strike far beyond his own person, silently and swiftly and with deadly accuracy. Therefore, the bow is a symbol of effectiveness in warfare.

Crown. Anciently royalty or people with ruling power wore crowns; therefore, the crown is a symbol of political position and power.

Conquest. This is not so much a symbol as it is a piece of information telling us that this person was successful in conquering.

We conclude that Enoch and his ministry best fit the known facts and the imagery. He lived in the first thousand years; he was a man of great righteousness (whiteness); he established a city called Zion, which eventually was translated (the crown of gold); and he led the people of God to battle (the horse) with great power (the bow). (See Moses 7:13-15.)[15]

While there is not space to examine fully the imagery of each seal and give its interpretation, a close examination of John's vision shows that the chronology is followed through from the times of Adam to the end of the world.

2. *The major emphasis of John's vision is only a small part of the chronology.*

Though we have established that the structural outline of Revelation is chronological, it would be a grave error to conclude that John's purpose was simply to give an overview of the history and destiny of the world. The Prophet Joseph Smith said: "The things which John saw had no allusion to the scenes of the days of Adam, Enoch, Abraham or Jesus, only so far as is plainly represented by John, and clearly set forth by him. John saw that only which was lying in futurity and which was shortly to come to pass."[16] And twice in Revelation we are told that the emphasis was to be a future one. (Rev. 1:1; 4:1.)

So, while the flow of Revelation is organized around a chronological outline, we are not suggesting that every part of the chronology receives equal emphasis. A brief examination of the number of verses used to describe what is seen in each seal quickly shows where the major emphasis was to be. The first four seals are covered in two verses each. (Rev. 6:1-8.) Remembering that each seal covers a thousand years of history, we can safely conclude that John could do no more than highlight or emphasize one aspect of that period of history. Even in the fifth seal, the seal in which John himself lived, only three verses are used to describe what is seen when the seal is opened. So we can safely say that the Lord was not going to emphasize even John's own time to John. Only when we come to the sixth seal does the detail start to expand. This seal (Rev. 6:12-17; 7:1-8) takes fourteen verses, a discussion that is seven times greater than each of the first four seals but still represents only a tiny part of the vision.

It is the seventh seal and the events thereof that comprise the vast majority of John's vision. We might expect that the Millennium with its thousand years of peace, harmony, and righteousness would be a major emphasis of John's vision, but such is not the case. Even if we include the binding of Satan in preparation for the Millennium and the calling forth of the righteous to join Christ at the beginning of the Millennium, only six verses describe the Millennium itself. (Rev. 20:1-6.) The final winding-up scenes of the earth's history, including the last great battle (Rev. 20:7-10), the final judgment (Rev. 20:11-15), and the celestialization of the earth (Rev. 21:1-27; 22:1-6), while given in some detail, comprise a total of only forty-two verses—still a small percentage of the total. Clearly John's major emphasis is on that tiny part of history that begins at the opening of the seventh seal and ends up with the second coming of Christ. Here again is dramatic evidence that Revelation is primarily a book for the Latter-day Saints. Though John had the stewardship for writing it (1 Ne. 14:18-28), most of it obviously deals with the times in which we are now living or will soon enter. It provides a vivid, detailed description of what saints can expect in preparation for the second coming of Christ.

3. *The chronological narrative of the vision is interrupted periodically with "teaching interludes."*

We have stated emphatically that the basic organizational structure of the Apocalypse is a chronological one. Immediately objections can be raised to that statement on the basis of the content. For example, in Revelation 12:7-9 we are given a brief description of the war in heaven, which took place before the world was even created. Yet chapter 12 is placed in that portion of the vision which is part of the seventh seal, or the last thousand years of the earth's history. For another example, Revelation 14:6-7 speaks of another angel flying through heaven with the everlasting gospel. This is a well-known reference to the restoration of the gospel in the last day. Since this took place in the early 1800s, this event would be part of the sixth seal, yet we find it in the midst of that part of the vision when the seventh seal is opened.

How do we explain these contradictions, these anachronisms in the chronological flow? As noted earlier, once we understand the purposes and organization of the Book of Mormon, the anachronisms of that book become clear and logical. So it is with the vision given to John. Consider this analogy to help explain why there are pauses or digressions in the chronological flow of Revelation. A master teacher moves through a presentation in an organized and logical fashion. He has a clear idea of the concepts he wants to teach. Occasionally, however, he pauses in the logical flow in order to lay the foundations for concepts important to the overall development of his theme. To one who does not see the overall unity of his thematic development, such digressions may seem illogical and off the point. But in fact, they are necessary to the better understanding of the concepts to follow. We could refer to such digressions as teaching interludes.

This analogy helps us not only to explain the supposed anachronisms in the chronological flow of Revelation, but also to better understand what is happening and why. Like a master teacher, the Lord occasionally pauses in the development of the vision as it is being given to John and shows him other things that will support, explain, or expand his knowledge so that he (and his readers) can better appreciate the overall impact of what he is seeing.

The idea of teaching interludes can most easily be seen in Revelation 10, the so-called "little book" chapter. It is inserted in the midst of the vivid imagery John is using to describe the vast army of Armageddon (Rev. 9:1-21), the last great battle in Jerusalem, and the two prophets who prophesy there (Rev. 11:1-3). The "little book" chapter at first seems totally out of place and not part of the chronological flow. A mighty angel appears, gives John a small book, and requests that he eat it. When John does so, he finds it as "sweet as honey" in his mouth, but it makes his "belly bitter." (Rev. 10:1-11.) Through latter-day revelation we are given the interpretation of the little book, which helps us understand why this chapter is inserted where it is. In the fifteen questions found in Doctrine and Covenants 77, we find that the Prophet asked the significance of the little book that John ate. He was told that "it was a mission, and an ordinance, for him [John] to gather the tribes of Israel." (D&C 77:14; 7:3.) In other words, in the midst of the vision of the last days, it is as if the Lord pauses and says to John, "Since you will live during these times, you may wish to know what you'll be doing. Here is your mission and calling."

There are five such interludes in the vision given to John. I believe that the teaching interlude concept explains the so-called anachronisms of Revelation. For example, the reference to the war in heaven (Rev. 12:7-11) comes in the midst of the kingdoms interlude and explains that Satan's opposition to the kingdom of God really began before the creation of the world. And the reference to the angels of the restoration (Rev. 14:6-7) shows that it is through the restoration in the latter days that Christ's kingdom will triumph over Satan's.

Notes

1. *Thayer's Greek-English Lexicon of the New Testament*, pp. 57, 323.

2. *Teachings of the Prophet Joseph Smith*, comp. Joseph Fielding Smith (Salt Lake City: Deseret Book, 1938), p. 290.

3. Bruce R. McConkie, "Understanding the Book of Revelation," *Ensign*, September 1975, p. 87.

4. Ibid., p. 89; emphasis added.

5. Ibid., p. 86.

6. Bruce R. McConkie, *Mormon Doctrine*, 2nd ed. (Salt Lake City: Bookcraft, 1966), p. 553.

7. *Teachings of the Prophet Joseph Smith*, p. 291.

8. Ibid., p. 289.

9. James E. Talmage, *Articles of Faith*, 3d ed. (Salt Lake City: The Church of Jesus Christ of Latter-day Saints, 1916), p. 308; Bruce R. McConkie, *Doctrinal New Testament Commentary*, 3 vols. (Salt Lake City: Bookcraft, 1965-73), 3:527-29.

10. Joseph Fielding Smith, *Church History and Modern Revelation* 1 (Salt Lake City: The Council of the Twelve Apostles of The Church of Jesus Christ of Latter-day Saints, 1953): 264; see also D&C 133:23.

11. Eldred G. Smith, *Conference Report*, April 1970, p. 142; see also 1 Nephi 22:26.

12. *Teachings of the Prophet Joseph Smith*, p. 290.

13. H. M. S. Richards, Jr., *What Is in Your Future* (Los Angeles: Voice of Prophecy, 1972), pp. 23-24; emphasis added.

14. Fallows, *Bible Encyclopedia*, s.v. "horse"; James Hastings, *Dictionary of the Bible* (New York: Scribner, 1963), s.v. "horse."

15. See also McConkie, *Doctrinal New Testament Commentary* 3:476-78.

16. *Teachings of the Prophet Joseph Smith*, p. 289.

19

WHITHER THE EARLY CHURCH?

S. KENT BROWN

The one fact uniformly attested by the early Christian writers themselves was that the church would not survive. The New Testament authors, as well as those of succeeding decades, continually underscored this theme. The earliest Christian writer, Paul, was one of the best witnesses of the eroding forces that were already washing away the foundations of the church. In one letter we read that within two or three years after he had spent considerable time in central Asia Minor, many Christians there had turned from the gospel he had preached to something else. (Gal. 1:6-12; 3:15.) Near the end of his ministry, Paul wrote to Timothy that "all they which are in Asia" had turned away. (2 Tim. 1:15.) His epistles to the church at Corinth illustrate how unstable were the Christians there. When we read his letters to the saints in Colossae, Thessalonica, and Ephesus, we sense that an intra-Christian struggle over points of doctrine and policy persisted and festered continuously. Further, a great portion of chapters 2 and 3 of Hebrews is devoted to warning the Christianized Jews lest they lose what they had received from the Savior's atonement.

In a related vein, as we read the first letter to Timothy we are impressed that here Paul was calmly laying down straightforward instructions to his longtime friend who had recently been called as an ecclesiastical authority in Ephesus. However, in 2 Timothy we sense

S. Kent Brown is professor of ancient scripture and director of publication for the Religious Studies Center at Brigham Young University.

that Timothy had by now become deeply discouraged because of the severe problems that faced the church, for people were turning away from the true path in droves.

One cumulative impression we receive from reading these letters, then, is that Paul and his companions spent considerable time and energy trying to smother the flames of apostasy. The writings of Paul and the book of Acts, however, sketch only the briefest outline of what happened during a few short decades in Palestine, Syria, Asia Minor, and eastern Greece. And these areas comprise but a modest segment of the territory around the Mediterranean Sea. Thus, the question comes to mind: What about the rest of the church during this and later periods?

At best, our sources of information about the church in other areas are meager and, frequently, rather late. Although the Christian movement had its origins among Galileans, we know most about the Jewish Christian community in Jerusalem from the early chapters of the book of Acts. Of Gentile converts, Cornelius was the most notable (Acts 10), but he was not the first. Nicolas of Antioch, one of the seven men chosen to manage temporal affairs among Christians in Jerusalem (Acts 6:2-6), seems to have had that honor, although one could build a case that the man possessed by the "legion" of demons in the country of the Gadarenes was probably a Gentile (Luke 8:26-39). In Acts 6:5, Nicolas is called "a proselyte." This means that he had once been a convert to Judaism from paganism. Only afterward did he become a Christian.

It was in Nicolas's hometown, Antioch, the capital of the Roman province of Syria, that Gentiles first joined the church in large numbers. We are told that Christian missionaries in Antioch initially preached only to Jews. (Acts 11:19.) A short time later, Jewish Christians from Cyprus and Cyrene began preaching there and "spake unto the Grecians, preaching the Lord Jesus. And the hand of the Lord was with them: and a great number believed, and turned unto the Lord." (Acts 11:20-21.) Subsequently, Barnabas and Paul preached at Antioch for a year, a period during which members of the church there came to be known for the first time as Christians. (Acts 11:25-26.) It was the success of proselyting efforts among Gentiles in Antioch that formed one key point in the official decision of the church to allow

Gentile converts to become members without having to live the law of Moses. (Acts 15:1-29; Gal. 2:1-10.)

When this decision was made at the Jerusalem Conference, it was also agreed that Paul would go to the Gentiles and Peter would preach among Jews. (Gal. 2:7-9.) A question arises in this connection: What about Paul's habit of preaching in Jewish synagogues when he first arrived in a city, even after the agreement? Was he breaking this understanding with Peter and others? To understand his actions, we must determine whether the agreement applied to proselyting among Jews in contrast to Gentiles or whether their agreement involved a geographical division of labor. That is, was Paul to preach in localities that had few Jewish inhabitants and Peter in those where large Jewish communities were established? From what Luke narrated in Acts about Paul's missionary efforts after the agreement was made, Paul and Peter must have understood that their division of labor included a division of territory. For it was rare indeed that Peter, or any of the twelve apostles, spent time in areas where Paul was proselyting. Even when Peter visited Antioch (Gal. 2:11), he did not appear to be engaged in missionary work.

Peter's part of the agreement would have pertained to the members of the Twelve. (Gal. 2:9.) Though we have to rely principally on apocryphal works to learn where some of these apostles preached,[1] it is worth noting that only in the case of John was there any real overlapping of the territory assigned to Paul, namely, in and near Ephesus. And this exception arose only after Paul's death.

Later tradition unanimously agrees that John worked out of Ephesus during the last half of the first century. Hence, we can feel reasonably safe in understanding that the three letters of John also reflect conditions among Christians of western Asia Minor after the death of Paul. These three epistles outline a portrait almost identical to that in Paul's letters: the church was riven with competing factions.

Among John's letters, we can also include the seven short notes in chapters 2 and 3 of the book of Revelation. These were addressed to specific congregations in cities near the west coast of Asia Minor. Moreover, they allow us a glimpse of how the church fared there until about A.D. 90. Interestingly, Paul had preached in many of these cities some thirty or forty years earlier. The fact that, when John was instructed to write these letters, he had been exiled to Patmos, an island fifty or so miles southwest of Ephesus, indicates that the churches in western Asia Minor had been undergoing serious persecutions. And the evidence from these brief letters themselves supports this. What is more, the Lord accused some of these churches of having fallen headlong into apostasy.

Except for the letters of Paul and John, the remaining letters in the New Testament leave us to guess concerning Christian activities in various places during the first century. The only possible exception is the first epistle of Peter, which was written "at Babylon." (1 Pet. 5:13.) Since we know from Revelation 17:5-18 that the name of Babylon was often used by Christian writers to refer to Rome, we are apparently safe in believing that Peter wrote his letter from Rome in A.D. 63 or 64, near the time of the persecution of Christians there under Nero. We know from 1 Peter 1:1 that this document was written to the saints in central and northern Asia Minor. We learn of no serious defections or schisms in the church there, but it is clear that the Christians had been enduring a period of local persecutions that Peter encourages them to bear. (1 Pet. 1:6-7; 3:14; 4:12, 14.)

We also discover that such persecutions had been borne by various congregations in many different localities prior to the writing of Peter's letter. (1 Pet. 5:9.) This can be seen in other New Testament sources as well. In addition to the persecutions Jews heaped upon Christians in Judea (Acts 8:1-3; 1 Thes. 2:14), we also know that Jewish opponents of Paul hounded his footsteps during much of his ministry (for example, Acts 9:23-25; 13:50; 14:19; 17:13; 21:27-30; 2 Cor. 11:24). On the other side of the coin, Paul also suffered at the hands of the Gentiles. (For example, Acts 16:19-23; 19:23-31; 2 Cor. 11:26.)

Persecution was thus the frequent lot of early Christians from the time of Jesus, and such continued to the last great empire-wide pogrom begun under Diocletian in A.D. 303. Often, Christians would meet resistance as soon as they joined the church. For example, we read in Hebrews 10:32-33: "Call to remembrance the former days, in which, after ye were illuminated, ye endured a great fight of afflictions; partly, whilst ye were made a gazingstock both by reproaches and afflictions; and partly, whilst ye became companions of them that were so used." From this, it is apparent that some, as soon as they joined the church, became a public spectacle, or "gazingstock," through public harassment.

No full-scale persecution was initiated against Christians in the Roman empire until A.D. 257 under the emperor Valerian. Before this time, all Roman persecutions, as well as Jewish, were limited to certain localities. In the first century, the most severe of the devastations suffered by Christians was that under Nero. During the night of July 19, A.D. 64, a fire broke out in some shops in the southeast portion of the Circus Maximus in Rome. The fire burned out of control for seven nights and six days, sweeping generally northward through the city. The blaze then broke out afresh on the estate of Tigellinus, a close associate and friend of Nero. Because of this and because of Nero's reported happiness over the conflagration, he was accused by Seutonius and Tacitus, two notable Roman authors, of having started the blaze so that he could rebuild the crowded city according to a grander and more organized scheme.

Naturally, Nero did not want to be thought of as the instigator of the blaze, so he blamed the destruction on the city's Christians, a hated and misunderstood sect who were thought to have broken away from the ancestral religion of the Jews. Nero was condemned for this unjust action, again by Tacitus. This famous Roman historian, along with the Christian writer Clement of Rome, described in some detail the horrible sufferings of the Christians in this period. Clement, in fact, reported that it was in connection with the persecution by Nero that Peter and Paul were martyred on account of their testimonies. (I Clement 4-5.)

The earliest mention of the Christian community at Rome occurs in the epistle Paul wrote to the Romans about A.D. 58 or 59. By this time, there was a substantial group of Christians in the city. Although we have no account of the first missionaries who preached there, we can infer from the way Paul arranged his greetings that by the time he wrote, at least five separate congregations or branches were meeting in the homes of various members. (Rom. 16:3-5, 10, 11, 14, and 15.) Since no Christian chapels were built until after the first century, it was natural for branches to meet in private homes for worship.

It is clear from Paul's letter to Rome that the church there was made up of both Jews and Gentiles. The church would not have been firmly established there until after A.D. 54, when Jews, who had been banned from the capital city by an imperial edict in 49, were allowed to return. From this time the church grew in size and importance until Nero took serious notice of it in A.D. 64. After the Gospel of Mark was written in Rome about A.D. 68-69, the sources fell silent on the Christian movement in that city until Clement wrote his letter from Rome to the church at Corinth about A.D. 96. This letter, called I Clement, hints that the Roman church had gone through sporadic persecution in recent years but that, in Clement's view, the saints had increased as a result in both numbers and devotion.

Although Clement did not comment much on the internal situation of the church at Rome, the reason for his writing was that a serious schism had arisen in the Corinthian congregation, concerning which Clement and other leaders in Rome had been consulted. Clement claimed that the schism arose because of jealousy and envy on the part of apostates. (I Clement 1-4.) But in another place it is evident that the interpretation of the Resurrection had been a central issue: some were denying the bodily resurrection while others were affirming it. (I Clement 24.)

A different misunderstanding of the resurrection had occurred some thirty years earlier in Ephesus. Paul wrote to Timothy concerning two men, Hymenaeus and Philetus, "who concerning the truth have erred, saying that the resurrection is past already; and overthrow the faith of some." (2 Tim. 2:17-18.) Rather than denying the resurrection, as did those about whom Clement later wrote, these men were teaching that Christians had already experienced this renewal of life, presumably through baptism, and that they did not need to look forward to it at all since it was now past.

Much of the misunderstanding about the resurrection must be attributed to erring notions of docetism that came to be more and more influential during the second century. The term *docetism* derives from the Greek infinitive *dokein*, which means "to seem." Adherents of docetism, known as docetics, maintained that Jesus only seemed to live among men, to suffer, and to die. In reality, they said, the heavenly Christ did not come into contact with the world of matter, for that would have defiled his divine nature. We can readily see that such a view of the Messiah negates the idea that salvation came as a result of Jesus' suffering, death, and resurrection. In fact, in place of this concept of salvation, the notion evolved that the Christ was merely a messenger or teacher who had brought to earth a special, secret knowledge that would allow the elect to escape the evil and corrupt world and to make their way back to the presence of the Father. This special knowledge was denoted by the Greek word *gnosis* and those who championed such a view of the Messiah became known as gnostics.

There were indications in the New Testament that the apostles were already trying to combat these false conceptions about the Savior. Both 1 and 2 John were written partly to correct such ideas. For instance, in John's first letter we read: "Many false prophets are gone out into the world. Hereby know ye the Spirit of God: Every spirit that confesseth that Jesus Christ is come *in the flesh* is of God: and every spirit that confesseth not that Jesus Christ is come in the flesh is not of God: and this is that spirit of antichrist, whereof ye have heard that it should come; and even now already is it in the world." (1 Jn. 4:1-3; emphasis added.) Later, John repeated the following in his second epistle: "Many deceivers are entered into the world, who confess not that Jesus Christ is come in the flesh. This is a deceiver and an antichrist." (2 Jn. 1:7.) In addition, we should note that many modern interpreters of John's Gospel believe that the sentence "And the Word was made flesh, and dwelt among us" (John 1:14) was directed against those who were then denying that Jesus had possessed a mortal body that was later resurrected. These illustrations, then, demonstrate that docetism had made deep inroads into areas of Christian thinking well before the end of the first century.

In its earliest forms, gnosticism had begun to make an impact within certain areas of Christianity even before Paul's death. Some modern students of Paul's letters have observed that Paul employed many terms familiar to Gnostics in his letters to Ephesus and Colossae in an effort to reverse their errant understanding of the Savior's mission and of the nature of the church. In addition, we can look to his first letter to Timothy for an explicit attack on Gnosticism. In the Revised Standard Version, which is clearer than the King James translation at this point, we read: "O Timothy, guard what has been entrusted to you. Avoid the godless chatter and contradictions of what is falsely called knowledge [*gnosis*], for by professing it some have missed the mark as regards the faith." (RSV, 1 Tim. 6:20-21.) Here Paul sounds a warning against the gnosticism that would develop into such a powerful influence in many Christian circles during the second century.

What we see at the end of the first century is a church full of problems and dissensions. All of the apostles were now gone, and no one could appeal to the "living voice" of God that came through his appointed servants. It is interesting to note that Eusebius, writing in the fourth century, knew of only one person, a man named Quadratus, who possessed the gift of prophecy as late as the middle of the second century.[2]

We lack information about the first-century church in places such as Egypt, Spain, and North Africa. We are dependent solely on apocryphal traditions to color in the Christian portraits of these areas. Paul supposedly spent time in Spain after his imprisonment in Rome and, according to information repeated by Eusebius,[3] Mark, the Gospel writer, established the first church in Egypt at Alexandria. The major doctrinal disputes centered on the resurrection and the nature of the mission of the Savior. These items were the very issues concerning which the apostles were to stand as witnesses. (Acts 1:8, 21-22.) We can see how serious the absence of the apostles became, since such questions continued as whirlpools of controversy among Christians until the fifth century A.D.

Most of the difficulties arose from within the church, as Paul said they would. (Acts 20:29-30.) Clement of Rome, for instance, implied that in his day it was impossible to tell a true Christian from a false one unless his attitude toward the resurrection was known. (I Clement 14, 24ff.) Persecutions against the church must have had some effect as well. We possess evidence from a letter written to the emperor Trajan by Pliny the younger, when the latter was proconsul of Bithynia and Pontus in A.D. 111-112, that many Christians had turned against the church when threatened with death; they were obviously unwilling to remain true to the faith. This situation was repeated in numerous instances after Pliny's time and, no doubt, had occurred occasionally before. Persecution also had an opposite effect: those who were committed to the Lord became even more firm in their devotion.

In summary, early Christians suffered much at the hands of persecutors, a fact attested to by both Christian and Roman writers. Moreover, although such persecutions were severe and led to loss of life, they were limited to specific geographical regions until that begun by Diocletian in A.D. 303. Naturally, such outbreaks both drove some out of the church and cemented the faith of others. Internally, however, the early Christian movement overflowed with serious difficulties, difficulties that split congregations and led to compromises in doctrine and worship. In the New Testament, problems like these not only were prophesied as being future by the early apostles and disciples but were also attested to as already having a disabling presence in the Christian communities of the first half of the first century A.D., less than fifteen years after Jesus' death and resurrection. And the crippling difficulties within the church did not cease. On the contrary, they continued until the church was transformed into something other than what it had been in the days of the apostles. For after the deaths of these leaders, the church was left to wander, making its way haltingly until its original form and makeup were lost.

Notes

1. See S. Kent Brown and C. Wilfred Griggs, "The 40-Day Ministry," *Ensign,* August 1975, pp. 6-11.

2. Eusebius, *History of the Church* III.37.1.

3. Ibid., II.16.1.

SCRIPTURE INDEX

THE OLD TESTAMENT

GENESIS

1:26	195
9:27	123
10:1-5	25
10:5	123
14:34-36, JST	202
15:6	91
17	91
22:15-18	91
24:60	91
26:1-4	91, 95
26:24	91
28	91
35:9-13	91
48:3-4	91

EXODUS

19:5-6	228
19:6	198
20:3	216
25:31-40	203
28:29	198
28:38	198
34:1, JST	93

LEVITICUS

11:44	227
13:2	198
16	199
16:3	198
16:12-13	198

16:32	198
18:8	65
19:18	104
20:11	65
24:11-16	30

NUMBERS

6:22-27	148
6:23	198

DEUTERONOMY

6:5	104
18:15	196
27:15-26	101
32:7-8	228
32:8	108
33:9-10	198

JOSHUA

22:22	160

JUDGES

6:23-24	201

1 SAMUEL

16:7	33

PSALMS

18:2	194
22:22	194
95:7-11	200

118:22	228
141:2	204

ECCLESIASTES

7:20	89

ISAIAH

8:18	194
29:14	68
40:6-8	227
45:22-23	131
49:6	3
53:4-11	229
54:1	103
54:5-6	217
64:4	68

JEREMIAH

3:14	217
3:20	217
31:31-33	75
31:31-34	111, 115
31:32	217

EZEKIEL

11:19	75, 79
16	217
18:21-23	222
36:26-27	75

HOSEA

2	217

THE NEW TESTAMENT

MATTHEW

4:19	217
5:11-12	160
5:17	30, 111
5:18	94
5:48	217, 241
6:33	216
7:1-5	214
7:12	214, 229
10	1
10:5-6	3, 26
12:37-39, JST	121
13:13	263
13:33	65-66
13:55	244
15:24	3
16:16-18	2
16:18-19	226
16:19	1
17:1-8	1
17:1-9	226, 233
18:17-18	226
19:16-26	218
24	30
24:24	246
24:43-44	156
28:19	16, 26
28:19-20	3

MARK

16:15	16
16:15-16	113

LUKE

2:14	169
6:12-16	26
6:16	244
6:22-23	160
8:26-39	277
10:1-17	26
12:39	156
16:19-31	36
17:7-10	111
21:24	115
21:34	157
24	4
24:45	14
24:46-49	16
24:47	16

JOHN

1:14	138, 282
1:42	63, 100
3:3	51
3:5	51
3:5-8	118
4:3-43	26
4:22	6
4:34	241
5:12	241
5:17	241
5:19	193
8:28	193
10:3-5	109
10:10	250
10:14	109
10:27	109
12:35-36	156
13:34	241
13:34-35	80
14:7	193
14:9	193
14:16	240
14:26	240
14:27	133
14:28	128
15:26	240
16:7	240
17:3	118, 159, 240
17:11	139
17:20	139
17:20-22	128
17:20-23	118
17:21	80
18:15-27	28
20:17	128
20:30	14
21:25	13

ACTS

1:1-2	24
1:2-3	2
1:3	13, 14, 25
1:4-5	16
1:5	26
1:8	1, 16, 26, 31, 283
1:11	160
1:13	244
1:15-26	2
1:17	99
1:21-22	27, 283
1:22	16
1:23-26	98
2:6-12	27
2:10	27
2:24	28
2:29-32	28
2:31-36	28
2:32	16, 27
2:36	28
2:38	105
2:41	27
2:44-45	239
2:47	27
3:1-8	5
3:13-15	28
3:15	27
3:20-24	28
3:21	116
4:4	27
4:8-12	28
4:33	27
5:32	5
5:14-15	6
5:28-41	7
5:29-30	5
5:29-32	27, 28
5:34	32
6:1-5	3
6:1-6	28
6:2-3	28
6:2-6	277
6:5	27, 29, 277
6:7	27
6:8	29
6:10	29
6:11	30
6:11-13	30
6:13	30
6:14	30
7	7
7:51-52	30
7:54	30
7:55-58	30
8:1-3	279
8:4	30
8:14	30

8:15-17	31	14:4	98	19	122
8:18-23	6	14:8-10	84	19:10	175
8:25	31	14:8-12	5	19:11-12	6
8:27	31	14:14	98	19:21	149
9	32, 33	14:19	84, 279	19:23-31	279
9:1-2	98	14:22	84	20:1-3	149
9:3-7	98	14:23	38, 84	20:4	137
9:7	33	15	6, 207	20:7-12	6
9:10-16	34	15:1	38, 85, 87	20:20-30	179
9:13-16	33	15:1-29	278	20:28-31	115
9:17-19	33	15:4	99	20:29-30	242, 283
9:23-25	279	15:5	39, 85	21	207
9:26	32	15:10	85, 112	21:17-25	39, 40
9:29	33	15:13-19	105	21:20	40
9:30	33	15:22-23	147	21:27-30	279
9:36-42	6	15:23	176	22	33
10	3, 277	15:27	147	22:3	32, 100
10:10-16	34	15:29	39, 85, 176	22:4	98
10:14-15	87	15:36	147	22:6-11	98
10:24	35	15:41	147	22:9	33
10:34	109	16:1-3	41, 99, 178	22:12-16	33
10:38-42	28	16:7	147	22:16	49
10:44-47	35	16:9	147	23:26	176
10:44-48	100	16:9-10	146	23:30	176
10:45	36	16:12	125	24:27	168
11:19	36, 277	16:16-40	125	25:11	107
11:20	36	16:19-23	279	26:5	98
11:20-21	277	16:25-26	6	26:13-15	98
11:25-26	277	17:1	148	26:28	43
11:25-30	37	17:1-2	42, 148	26:29	43
11:26	37	17:3	148	28:30	168
11:29	71	17:4	148		
11:29-30	77, 99	17:5-9	149	**ROMANS**	
11:30	38	17:6	148	1:1	47, 98
12	105	17:7	149	1:16	55, 110
12:1-2	100	17:10	148	1:17	47
12:2	208	17:13	279	1:19-21	159
12:6-7	6	17:13-14	148	1:21	159
12:25	38	17:23	42	1:28-29	159
13	38	17:26	194	3:1-2	54
13:1	195	18	58-59	3:10	89
13:1-4	98	18:5	150	3:20	48, 89
13:2	38	18:5-8	59	3:20-28	91
13:6-11	6	18:8	59	3:23	89
13:13	38	18:11	58, 150	3:23-24	48
13:16	27	18:13	59	3:24, JST	89
13:23-42	38	18:14-16	59	4:1-9	91
13:44	37	18:21	59	4:4, JST	111
13:45-46	84	18:24	59	4:16, JST	48, 90
13:48	84	18:26	59	4:25	91
13:50	38, 279	18:27-28	59	5:1	110

5:1-21	91	**1 CORINTHIANS**		7:29-31	123
5:2	114	1:1	63, 98	8:1	68
5:11	48	1:1-3	60, 62	8:4-6	68
6:3-5	113	1:1-9	60, 61	8:7	68
6:3-11	110	1:2	62	8:8	68
6:8	49	1:3	62, 63	8:9	68
6:23	49	1:4	63	8:12	68
7	50	1:4-9	60, 62	9:1-2	98
7:4	50	1:5	62	9:25-27	120
7:14	50	1:7	62, 80	10:1-4	69
7:14-16, JST	51	1:8	62	10:4	92
7:17	50	1:9	62, 63	10:5-12	69
7:18-19, JST	51	1:10	63	11:2-16	61
7:22-23	105	1:10-17	60	11:11	118
7:25	105	1:11	59	11:17-34	61
8	52	1:13	63	12:2	81
8:2	105	1:18-21	64	12:4-10	69
8:7	105	1:19	68	12:9	213
8:13-16	52	1:22-23	64	12:13	167
8:15	52	1:24	64	12:25-26	70
8:16-17	194	1:26	64	12:27	70
8:17	52, 119, 128	1:27	64, 80	12:28	114
8:26	52	2:2	45	12:28-30	70
8:29-30	123	2:4-5	64	13	61
8:29-30, JST	53	2:9	68, 108	13:1	70
9:4	92	2:10	108	13:6-7	70
9:6-8	96, 102	2:12	64	13:12	80
9:8-21	123	2:14	64	13:13	70
9:31-32	53	3:1-3	65	14	61
10:2	40	3:2	65	14:1	70
10:4	53	3:6-9	65	14:40-41	71
10:17	212	3:9-15	65	15	61, 66, 74
11:5-6	110	3:16-17	121	15:3-7	71
11:11-26	115	3:21-23	65	15:7-9	98
11:13	41	4:17	147, 179	15:8-9	71
11:13-26	123	5	61	15:12	71
11:16-24	54	5:1-5	65	15:20-23	110
11:17-25	96	5:6	65	15:22	71, 213
11:20-21	54	5:6-7	66	15:29	14
11:25	54	5:7	102	15:32	175
15:24-28	41	5:7-8	69	16:1-4	77
15:24-29	77	5:9	59	16:1-8	61
15:26	149	6:1-8	61, 66	16:8	60, 72
16:1	167	6:9-10	113	16:10	71, 147
16:3-5	280	6:9-20	61, 66	16:10-11	60, 72
16:10	280	6:19	66, 69	16:14	71
16:11	280	6:20	69	16:17	59, 167
16:12	167	7	61, 66, 123, 124	16:19-20	71, 79
16:13	167			16:19-24	61
16:14	280	7:1	59, 61	16:22	72
16:15	167, 280	7:25	67	16:22-24	71
16:21	149	7:26	67	16:24	72
16:25	54	7:29	67		

2 CORINTHIANS

1:1	98
1:1-2	73. 74
1:1-14	73
1:3	74
1:3-4	74
1:3-11	73
1:5-7	74
1:8	74
1:9	74
1:17-18	78
1:22	114
2:1	60, 72
2:4	72, 75
2:4-11	75
2:7	75
2:11	75
2:12-13	72
2:14	75
3:3	76
3:4	76
3:6	76, 82, 115
3:6-8	111
3:13	76
3:14	76
3:15	76
3:17	76
3:18	76
4:1-2	78
4:4	120
4:8-10	7
5:5	114
5:17	76
5:18	76
5:19	76
5:20	77
5:21	199
7:4-9	77
7:6-7	72
7:8	72
7:8-12	72
7:9	77
8:1-5	77, 149
8:8	77
8:9	77
9:2	79
9:6	77
9:6-15	77
10:1-18	73
10:2	78
10:10	78, 103
10:18	78
11:9	149

11:23	168, 175
11:24	279
11:24-25	7, 84
11:24-33	78
11:26	279
11:32	99
12:1-4	119
12:1-7	78
12:7	103
12:10	78
12:12	78
12:13	78
12:14	60, 72
12:17-18	72
12:19	78
12:20-21	78
13:1-2	60, 72
13:11	79
13:11-14	73, 74
13:14	79

GALATIANS

1:1	98
1:3	98
1:4	98
1:6	83, 85, 161
1:6-9	98
1:6-12	276
1:7-9	84
1:8-9	88
1:11-12	83
1:12	98
1:13	84, 98
1:14	67, 98
1:16	99
1:17	98
1:17-18	32
1:19	99, 204, 244
1:21	99
2	6
2:1-3	41
2:1-5	179
2:1-10	278
2:2	99
2:3	99
2:7	99
2:7-9	278
2:9	41, 99, 100, 207, 278
2:11	278
2:11-12	100
2:14	100
2:15	100

2:16	88, 90
2:19	100, 111
2:20	100, 119
2:21	110
3	91
3:1	100
3:2	115
3:2-5	111
3:3	101
3:4	92
3:5-18	111
3:6	91
3:7	101
3:7-8	91
3:8	93, 101
3:10	101
3:11	91
3:13	101
3:13-25	111
3:14	101, 111
3:16	196
3:16-29	101
3:17	91, 94, 101
3:19	94, 101
3:21	94, 101
3:24	91, 94
3:27	84, 87, 95, 105
3:28	116, 167, 173
3:28-29	101
3:29	84, 87, 95, 105, 208
4:1-2	102
4:4	102
4:5-6	102
4:7	102
4:9	102
4:10	102
4:12	103
4:12, JST	103
4:13	87
4:13-15	103
4:19	103
4:20	103
4:22-26	103
4:27	103
5:1	88, 103
5:3	103
5:4	96
5:6	96
5:7	103
5:11	96
5:12	96

5:13	103	5:25	117	4:7	133
5:14	104	5:28-29	117	4:8	132
5:16	96	5:30-31	118	4:9	134
5:16-26	104	5:33	117	4:11	134
5:17	96, 104	6:1-4	117	4:13	134
5:19-21	97, 113	6:5-9	116	4:18	126
5:21	97	6:10-18	216		
5:22-23	96, 133	6:11	121	**COLOSSIANS**	
6:1	104	6:12	19	1:1	98
6:1-5	97	6:12-13	246	1:3	137
6:7	97	6:21	122	1:3-8	170
6:8	104	6:21-22	137	1:4	136
6:9	104	6:23-24	122	1:5	137
6:12	104			1:6	138
6:15	96, 97, 105	**PHILIPPIANS**		1:7	165
6:17	105	1:1	182	1:7-8	136
		1:3	126	1:9	138
EPHESIANS		1:9	127	1:10-11	138
1:1	98	1:12	127	1:12-14	138
1:4	108, 112	1:13	127	1:15	138
1:5	108, 123	1:13-14	127	1:16	138
1:10	115	1:17-19	127	1:16-18	110
1:11	108, 123	1:23-25	127	1:18	138
1:13	122	1:27	127	1:19	118, 139
1:13-14	114, 233	1:28, JST	128	1:20-22	139
1:15	122	1:29	128	1:21	115
1:15-18	108	1:30	128	1:22	139
1:17	110	2:1-3	128	1:22-23	139
1:19-23	110	2:5-6	128	1:23	139
2:1-3	115	2:8-9	129	1:26-27	139
2:8-10	110	2:10, n.	243	1:27	118-19
2:10	112	2:10-11	130	2:1	136, 166
2:12	115	2:12	120, 131	2:2-3	140
2:13-19	115	2:13	131	2:4	137, 140
2:20	114, 141	2:14	131	2:6-7	140
2:21	114, 161	2:16	131	2:8	137, 140
3:1	168	2:19	147	2:9	118, 139,
3:2-8	115	2:20	147		140, 141
3:3-4	122	2:22	147	2:10	141
3:3-6	54	2:29	131	2:11	142
3:19	119	2:30	131	2:12	142
4:1	168	3:4-6	32	2:14-16	141
4:4-6	108	3:5	100	2:17	141
4:11	182	3:6	67	2:18	141
4:11-12	114	3:8	132	2:18-19	137, 141
4:11-14	2	3:9	132	2:19	141
4:12	113	3:10	132	2:20	141, 142
4:13, JST	118	3:11	132	2:23	141
4:24	113	3:12-15	103	3:1	142
5:3-6	113	3:13-14	120	3:1-4	142
5:5	121	3:14	132	3:5-9	142
5:22-23	117	3:17	132	3:9-10	142
5:22-24	117	3:20	132	3:11	142, 167

3:12-15	142	4:3	155, 163	3:6-15	158
3:16	142	4:3-4	155	3:10	162
3:18-21	143	4:4	155	3:10-11	162
3:22-23	167	4:7	113, 155	3:13	162
4:3-5	143	4:8	155	3:14-15	162
4:6	143	4:9-10	155	3:16	158, 162
4:7	122, 167, 175	4:9-12	151, 155	3:17	71, 162
4:7-9	137	4:11	155	3:17-18	158
4:9	175	4:11-12	162	3:18	162
4:9-17	174, 175	4:12	155		
4:12	165	4:14-17	156	**1 TIMOTHY**	
4:13	165	4:15	156	1:1	98
4:16	122	5:2	156	1:2	179
4:17	169	5:5	156	1:3	179-80
4:18	71	5:8	157	1:3-11	180
		5:8-22	151	1:4	186
1 THESSALONIANS		5:9	154	1:6	180
1:1	150, 151	5:23-24	151	1:19-20	179
1:2-5	170	5:25-28	151	2:1-2	186
1:2-10	150, 151	5:26	157	2:5	185
1:3-4	151			2:9	186
1:4-5	152	**2 THESSALONIANS**		2:9-15	123
1:6	149, 152	1:1-2	158	2:15	186
1:7	148, 152	1:2	162	3:1-7	2, 182
1:7-8	152	1:3	158	3:2	182
1:9	152	1:3-4	158	3:6	182
2:1	153	1:4	149, 158	3:8	182
2:1-12	150	1:5	159	3:8-13	182
2:2	153	1:5-12	148	3:10	182
2:3-6	153	1:6	159	3:11-12	182
2:5	153	1:8	161	4:1-3	187
2:6	153	1:8-9	159	4:8	187
2:7	153	1:9	159	4:12	187
2:8	153	2:1-3	158	4:14	181
2:9	153	2:1-12	115	5	183
2:10	153	2:2	160	5:8	183
2:11	153	2:3	160	5:10	184
2:13-16	150	2:3-4	160	5:13	184
2:14	279	2:4-12	158	5:14	184
2:14-16	153	2:7	161	5:16	184
2:17	149	2:9	161	5:17-18	184
2:19	154	2:10	161	5:22	181
3:1-2	150	2:12	161	6:1-2	167
3:1-6	149	2:13-14	158	6:7	184
3:2	147	2:13-17	161	6:9-10	184
3:3-4	154	2:15-17	158	6:11	187
3:6-7	150	3	183	6:17	184
3:9-12	154	3:1-5	158	6:20	181, 242
3:9-13	150	3:3-4	162	6:20-21	283
3:13	154, 163	3:4	158		
4:1-2	155	3:4-5	162	**2 TIMOTHY**	
4:1-4	155	3:6	162	1:1	98
4:1-8	151	3:6-13	162	1:2	179

1:5	178	1:11	171	11:24-26	92
1:7-8	185	1:12-13	171	12:10	113
1:8	168	1:14	171	12:23	110
1:10	45	1:15-16	171, 173	13:20-21	205
1:11	41	1:16	166, 167		
1:13	185	1:17	171	**JAMES**	
1:15	276	1:20	172	1:1	176, 208
2:1	185	1:21	173	1:2	210
2:3	185	1:21-25	168	1:2, JST	224
2:17-18	281	1:22	136, 173, 175	1:3-4	211
2:24-25	187	1:23-24	172	1:5	223
3:1-7	188	1:23-25	176	1:5-6	217
3:15	185	1:25	174	1:8	223
3:16	185			1:9-11	219
4:3-4	188	**HEBREWS**		1:12, JST	224
4:5	2	1:2	194	1:14	212
4:6-8	189	1:3	138, 193, 194	1:17	212
4:7	121	2:9	194	1:19	223
4:7-8	120	2:11	194	1:19-21	212
4:10	179, 189	2:12	194	1:21, JST	224
4:11	189	2:13	194	1:22	212
4:12	137	2:16	194, 196	1:23	223
4:13	189	2:17	194, 197	1:25	103
		3:1	197	1:26	213
TITUS		3:8-11	200	1:26-27, JST	213
1:1	98	3:14-19	93	1:27	209, 223
1:2	108	4:1-2	93	1:27, JST	224
1:4	179	4:2	93	2:1-9	218, 219
1:5-8	182	4:11	200	2:1-13	219
1:6	182	4:14	197	2:2, JST	224
1:7-9	2	4:15	89, 197	2:4, JST	224
1:15	187	5:1	197	2:8	209, 223
1:16	180	5:4	181, 196	2:10	218
2:1	180	5:6	197	2:10, JST	224
2:9-10	167	5:7-8	206	2:14, JST	224
2:13-14	228	5:8-18	197	2:14-15, JST	224
3:1-2	186	5:10	197	2:14-26	112
3:9	186	6:1	113	2:15, JST	224
		6:20	197	2:16, JST	224
PHILEMON		7:2	201	2:17	223
1:1	168, 169	7:3	201	2:19, JST	224
1:1-3	168, 176	7:3, JST	201, 202	2:22	212, 223
1:2	169	7:26	197	2:22, JST	224
1:3	169, 174	8:1	197	2:25, JST	224
1:4-5	170	8:8-13	115	2:29, JST	224
1:4-7	168, 170	8:12-14	111	3:1	220
1:5	172	9	203	3:1, JST	224
1:6	170	9:11	197	3:3-7	213
1:7	172	9:24	199	3:6	213, 223
1:8-20	168, 170	10:4	111	3:8	213
1:9	107, 171	10:19-22	200	3:9-12	213
1:10	166, 171, 172	10:21	197	3:10	217
1:10-12	175	10:32-33	279	3:13-17	213

4:1-4	217
4:2-3	223
4:4	217, 223
4:6-7	217
4:6-10	217
4:7	217, 223
4:11-12	214, 217
4:12	223
4:17	220, 223
5:1-3	219
5:1-6	219
5:4	219
5:5-6	219
5:7-11	212
5:14	222
5:15	222
5:16	222, 223
5:19-20	222
5:20	209, 222

1 PETER

1:1	98
1:2	54, 108
1:2-9	227
1:6-7	279
1:9, JST	228
1:10-12	227
1:13-16	227
1:17	227
1:17-21	81
1:20	123
1:22	227
2:1-3	228
2:4-9	228
2:6	228
2:7-8	228
2:9	228
2:11-12	229
2:13-16	229
2:18-23	116
2:18-25	229
3:1-4	229
3:5-6	229
3:7	229
3:8-17, JST	229
3:14	279
3:18-21	226
3:18-22	229
3:19	14
3:20, JST	230
4:1, JST	230
4:6	14, 226
4:6, JST	230

4:7-10, JST	230
4:8, JST	252
4:11	230
4:12	279
4:12-19	230
4:14	279
5:1-4	230
5:9	279
5:13	279

2 PETER

1:1	98
1:4	231
1:5-7	231
1:10	232
1:19-20, JST	233
1:21	233
2:3	233
2:9	233
2:10	233, 247
2:11	248
2:13	251
2:13-14	248
2:17	249
2:18	251
2:20-21	234
3:2	234
3:3	234
3:8-10	234
3:11-14	234

1 JOHN

1:1-4	237
1:5-7	239
1:7	240
1:7-9	239
1:8	89
2:1	240
2:3-5	240
2:18-23	241
3:1-3	118, 129
3:2	240
3:2-3	240
3:3	240
3:3	241
3:11	241
3:20	240
4:1	242
4:1-3	241, 282
4:2	141
4:14	237
4:16-21	241
4:18	241

5:4-5	242
5:7-8	238

2 JOHN

1:5	241
1:7	141, 282

JUDE

1:1	244
1:1, JST	244
1:1-2	245
1:5-11	246
1:6	246
1:8	247
1:9	247
1:10	247
1:12	248
1:12-13	249
1:14	250
1:14-16	250
1:15	249
1:15-16	251
1:16	249
1:18	251
1:20-21	252
1:21	245
1:22-24	252
1:24-25	253

REVELATION

1:1	272
1:12	264
1:12-13	266
1:20	264, 265, 266
1:20, JST	265
2:17	265
2:27	265
2:28	264
3:21	119
4:1	268, 272
4:2-3	269
5:1	269
5:2-4	269
5:5-14	269
5:6	265
5:7, JST	265
5:8	264
6:1-8	272
6:2	271
6:12-17	272
7:1-8	272
7:3	262
9:1	266

9:1-21	274	12:9	264	17:9	264
9:4	270	13:1	264	17:15	264
10:1-11	274	13:1-5	265	19:8	264
11:1-3	274	13:16	261	20:1	266
11:15	8	14:6	266	20:1-6	272
12:1-5	265	14:6-7	273, 274	20:2-3	266
12:3	264	14:8	265	20:7-10	272
12:7	265	16:19	265	20:11-15	272
12:7, JST	265	16:20	266	21:1-27	272
12:7-9	273	17:1	264	22:1-6	272
12:7-11	274	17:5-18	279	22:16	264

THE BOOK OF MORMON

1 NEPHI

10:12-14	115, 123
10:14	54
11:25	265
13:28-29	256
14:18-28	273
15:36	111
22:16-19	230
22:25	109

2 NEPHI

1:15	250
2:8	111
2:11-13	211
5:24	162
9:5-9	111
9:10	249
9:21	89
9:26-27	220
9:28	141
25:23	90, 112, 213
25:24-27	40
26:30	250
26:33	173
29:11-12	113
30:1-2	96
31:19	111
31:20	55, 120

JACOB

2:13	186
2:17-18	220
4:5	94
4:10	210
4:18	54, 253
5:17	8

JAROM

1:11	94

MOSIAH

2:21	111
3:19	216
4:27	219
5:7	105
7:27	195
12:24-32	40
13:28	94
13:29-30	94
15:18	133
16:14-15	40
26:21	109
27:25	102

ALMA

1:6	186
1:32	186
4:6	186
5:14	97
5:53	186
5:54	119
7:20	210, 212
7:21	121
11:36-37	113
13:2	195
13:3	196
13:7-9	228
13:17-18	202
14:11	211
22:15-18	213
24:10	111
25:16	94
29:3-4	253

29:7-8	253
31:27-28	186
32:27	213
34:40	248
38:10	248
38:12	248
39:3-4	221
42:13	110
42:14	210
42:14-15	89
42:21-25	110, 123
42:25	89
60:13	211

HELAMAN

5:10	113
10:5	52
14:13	111
14:19	220
15:7-8	212, 216

3 NEPHI

6:10-14	219
9:17	40
12:46	40
15:2-8	40
15:4-5	94, 111
15:16-24	40
15:21-24	26
16:4	40
18:24	266
18:31	109
19:23	140
27:19-20	89
27:20	119
27:27	217

4 NEPHI

1:23-26	220
24	186

MORMON

8:31	214
8:36-37	186

ETHER

12:4	216

MORONI

6:4	111
7:47	70
8:8	94

10:21	252
10:32-33	112, 254

THE DOCTRINE AND COVENANTS

1:19	80	50:41-42	109	84:73	215
1:22-23	91	52, Preface	1	86:10	116
1:35	109	56:17	162	88:3-4	114
3:7-8	221	58:42	89	88:20-21	113
3:11	221	59:16-20	219	88:29	130
3:20	111	59:23	134	88:34-35	90, 250
4:2	216	60:13	162	88:35	113
4:5-7	253	63:64	215	88:36	88
7:3	274	66:2	91	88:38	88
7:7	226	68:2-5	265	88:39	88
13, Preface	226	68:30-31	162	88:68	55
14:7	111	75:24	184	91	15, 277
18:9-16	154	75:29	162	91:1-2	16
20:2-3	1	76:31	231	91:4-6	23
20:18	195	76:35	231	93:17	194
20:26	115	76:52	218	93:19	195
20:32	233	76:53	113	93:20	119
20:34	233	76:54-59	118	93:22	108
20:38	238	76:54-60	52	93:35	121
21:5	226	76:58-60	130	98	211
27:6	116	76:71	116	101:4-5	211
27:12	226	76:77-78	116	101:32-34	139
27:13	116	76:94	110, 118	101:39	91
27:14	109	76:94-95	194	103:3-4	211
27:15-18	121, 216	76:95	195	105:24	215
29:11	116	77	269, 270, 274	106:4	234
29:30-32	109	77:6	269	106:4-5	157
29:44	112	77:7	270	107:1-4	228
38:26	109	77:13	271	107:3	92
28:27	80, 114, 128, 193	77:14	274	107:52	183
		81, Preface	1	107:54	265
38:39	219	82:3	220	112:23-26	230
39:11	91	82:10	212	121:41-43	75
45:9	91	83:2	183	128:18	116
45:25-30	115	84:17	201	128:21	259
45:59	116	84:19-25	201	130:10-11	265
49:2	113	84:24-25	93	130:20	210
49:15	188	84:38	218	130:20-21	222
49:18	188	84:63	109	131:1-4	118

132	92	132:26	233	138	230
132:19	195	132:29-50	91	138:1-11	226
132:19-25	118	133:14	265	138:20-22	230
132:20	130	133:57	91		
132:24	159	136:31	211		

THE PEARL OF GREAT PRICE

MOSES

		7:60	251	2:11	90, 101
1:33	138	7:63	251	3:22	109
5:58	93	7:65-66	251	3:25	211
5:58-59	92	8:19	93		
6:52-62	93	8:24	93		
6:59	108				
7:13-15	271	**ABRAHAM**			
7:31	116	2:6-11	91		
7:53	254	2:8-11	197		

JOSEPH SMITH–HISTORY

1:12	209
1:70-72	31

ARTICLES OF FAITH

5	78

SUBJECT INDEX

Aaron, 196; rod of, 204

Abraham: was justified without law of Moses, 90-91, 111; covenant of, 91-96; family of, as metaphor for old and new covenants, 95; Messiah to be seed of, 196, 197. *See also* Abrahamic covenant

Abrahamic covenant: equated with fullness of gospel, 91, 92; elements of, 91-92; predated law of Moses, 92, 93-94; method of entering, 95, 101

Acts, book of: written by Luke, 24; general makeup of, 24-25; major messages of, 43

Adam, 48-49

Adoption into God's kingdom, 51, 102

Afflictions, rejoicing in, 210-12. *See also* Persecution of Christians

Agrippa, 43

Airplane, view from, analogy of, 258-59

Alexander the Great, 8

Alma, 195-96, 202, 248

Ananias, 32, 33

Anarchists, 247

Anderson, Richard L.: on Christ's physical body, 141; on church as temple, 160-61; on Timothy, 179; on Gnostics, 181; on self-appointed leaders, 181-82; on productive labor, 183; on Paul's courage, 189; on James, 208

Angels: worshiping, 141; rebellion of, 246-47

Anti-Christ, 241-42

Antioch, 36-37, 277

Apocalypse, or Revelation, 256. *See also* Revelation, book of

Apocryphal writings: problems of, 13-15; postresurrection, 14; determining

authenticity of, 15; Joseph Smith's revelation concerning, 15-16; missionary labors described in, 17-18; creation accounts in, 19-20; secrecy enjoined in, 20-21; references in, to rituals, 21; persecution predicted in, 21-22; potential value of, 22-23; Jude's apparent use of, 246-47, 248, 250-51

Apollos, 59, 63

Apostasy: criticism as sign of, 78; among Galatian saints, 83-84; caused by adherence to dead tradition, 87-88; beginnings of, 137; to precede Second Coming, 160-61; costly clothing as sign of, 186; personal, in last days, 187-89; was caused from within church, 242, 283; mentioned by Jude, 245-46, 251; analogy for, from nature, 249; battling against, 252-53; was uniformly attested by early Christian writers, 276-77. *See also* Heresies

Apostles, Twelve: filling vacancy in, 2; Jesus' final instructions to, 16; missionary labors of, 16-17; as special witnesses of Christ, 26-27

Apphia, 169, 172

Aquila, 58-59

Archippus, 169, 172

Armor of God, 121, 157

Atonement: justification comes through, 89; as act of mediation, 199; removed effects of Fall, 200

Augustine, 109-10

Authority: need for 78, 181-82; comes from God, 196; rejection of, 247

297

Baptism: of Ethiopian proselyte, 31; all have need of, 33; symbolism of, 49; to enter Abrahamic covenant, 95, 101, 105 n. 7; of Holy Ghost, 118-19
Barnabas, 32, 36-37, 98
Benson, Ezra Taft, 186
Bishops, qualification of, 182
Body: as temple of Holy Ghost, 69, 121; metaphor of, for diversity of gifts, 70; natural and spiritual, 104; Gnostics' view of, 140; Christ possesses, 141, 242; of Christ, denying reality of, 242, 281-82
Born of Spirit, 5, 49, 51, 54-55, 105
Burton, Theodore M., 132

Caesar, Claudius, 37
Calling and election made sure, 119, 142, 232-33, 234
Calvin, John, 109-10
Charity, 70-71
Chronological flow of John's Revelation, 268-71; varying emphasis in, 272-73; interruptions in, 273-74
Church of Jesus Christ (meridian): organizational development of, 1-3; officers in, 2, 114; challenges faced by, 6-9; Greek influences on, 8-9; value of studying, 10; divisions in, 63-65, 281-84; Paul compares, to a building, 65; metaphor of body as, 70; need for establishing, 114; Peter as president of, 226
Church of Jesus Christ of Latter-day Saints: gradual organization of, 1-2; three main missions of, 225
Circumcision: issue of, resolved at Jerusalem council, 38-41, 85; irrelevance of, 53, 95-96; Jews' adherence to, 87-88
Clark, J. Reuben, 142-43
Clement of Rome, 280, 281
Clothing, costly, 186
Colossae, 136, 165-66
Colossians, heresies circulating among, 137
Consequences, inescapability of, 97
Converts, missionaries' love for, 83
Corianton, 220-21
Corinth, 57-58, 72, 150; dating of Paul's arrival at, 81 n. 3
Corinthians, epistles to: reasons for writing, 59-60; structure of first, 60-61; historical background and structure of second, 72-73
Cornelius, 34-36, 87
Court disputes, Paul decries, 66

Covenant, new: Old Testament types of, 69; written on tables of heart, 75-76; equated with Abrahamic covenant, 91
Cowdery, Oliver, 154
Creation, apocryphal accounts of, 19-20

Deacons, 182-83
Depravity of man, misconceptions concerning, 50
Diocletian, 284
Discipleship, costs of, 47
Dispensation, definition of, 123 n. 9
Dispensation of the fulness of times, 115-16
Divine nature, partakers of, 231
Divisions in church, 63-65, 281-84
Docetism, 242, 281-82
Domitian, Roman emperor, 245
Double-mindedness, 216-17
Druze, esoteric language of, 262-63
Dummelow, 126

Election: unconditional, apostles did not teach, 52, 122 n. 3; of grace, 53-54; of noble spirits, 108-10, 227; calling and, made sure, 119, 142, 232-33, 234
Enoch, 246-47, 250-51, 254, 271
Epaphras, 136-37, 165, 172, 173
Epaphroditus, 126, 131
Ephesians, epistle to, theme of, 107-8
Epistles of Paul: purpose and audience of, 46; organized by length in New Testament, 46; several, written from prison, 107, 122 n. 2
Esoteric language, 262-67
Eternal life, 159, 240
Ethics, 132, 133
Eusebius, 16-17, 208, 245, 283
Exaltation, 119, 128-30; involves keeping whole law, 218

Faith: justification by, 47-48; combined with works, 112, 212-13; fear is antithesis of, 185
False teachings. See Heresies
Families, 143; providing for, 183; Satan's attempts to destroy, 188
Famine in Judea, 37
Fear, 185, 243 n. 6
Feasts of love, 248
Fellowship: of sinners, 65-66; with God, 239-40
Firstborn, Christ as, 138

Foreordination, 52-53, 108-10; versus predestination, 109, 123 n. 5; to good works, 112; to priesthood callings, 196
Forgiveness, 75, 97, 171; associated with healing, 221-22; saving souls brings, 222
Fornication, 155
Freedom, 190.
Fruits of the Spirit, 132-33, 151
Fulness of times, dispensation of, 115-16

Galatians: apostasy of, 83-84; background of epistle to, 86-87
Gallio, 59, 81 n. 3, 150
Genealogy, 186-87
Gentiles: ministry among, hints of, 3-4; definition of, 25, 123 n. 8; first converts among, were proselytes, 27; gospel extension to, came through Peter, 35; as "true Israelites," 53-54, 102; from Galatia, 84; Paul's call to preach to, 99-100, 278; became one with Jews, 115
Gifts, spiritual, diversity of, 69-70
Gnosticism, 140, 141, 180-81, 237-38, 282
God the Father: Greek misconceptions of, 9; false doctrine about, was original heresy, 9; reconciliation to, 76-77; justice and sovereignty of, 123 n. 6; being equal with, 128-29; is exalted man, 129; refusing to know, 159; is revealed through Jesus, 193; fellowship with, 239-40; love of, 245-46, 252-53
Godhead, oneness of, 139, 140
Golden rule, 229
Gospel, fullness of: equated with Abrahamic covenant,91-92; availability versus acceptance of, 92-93; higher laws of, 96; fruits of, 132-33; broad knowledge of, aids scripture study, 258-59
Gospels, four, 12-13
Gossip, 214
Grace: definition of, 110; role of, in salvation, 110-11; in Paul's salutation, 169; fall from, 233
Grecians contrasted with Greeks, 28, 36
Greeks, influence of, on church, 8-9

Harris, Martin, 221
Healing, 221-22
Hebrews, epistle to, 192
Hegesippus, 237-38
Hellenistic influences on church, 8-9
Heresies: concerning nature of God, 9; circulated in Galatia, 83-84; Paul urges

Galatians to forsake, 88; taught in Colossae, 137; Paul warns Timothy and Titus against, 180-81; of "private morality," 188; John warns against, 238; denying Christ's physical body, 242, 281-82. See also Apostasy
Hinckley, Gordon B., 185
Holiness: code of, 155; in conversation, 234
Holy Ghost: gift of, men changed by, 4-5, 28; effect of, on Peter, 28; conferring of, is Melchizedek Priesthood function, 31; fell upon Cornelius and Gentiles, 35; directs prayers of righteous, 52; body as temple of, 69, 121; seal of, 113-14; being baptized of, 118-19; becoming receptive to, 142; aid of, in understanding scriptures, 258
Homosexuality, 189
Hope, 240-41
House, spiritual, metaphor of, 228

Idleness, 155, 162
Idols: eating meat sacrificed to, 67-68; turning away from, 152
Ignatius, 174, 239
Immorality: among saints, Paul denounces, 65-66; in last days, 188-89
Imprisonment of Paul, 126-27, 168-69, 175 n. 8
Infancy Gospels, 13
Irenaeus, 237
Israel: chosen stature of, 3, 53-54; gospel preached first to, 27; expanding definition of, 53-54; redemption of, from slavery, 69; possessed but lost fullness of gospel, 93; "marriage" of, to Jehovah, 103; Melchizedek Priesthood taken from, 200-201; as a peculiar people, 228

James, brother of Jesus, 100, 105 n. 2, 207-8
James, epistle of: audience for, 208; dating of, 208; reasons for writing, 208-9; impressive statements in, 223
Jason, 149
Jerusalem council, 6, 38-41, 85
Jesus Christ: proselyted among house of Israel, 3; resurrection of, 4; postresurrection teachings of, 14, 16, 25-26; final instructions of, to apostles, 16; faith in, salvation is through, 47-48, 140; compared with Adam, 48-49; fulfilled law of Moses, 50, 94, 111; becoming joint-heirs with, 51-52, 82 n. 14, 139, 194-95; foreordination of, 52-53, 196; Old

Testament types of, 69; justification comes through, 89-90; knows his sheep, 109; preeminence of, 110, 118, 137-39; millennial role of, 116; analogy between husbands and, 117; knowledge of, obtaining, 118; equality of, with Father, 128-29; all people must look to, 130-31; peace offered by, 133-34; Colossian heresy concerning, 137; possesses fullness of Godhead bodily, 140-41; becoming like, 142-43; Second Coming of, 146, 155-57, 160; God is revealed through, 193; keys to recognizing, as Messiah, 197; as "great high priest," 197-98; as Mediator, 199, 240; Mosaic symbols pointing to, 203-5; as chief cornerstone, 228; ministry of, in spirit world, 229-30

Jews: apostasy of, 6; Christian, 6; "by nature," 100; as heirs not yet of age, 102; became one with Gentiles, 115. See also Israel

Johannine Comma, 238-39

John, epistles of: authenticity of, 236-37, 238-39; first, dating of, 237

John the Baptist, 27

Joint-heirs with Christ, 51-52, 82 n. 14, 139, 194-95

Judaizers, 6, 85

Jude, 244-45; epistle of, 245

Judea, famine in, 37

Judgment according to light given, 220-21

Justification, 88-91, 105 n. 6

Kimball, Spencer W.: on Paul, 127, 134-35; on families, 143; on self-sufficiency, 183; on welfare responsibility, 184; on wealth, 184; on praying for leaders, 186; on disobedience to parents, 188; on homosexuality, 189; on gossip, 214; address given by, about Peter, 226

Kingdom of God, seeing, versus entering, 51

Knowledge: of Christ, obtaining, 118; secret, 140; false, of Gnostics, 181, 282-83; brings responsibility, 220-21; is principle of salvation, 231, 240; of gospel aids scripture study, 258-59

Law: whole, keeping, 218; of man, submitting to, 229; becoming, unto oneself, 250

Law of Moses: Stephen's teachings concerning, 30; discussed at Jerusalem council, 38-39, 85; Nephite understanding of, 40; establishes need for Reedeemer, 48; fulfilled in Christ, 50, 94, 111; replaced

by new covenant, 75-76; does not bring justification, 88-91; Abrahamic covenant preceded, 92, 93-94; as schoolmaster, 94; explained in epistle to Hebrews, 192; symbols in, pointing to Christ, 203-5

Language, esoteric, 262-67

Leaven, symbol of, as evil influence, 66, 68-69

Lee, Harold B., 98, 101-2, 188

Light: children of, 156-57; judgment according to, 220-21

Love: Paul's discourse on, 70-71; following rebuke, 75; between saints, Peter encourages, 227-28; characterizes Christ's disciples, 241; God's, 245-46, 252-53; feasts of, 248

Luke, 24

Lust, 248-49

Luther, Martin, 112, 224 n. 4

Lyman, Francis M., 128

Macedonia, 146-47

Marriage: Paul's views on, 66-67, 116-19; metaphor of, for Israel, 103; celestial, 118; forbidding of, as sign of apostasy, 187-88; Peter's admonitions regarding, 229

Matthias, 2, 26

Maxwell, Neal A., 188

McConkie, Bruce R.: on heresy concerning God's nature, 9; on converting peoples to Christ, 47; on becoming joint-heirs with Christ, 52; on election of grace, 53-54; on spiritual rebirth, 54-55; on Peter and Paul, 100; on looking to Christ, 130-31; on ethics tied to doctrine, 132, 133; on spiritual understanding, 138; on Christ's eternal birthright, 138; on Christ dwelling in us, 140; on teachers in Church, 181; on temporal assistance for elders, 184; on costly clothing and apostasy, 186; on apocryphal book, 247; on book of Revelation, 257; on understanding prophecies, 258; on Lord's use of parables, 263

McKay, David O., 104, 216, 226, 231

Meat offered to idols, 67-68

Mediator, 198-99, 240

Melchizedek, 201-2

Messiah, keys to recognizing, 197

Michael, 247-48

Missionary work: apostles assigned to do, 16, 25-26; apocryphal accounts of, 17; scope of, expanded past Israel, 26; stimulated by persecution, 30; among Samaritans, 31; of Paul and Barnabas, 36-38; of Paul, 41-43; responsibilities to do, 143; of Thessalonian converts, 152; false, contrasted with true, 153; saving effects of, 222; in spirit world, 230; must be done God's way, 252-53; division of labor in, 278

Mohammed, 270

Money, love of, is root of evil, 184

More sure word of prophecy, 232-33

Moses, 200, 248. *See also* Law of Moses

Music, 142-43

Mystery, 114-15; of salvation of Gentiles, 115; of fulness of times, 115-16; of marriage and church, 116-19; of nature of Godhead, 139-40

Nephites, 40, 219-20

Nero, 107, 180, 245, 280

Nibley, Hugh, 251

Nicknames of slaves, 167

Nicolas, 27, 277

Noah, 183

Oaks, Dallin H., 214-15

Obedience: cycle of, 212; total, 218; to laws of man, 229

Offices in early church, 2, 114

Old Testament, Paul's allusions to, 68-69

Olive tree, allegory of, 54, 102

One: becoming, as saints, 80, 128; Godhead is, 139, 140. *See also* Unity

Onesimus, 137, 166-74

Opposition in all things, 211

Order, doing things in, 219

Ordinances, 113

Organization: of early church, 2, 26, 114; of Paul's epistles in New Testament, 46; of book of Revelation, 267-68

Packer, Boyd K., 211

Parables, 263

Pastoral epistles, 178

Patience, 134; in suffering, 211-12

Paul: change wrought in, by Spirit, 5; persecutions endured by, 7, 37, 74, 78, 84, 127; early life of, 31-32, 131; conversion of, 32, 45; first Jerusalem visit of, 32-33; vision of, 33, 98; temperament and training of, 34; Joseph Smith's description of, 34; goes to Antioch with Barnabas, 36-37; first missionary journey of, 37-38, 84; attends Jerusalem council, 38-39, 85; missionary labors of, 41-43; epistles of, 45-46; ministry of, at Corinth, 58-59; teachings of, on marriage, 66-67, 116-19; defends his ministry and authority, 77-78, 152-53; apostolic authority of, 98; as apostle to Gentiles, 99-100, 278; physical affliction of, 103; "letters of imprisonment" written by, 107, 136, 168; enjoins working out one's salvation, 120, 131; experiences of, in Philippi, 125; imprisonment of, in Rome, 126-27, 168-69, 180; sacrifices made by, 131-32; testimony of, 133; sees vision of Macedonian, 146; second missionary journey of, 147; intercedes for runaway slave, 170-72; courage of, 189

Peace: offered by Christ, 133-34; Paul exhorts saints to seek, 155; in Paul's salutation, 169

Pentecost, effects of, 4, 27-28

Perfection, 103, 118, 119-20; attained by seeking good things, 132; mentioned by John, 241

Persecution of Christians: by Jews, 7, 279-80; by Romans, 7-8, 180, 279; apocryphal predictions of, 21-22; stimulated missionary activity, 30; for sake of Christ, 128; mentioned in Thessalonian epistles, 152, 153-54, 158-59; Peter warns of, 230, 279; caused many to renounce faith, 283

Peter: change in, after receiving Holy Ghost, 5, 28; receives vision of unclean beasts, 34, 87; seemingly hypocritical action of, 100; as president of church, 226; preached among Jews, 278

Peter, epistles of: frequent neglect of, 225; presidents of Church inspired by, 226; first, admonitions in, 227-30; second, major theme of, 230-31; keys to understanding, 231-32; Jude's apparent quotation from, 245, 249

Philemon, 166-73; structure of epistle to, 168

Philip, 3, 30-31

Philippi, 125

Philippians, 125-26

Philosophy: mingling, with doctrine, 137; false superiority generated by, 141

Plato, 239

Pliny the younger, 283

Politarchs, 148, 149

Poor, collection for, 28, 37, 71, 77

Prayer: role of Holy Ghost in, 52; for government leaders, 186

Predestination versus foreordination, 109, 123 n. 5

Premortality: righteousness in, 108-9; doctrine of, in apocryphal writings, 247

Pride associated with riches, 221-22

Priesthood, 228; Aaronic and Melichizedek, distinction between, 31; bestowal of, 181-82; ordination to, as type for Messiah, 195-97; prepares saints to enter Lord's presence, 200-201; Melchizedek, 201-2

Priests, Levitical, as types for Messiah, 195, 197-99

Priscilla, 58-59

Profanity, 214-15

Prophecy, more sure word of, 232-33

Proselytes, definition of, 27

Quadratus, 283

Questions answered in 1 Corinthians, 66-71

Race, metaphor of, 120

Reconciliation, 76-77, 139

Relationships: Paul's advice on, 116-17, 143, 167; shared by church members, 172

Repentance, 112-13

Rest of the Lord, 200

Resurrection: of Christ, faith-promoting power of, 4; Paul testifies of, 71; schism in church over, 281

Revelation, 138; real knowledge comes by, 140; constraint in speaking of, 215-16

Revelation, book of: message in, of enduring persecution, 8; meaning of title of, 256; three keys to understanding, 257; difficulty of following, 257-58; spiritual promptings in study of, 258; diligent study of, 260-62; understanding cultural background of, 260-62; esoteric language in, 262-67; interpretations of, in scriptures, 264-66; organizational structure of, 267-68; reveals chronological history of earth, 268-71; Joseph Smith's revelation concerning, 269-70; emphasis of, is future, 272-73; "teaching interludes" in, 273-74

Richards, George F., 253

Riches. See Wealth

Romans, epistle to, 45-56

Rome: Paul's imprisonment in, 126, 168-69, 180; letters written from, 107, 136, 168, 279; Christian community at, 280-81

Romney, Marion G., 190

Saints: unity among, 80, 128; spiritual understanding of, 138; as brothers and sisters, 172; as a peculiar people, 228; traits to be sought by, 231

Salutations in Pauline epistles, 62, 74, 151, 169-70

Salvation: role of grace in, 110-11, 213; role of works in, 112-13; involves continued effort, 119-20; working out, with fear and trembling, 131; different levels of, 213; depends on knowledge, 231

Samaritans, 30-31

Satan: as god of this world, 120; as spiritual enemy, 121; apostasy wrought by, 161; fights against marriage, 188; promotes profanity to discredit God's name, 214; will flee if resisted, 217; substitutes himself for Christ, 241; contended against Michael, 247-48; deceives many through desire, 249

Saul of Tarsus. See Paul

Schoolmaster, law of Moses as, 94

Scriptures: value of, 185-86; searching, for truth, 210; studying, with Spirit, 258; reading, versus absorbing, 260

Second Coming of Christ, 146; confusion of Thessalonians over, 155-56, 160; Paul's teachings concerning, 156-57, 159, 160; testimony of, sustains saints, 163; as thief in night, 234

Secrets, keeping, 215-16

Seven, calling of, as welfare assistants, 2-3, 28-29

Silas, 147, 158

Sin: casual acceptance of, 65; all people commit, 89; payment for, 89-90; various types of, 96-97, 104, 120-21, 188; becoming dead to, 142; salvation from, for missionary and convert, 222

Slavery, 166-67, 173, 229, 261

Smith, Joseph: on Paul's physical appearance, 34; on kingdom of God, 51; on unity in cause, 70, 79-80; on law of Moses added to gospel, 101; on not accusing others, 104; on calling and election, 119, 122 n. 3, 232, 234; on becoming like God, 129; on growing from grace to grace, 139; effect on, of passage in James, 209-10; on keeping secrets, 215; on abiding whole law, 218; gave manuscript to Martin Harris, 221; on Peter, 226; on knowledge and salvation, 231; on keys to Peter's writings, 231-32; on plainness of John's Revelation, 257; revelation given to, about book of Revelation, 269-70; on future emphasis of Revelation, 272

Smith, Joseph F.: on disciples' receiving Holy Ghost, 4-5; on heirs of God's kingdom, 102; was impressed by Peter's writing, 226; sees vision of spirit world, 226, 229-30

Smith, Joseph Fielding, 186, 221-22

Snow, Lorenzo, 129-30

Souls: worth of, 154; saving, 252-53

Spirit world, Savior's ministry in, 229-30

Spiritual world, Savior's ministry in, 229-30

Spiritual progress, 54-55

Stephen, 3, 7, 29-30

Symbols: Mosaic, pointing to Christ, 203-5; use of, in Revelation, 262-63; keys to, in other scriptures, 264-66; nature of, gives key to meaning, 266-67; in first seal of John's book, 271

Syncretism, 137

Tabernacle, symbolism of, 203

Tacitus, 280

Talmage, James E., 7-8

Taylor, John, 101, 134

Teachers, responsibility of, 181

"Teaching interludes" in Revelation, 273-74

Temple: body as, 69, 121; as image for church, 161

Temptations, avoiding, 234

Testimony, loss of, 101

Thessalonians, epistles to: dating of, 150; first, structure of, 150-51; second, structure of, 157-58

Thessalonica, 147-49

Thief in night, Second Coming is as, 156, 157, 234

Thorn in the flesh, 103

Timothy, 147, 149, 276-77; circumcision of, 41, 99, 179; accompanies Paul to Rome, 126; Paul sends, to Thessalonica, 154; as Paul's close companion, 178-79; takes charge in Ephesus, 179-80; Paul admonishes, to strengthen faith in Christ, 185

Timothy, epistles to, 179-80, 189-90

Titus, 38, 40-41, 72, 99, 179

Tongues, loose, 213-16

Tradition, resistance of, to change, 3-4, 39, 87

Transfiguration, Mount of, 232-33

Trials: rejoicing in, 210-12; Peter warns of, 230. See also Persecution of Christians

Truth, 113; turning away from, 188; pattern for finding, 209-10

Unity: Paul pleads for, 63-65, 128; priority of, 68; despite diversity of gifts, 70; Joseph Smith's injunctions on, 79-80; is power of weak, 80; as theme of Ephesians, 107-8; salvation depends on, 193, 195

Urim and Thummim, 198

Valerian, Roman emperor, 280

Vision: of Paul on road to Damascus, 33, 98; Peter's, of unclean beasts, 34, 87; Paul's, of Macedonian, 146; of Joseph F. Smith, 226, 229-30; of George F. Richards, 253

War, peace in midst of, 134

Wealth, 184; inability to give up, 218; potential evils of, 219-20

Welfare system: assignments in, 2-3, 28-29; principles of, 183-84

Whitmer, David, 154

Widows, Paul's advice concerning, 183-84

Wisdom: worldly, versus spiritual, 64; pattern for finding, 209-10

Witnesses, 26-27, 153

Wolves among the flock, 98, 242

Women, 186, 229

Work: importance of, 155, 162; Paul's commitment to, 183

Works: insufficiency of, to save, 47-48, 89-90, 110-11; necessity of, 90; role of, in salvation, 112-13; combined with faith, 212-13

World, allegiance to, 217

Young, Brigham, 100-101, 104, 163, 215-16

ABOUT THE EDITOR

Robert L. Millet, professor of ancient scripture and former dean of Religious Education at Brigham Young University, taught in the Church Educational System before joining the faculty at BYU in 1983. He earned a master's degree in psychology from BYU and a Ph.D. in religious studies from Florida State University. Brother Millet and his wife, Shauna, are the parents of six children.